Heart Power

Inspiring the Courage to Heal and Love Yourself One Day at a Time

Ed Conrad

BALBOA.
PRESS
A DIVISION OF HAY HOUSE

Photo Credit: Sunny Wood

Balboa Press books may be ordered through booksellers or by contacting:

Balboa Press
A Division of Hay House
1663 Liberty Drive
Bloomington, IN 47403
www.balboapress.com
1 (877) 407-4847

Printed in the United States of America.

ISBN: 978-1-4525-2229-6 (sc)
ISBN: 978-1-4525-2231-9 (hc)
ISBN: 978-1-4525-2230-2 (e)

Library of Congress Control Number: 2014916633

Balboa Press rev. date: 10/06/2014

In Dedication
to:
Hillary and Zach...
the greatest gifts a father could ever hope for

"The heart generates all of the earthly emotions as well
as the blissful emotions of the higher realms.
But it is so much more than just emotion. It is infinite awareness,
and the basis of all the higher consciousness you will ever assimilate.
It is from this power, within the center of your being, that the
entire script of your life is written. Live in your heart—not in
your mind—to fulfill the script of your life or to rewrite it.
Your mind is powerless to bring that about.
But every desire of your heart
will be fulfilled."

Glenda Green

Acknowledgements

I am incredibly grateful for all of my colleagues in Unity and for my countless supporters and teachers through my years in Unity spiritual communities. Without your presence and inspiration in my life, this book would not have been possible.

Many thanks go out to all my many friends, mentors, and readers over the years whose insistence helped to encourage me to take this on and carry it all the way through to the end. I appreciate all of you.

I wish to extend my thanks to Samuel Baseler for providing the perfect space at Tor Caerdich to get this project off to a grand start. Having the Grand Valley and Colorado National Monument of Western Colorado as my backdrop, I was able to access the energy and inspiration needed to give life to this project.

There are those who deserve special mention who have played key parts in the shaping of my life: my grandfather Doc whose care for me and service to others set an incomparable example; my mother Pat, who through the years was able to open her heart more and more. I thank you for your outpouring of love to me. I miss you; my father Earl, who showed me how to play and live fully in spite of his physical limitations; Marsha, who has been a loving mother to our children and helped me to open my inner door to my spiritual life; Kalia, for loving me in spite of my resistance, for riding the waves of the ministerial life with me, and for your constant encouragement to feel and express what was deep inside of me; Rev. Sallye Taylor, without whom I never would have become a Unity minister; and, Jonathan Stemer, my companion in heart discoveries for the past five years.

And, I deeply appreciate Susan White for her presence as my muse and constant source of love and support throughout the creation of this book. Thank you so much!

Finally, I'd like to express my endless gratitude to the wisdom teachers across so many traditions that have urged me to look beyond appearances, even if it was troubling, as well as open my heart and soul to unconditional love. Many of them are mentioned and referenced in this book. They have inspired me beyond words and confirmed for me that there will always be a home in my soul for deep connection with others and the Divine Presence in our midst.

INTRODUCTION

I had a dream. I was walking along a straight, narrow, well-worn path and singly focused on looking down to make certain I stayed on the path. I kept on walking with my head down. Eventually, the path ended. It was immediately obvious that I had come to the edge of a cliff. I was still looking down as my fear of heights kicked in. My heart started beating fiercely and my groin tightened. I very nervously peered over the edge. It was a bottomless abyss! I instinctively recoiled. I didn't know what to do. For some reason, I knew I couldn't turn around and go back from where I had come. Then, from deep inside I heard a very calm and matter-of-fact voice say, "Jump." My immediate reaction was, "Jump into an abyss?! I'm not insane!"

Then I felt this inner nudge like someone tapping me on my shoulder. For the first time in the dream, my attention shifted away from keeping my head down. I raised my head and looked up and out to the far-distant horizon. There was endless open space and blue sky. Awestruck by this vast expanse in front of me, I kept gazing into its immensity. I felt like I was being pried wide-open. I was no longer aware of my fear of the danger lurking below. Once again I heard that voice of certainty from deep within me say in a loud whisper, "Jump." I felt this irresistible pull to take one more step forward over the edge toward the vast open space awaiting me. It didn't seem to matter that there was an abyss. I took that step.

Next thing I knew, I was **not** falling to my death but enjoying a slow, effortless descent. I saw a suitable landing place below me and easily landed on both feet. As I looked around, I was feeling incredibly joyful and full of love. This place was beautiful and altogether new. I was no longer confined to one narrow path. It was clear that I was free to go in any direction!

We must have great heart to face the narrow madness and illusions of fear and keep going toward our deepest longings. A far more expansive and courageous way to live awaits us. This dream provided the courage and vision I needed to face previously paralyzing fears and move through a major life change. This book has been created to help you in much the same way.

I was born and raised in Fort Worth, Texas and observed the clash between the conservative Texas' values of my family and culture and the emergence of the civil rights' movement. The counterculture movement hadn't moved there yet. My childhood religious and cultural influences strongly highlighted the differences between groups and beliefs and why certain believers and races of people were more valued than others. Those messages, along with the fear-based silent conspiracy to keep everyone conformed to the established culture, were attempts to keep souls like me on one straight and narrow path. That didn't happen.

The cultural reality of discrimination and hierarchy were disturbing to me and flew in the face of what seemed obvious—that we all arise from the same Divine Presence and are of equal value. This was and still is deeply true for me. Fear-generated beliefs and customs that separate, categorize, and diminish others and ourselves are worthless. They only substantiate the false power of fear. I eventually left my boyhood home in search of my tribe and my soul.

Heart Power is a weaving of words, stories, vulnerabilities, and insights designed to inspire people of goodwill, like you, to live with great heart. What does it mean to live with great heart? It means accessing day by day the needed courage to feel and face fear and keep going, while, at the same time, expanding your capacity to give and receive love. Putting heart power into practice directly addresses one of life's foremost dehumanizing issues—fearful living.

You likely wouldn't be reading this if you didn't yearn to gain the courage necessary to fulfill the first part of what has been called the Prayer of St. Francis (the prayer actually originated in early twentieth-century France and the author is unknown)—turn hatred into love, injury into pardon, doubt into faith, despair into hope, darkness into light, and sadness into joy. You may get stuck on the fearful side of these polarities and feel powerless to cross over and experience love, pardon, faith, hope, light, and joy.

Mind power, I find, is very inadequate in the work of transforming fear. Heart power, through simple practices, generates greater alignment of body, mind, emotions, and spirit and therefore more potent energy to dismantle fear and pass through it. You're provided numerous examples of heart-power practices throughout this book.

Over time, we begin to recognize that there is a sacred current of love and wisdom flowing through us to guide our way and reveal glimpses into what is required to be a divine-human who is responsive to the evolutionary impulse within all life. Like a long-studied work of great art, in time we develop the ability to arrange these glimpses into a coherent whole of wisdom and beauty. We begin to see and resonate with our deep heart. I have written this book and offer it to you with this intent as well.

These daily readings can certainly be your companion for years to come. Read this book according to the date or follow your intuition and open to whatever page you are led to read. Use it more than once a day if you like—at the beginning of your day and at bedtime. Some writings coincide with a particular day or season such as Martin Luther King, Jr.'s birthday or Earth Day or holiday time or significant days in my personal life.

It is my profound hope that this daily companion book open you even more to the power of your deep heart and inspire your beautiful spirit when most needed, arouse courage in you when feeling small and fearful, ease your mind, and form real love in you to guide you wisely and well.

JANUARY 1

A Walkabout

"We have come to love, serve, and remember."

Writing this book has been like nothing else I've ever done. I have spent countless hours and days uncovering what is within me often late into the night. Unlike most other books, I have created 366 offerings, each one expressing a unique message from my deep heart to yours.

The closer I got to the end, the more slowly the writing progressed. It's been a marathon. I've been able to more fully appreciate the enormous gift of life as I've gathered in some of what I've experienced and learned in my parentheses in eternity. Much remains beyond my human experience and imagination. It has felt like a purposeful walkabout to get closer to my own soul.

We all could benefit from getting reacquainted with ourselves. It doesn't happen all at once. It's a gradual emergence, a lifetime calling, a grand cycle. It's our rare opportunity in this vast cosmos to peer through the grand design of our souls and somehow see and feel a Divine Presence looking back at us. We keep looking and finding something new, something ancient, something previously unimaginable.

You haven't wandered into this life by accident. Nor have you wandered into this book by accident. You are having a sacred encounter with the oneness of life.

Let your spiritual heart open to receive this simple prayer and may it empty into every stream flowing through your life this year. Rabbi Abraham Heschel, noted author and civil-rights leader, wrote, "Just to be is a blessing. Just to live is holy."

JANUARY 2

Alpha and Omega

"There is no place where love is not."

Countless times the alpha of love shows up in our lives. A first takes place—a new baby, a new friend or loved one, a new discovery, a new attitude, a new home, a new song, renewed health, new work. We push the pause button on everything else and turn our hearts toward appreciation. There is often celebration and a resurgence of hope and purpose. A resonant field of love permeates the space.

There is the omega of love. An ending occurs. A loved one passes on, a marriage ends, a project is completed, we leave our childhood home, our favorite book or movie comes to an end, we give away a priceless family heirloom. In these times, we push the pause button again and, even amid sadness or despair, we still turn our hearts toward appreciation, an appreciation for what we've received from that loved one or beloved thing. A resonant field of love simmers in our heart-space.

Both alpha and omega moments are portals to love and appreciation. The wisdom of the heart teaches us to learn from what we generate during these powerful transitions by fueling more moments of everyday life with love and appreciation. May all things turn you toward this ever-present field.

JANUARY 3

Heading for Deeper Waters

"You're no longer afraid of what's inside of you. It is only passing through."

At age two during a family vacation on the beaches of Biloxi, Mississippi, under the not-so-watchful eye of my mother, aunt, and two older sisters, I somehow made my way into the surf unnoticed. After a bit of time, they finally realized I was gone, but couldn't spot me anywhere. Thanks to my bright-blue bathing suit, they eventually spotted me floating face-down in waist-deep water.

Their screams alerted a passerby. He ran toward that bright-blue suit and pulled my limp body from the water. He knew just what to do and resuscitated me. After that life-saving moment, on a scale of one to ten, my terror of being near deeper water was a ten.

At age thirteen, I was able to find the courage to take swimming lessons. While flopping around in water over my head, my swim instructor simply let me feel the terror. Not only did I feel terror, I also felt anger and embarrassment in my helplessness. About the fourth lesson, the feelings of terror, anger, and embarrassment began to dissipate. At the end of the series of lessons, I still felt anxiety while in deep water, but no terror. I also was feeling happy, because I was realizing what had been underneath my terror of deep water all along: a love for water. It was this love which drew me to head for the gulf waters as that innocent two-year-old.

Yes, you can mine great wisdom and self-awareness by facing and integrating life's painful and frightening experiences. You can move from being frozen inside to being free. You have the capacity to be in the deeper waters of a mature and authentic spiritual life and live more fully even when fear is present.

By the way, my favorite color is blue.

JANUARY 4

Sacre-Coeur

"There is one heart beating."

High atop a hill in a northern district of Paris sits the magnificent Basilica of the Sacred Heart of Paris, known to Parisians simply as Sacre-Coeur (sounds like purr), meaning "sacred heart." Filing through its awe-inspiring interior with the moving mass of pilgrims, tourists, and worshippers, I was deeply moved by its great blue and gold dome mosaic of Jesus standing tall with outstretched arms and a shining gold radiating heart. I felt such deep emotion. The artist powerfully reminded me of what we all possess: a sacred heart.

Here's how I experience it and what I've learned about its presence through all the vulnerabilities and shifts of my human experience.

The sacred heart, or spiritual heart, or deep heart, as it is sometimes called, is a vibrational pattern which emanates from the lower center of our chest. It circulates through our bodies and extends out well beyond our physical shape into the space around us.

As a vibrational pattern, the sacred heart ignites a quality of self-awareness and presence which generates the inspiration and courage to self-express without hiding our true light. This quality gives birth to ways of communicating, serving, and creating that flow and radiate love, ingenuity, imagination, and new energy into every aspect of life. This sacred energy, expressed and understood in this light, is a one-of-a-kind manifestation of intelligence and generosity of spirit which can serve as the orchestrator for all that we are as spiritual humans.

Simply put, the sacred heart is the imprint of Divine Presence in our core which moves us in all the ways described above. It is my deepest conviction that the sacred heart is our greatest inner resource.

Wherever you are right now, if you can do it safely, after several deep breaths, focus on the lower center of your chest while you continue to breathe slowly and deeply. Keeping that focus, now gently lean back just a bit, if you can safely, and stretch your arms straight out from your side with your chest open wide. Notice what this feels like. Now, while holding this sacred pose, for as long as you are comfortably able, radiate love and compassion out to the world from your center, your **sacre coeur**. Be the heart of the world, a love without end. Namaste.

January 5

Take a Risk

"You're sitting on a planet spinning around in the
middle of absolutely nowhere. If you have to be here,
at least be happy and enjoy the experience."
—Michael Singer

Every day we awaken and it is faith that propels us ahead. Most of us learned as schoolchildren that we are hurling through space around our sun at a speed of nearly 67,000 miles per hour. We have faith that even at these dizzying speeds our planet will hold us on its surface via gravity without being launched into space.

Life on Earth has its risks. The question is this: how do we live when risks are a fact of life? The risk of being on a planet spinning around in the middle of absolutely nowhere hardly registers the tiniest blip on our fear screen. We faithfully assume that all forces are going to continue to work together in harmony to ensure our safety and the life of our planet.

However, other much smaller but personal matters can send the fear needle on our risk meter into our danger zone. On a road in a state park in Indiana, at the top of a hill I saw a sign with these words: "Caution. Steep Hill Ahead. Proceed at Your Own Risk." We all proceed through life at our own risk, unless we are small children.

Your experience is a reflection of what you tuck away in your deep heart, in the core of your being. You tuck away that the universe is either a friendly place or it's not. This earthly experience is largely for your enjoyment and learning as you progress on the wheel of life or for your fears to rule the day. Even with the risks as they are, which would you rather embrace?

Let this day point out to you how entrenched your fears may be and how they inhibit and determine your choices and behavior. Without putting yourself in real danger, be willing to take one fear and risk not allowing it to stop you. Go ahead! It's like a loving parent encouraging you to have faith and come down the slide. They assure you they will be at the bottom to catch you. Eventually you let go and discover how fun and safe it really is.

January 6

An Epiphany

"I realize that what I thought were still clouds straight overhead aren't clearing and aren't going to clear, because these are clouds of stars, the Milky Way come to join me. There's the primal recognition, my soul saying, yes, I remember."
—Paul Bogard

If Jesus himself were involved in the current day celebration of Christmas he might scoff at the notion that he is the reason for the season. The reason for the season could be more a celebration of the incarnation of the divine in all of life across all religious and spiritual belief systems. How about celebrating the universal light in this world that expresses in and through all?

I'm more drawn to the Feast of Epiphany which occurs on the twelfth day of (after) Christmas on January 6th and celebrates the revelation of the divine incarnation of Jesus brought to the whole world by the magi.

The global version of Epiphany would rejoice in the incarnation of divine light in and through everyone and every living thing. What a glorious celebration it would be! All peoples join on one day, as we are reminded in the first chapter of Genesis, to "call it good." Yes, declare all of creation good and rejoice that Divine Presence continues to create and express across the universe.

The spiritual DNA of Divine Presence shows up in the most unlikely places. It is not exclusive to beautiful temples or priestly individuals, but present and alive in what may appear to be the imperfect moments of simple everyday life. Divinity does not evaluate where it best belongs. It just is. May your vision come into focus so that you see Divine Presence everywhere and have your very own personal epiphany.

Salam, amani, maluhia, shanti, wolakota. To all in this world—peace.

JANUARY 7

Hillary's Heart

I've heard it said more than once recently that letter writing has almost become extinct. There is nothing like a letter written by one's own hand. It carries the weight of authentic transformative truth. Almost twenty years ago, my daughter Hillary wrote this letter to me. I've kept it close by since then. It's a beautiful example of heart-centered communication. May her words inspire you to write a letter to someone, yes, a letter, that is long overdue.

"Dear Dad,

Thank you so much for coming to Seattle and giving me a great amount of joy. Most of the last nine years I have wanted so much for us to be closer, for you to know that I don't feel any anger for what the past brought about and I see that life pulls souls in all directions.

Today I found out that a close friend of mine from school died in an accident last Thursday night. Thursday day we spent most of the day together, doing massage, and then he gave me a ride home on the motorcycle that killed him. There are feelings of regret that I never expressed how happy I was when we spent time together and that he was a great friend. I just thought he knew. Now I'll never know. I just hope he took that with him.

For years after you left I had the same nightmare that you were on a train waving goodbye and I knew that you would never come back. The nightmare went away after a few years, but in my heart I never knew if you knew how much I missed you and how much I wanted to be part of your life. Now that I've grown out of the pain, I see that we have the rest of our lives to be friends.

I always want you to know how much I love you, because some day fate will take us out of this world. I don't want there to be any regrets, only happiness and peace. You will always be my dad and I love you!"

January 8

A Divine Sculpture

"In truth, real love never dies.
It is always with us calling us home."

"The unexamined life is not worth living," Socrates bluntly declared. We are asked to take ownership of our actions and decisions.

This drumbeat is with me strongly right now. This is at the heart of my life. I'm looking closely. I've been experiencing both clarity and raw moments of questioning myself. I feel somewhat like Michelangelo's sculpture of David, simply allowing everything that is "not David" to be carved away. I am being shaped and formed into a new creature. That's the life I've chosen.

May each of us, when and where needed, be shaped and formed in new ways. At times it is clearly an unavoidable and blessed necessity. Those of us committed to following the ageless wisdom and power of the heart shall always be cast in the direction of what remains unfinished, unexamined, and unlike real love. As Jesus expressed, if we allow ourselves to be heart-led, we shall eventually "see God" in everything and everyone.

Remember, the starting point and ending point of any life change is always to remain steadfast in feeling and knowing the truth of who and what you are: a spiritual being, the light of the world with divine love at your core, empowered to live a life of purpose and joy. Many have come into my life to remind me. May this reminder serve you right where you are.

January 9

A Love Offering

"Turning tides, at the fulcrum of decision. Hope or destruction, which way will we go. All I know is if you want to love another, reach down in your soul and love yourself. Shine your light upon the world and love yourself. And love will come to you when you love yourself."
—Jenny Bird

Each day we come to the altar of our lives and decide what we shall place there as an inner offering. It could be anxiety or worry, forgiveness or willingness, fear or inadequacy, courage or serenity, playfulness or joy. This offering then becomes the leading edge of our experience.

What I may finally be getting about daily life is that it can be distilled down to one offering: love yourself. Some of the painful experiences we have gone through or soul impressions brought into this life have somewhat muted and masked how to love ourselves. We either reach down in our souls and love ourselves or not. This is the day-to-day-fulcrum of decision.

In recent days I have been experiencing the teeter-tottering of this fulcrum. I've felt uneasy. Yet, as I've recognized what's going on within me, I've been able to begin to see how I have endarkened the light of this love. There is some self-forgiveness to do, some honest looking at my choices, and some changes to make. I'm grateful.

Many of you are alongside in your need to transform your relationship with yourself. It is true. Love will come to you when you love yourself.

January 10

Flaws and Angels

"Imperfection(s)...are reminders that we're all in this together."
—Brene Brown, Ph.D.

Living in Western Oregon, I've become accustomed to long stretches of time in cloudy, foggy, rainy weather from November through June. Seasonal affective disorder (SAD) is an issue for many including me who live in this sun-deprived environment. While writing, I keep close at hand my light-box which is specifically designed to provide a natural spectrum of light and improve my mood and energy level. It does help.

When the sun finally does appear after a long period of being absent, locals respond like a hoard of rabid U2 fans discovering suddenly that a U2 concert has just begun in their neighborhood. An onrush of giddy people emerge from their caves and flood outside to take it in. Or, when the sun appears for a few moments, imagine thousands of people dashing to get next to the closest window and staring out at this bright object in the sky as if it were a UFO. It's like that here.

So how in the world can I offer words of inspiration for this day when thinking about seasonal affective disorder? I feel like I need to apologize for bringing up the subject of disorders. There are so many of them. You or someone you know has been diagnosed or labeled with a disorder.

Our human system gets out of order. So be it. We are all flawed human beings. This awareness is the taproot for compassion. These flaws are stories that lead us to the heart of living with each other and our shared imperfections and vulnerabilities. Having a flaw or seeing the flaw in another is never a good reason to close our hearts.

There is nothing more powerful in your shared human experience than when you open to let others see you as you are, flaws and all. It's as if angels hover nearby. There is a spectrum of light that shines into these moments that makes you glad to be a part of love's wild ride.

JANUARY 11

Have Mercy

In an interview, author and healer Stephen Levine said, "Our relationships are usually run like business: 'I'll give you two. You give me two. If you only give me one, I'm going to take my bat and ball and go home; I won't play anymore.' So this is the kind of totaling of accounts that's always going on with people. It's real easy to think that finishing business is, 'You forgive me, I forgive you. But, I'm not going to forgive you until you forgive me'—this always waiting for someone else to give you something.

We started to see that many people started to see that the end of business was no longer relationships as business. When I take you into my heart, our business is done. If you don't take me into your heart, that's your pain and I feel that, but it really doesn't affect my business. We started to see people heal their relationships towards the end of their lives, where they were really meeting other people with such mercy and such care for their well being, that even those who were angry were able to truly finish handling relationships like bargaining chips and become radiant examples of real love."

Further along in this interview Levine commented on those who resist healing and battle against an illness. At a time when they most needed mercy they had none for themselves. "And they pushed everybody away, and whether they lived or died, what they did is create schism in the family, judgment in the family, guilt in the family, feelings of unworthiness in those who loved them most, because nobody could help. And I've seen other people in the same situation—same pain in their body, same pain in their mind—say, 'I don't have a moment to lose. I can't stand to live a moment longer with my heart closed. Too much pain for me, too much pain. The world doesn't need another closed heart.'"[1]

Yes, the world doesn't need another closed heart.

January 12

Lengthening and Flowing

"The bamboo or willow survives by bending with the wind."
—Bruce Lee

Poet and scholar John O'Donohue writes about the wisdom of the wolf spider. It never creates its web between two hard objects like two stones or pieces of wood. It constructs its web between two blades of grass. Why? When the wind blows, its web would be destroyed if tied between hard objects. However, when tied between blades of grass, winds blow and the web moves with the bending blades of grass. When the wind stops, the web, like the grass, returns to its original balance point.

The expression "it will either make you or break you" is apropos. When, like a sudden gust of wind, someone delivers harsh or cruel words, or life throws at us an unexpected turn of events, typically our minds get fixed on fearful self-defense. We feel stuck between a rock and a hard place. Life becomes a battle that cannot be won. We eventually break in some way.

It's obvious that when stuff comes at you, you need to be able to bend and lengthen in order to not break. A wisdom and suppleness develops from literally stretching inside through creating a long standing conscious relationship with the rise and fall of your breath. Everything about you relaxes and stretches more easily rather than stiffening and breaking. In the practice of yoga, a good instructor will always remind you to breathe deeply. You lengthen and flow like a river rather than damn up in resistance. The debris flows on by. Take heed.

January 13

Turning Right Side Up

> "So, God created man in his own image...
> male and female he created them."
> —Genesis 1:27

Twenty-percent of the world is doing what they do well. The rest of us are doing something else. Many of us have become indoctrinated. We've been poured through a sieve. What's left has little juice. This is not a permanent condition.

Religious traditions have largely created and envisioned gods in human images with human shortcomings. How about we do the reverse and create and envision humans in divine images. Discoveries in physics and technology are leading the way. What previously was considered the realm of gods has now become the reality of the new revelations of who and what we are.

We are energy—particles and waves of light containing an infinite variety of possibilities. Certain artists, filmmakers, musicians, scientists, and writers live to break the chains of impossibility and point out our flat-earth beliefs and set-in-concrete primitive viewpoints. This crazy notion of inherent human brokenness is so upside down. Let's get with the program we are here to complete.

Imagine that you are a god-in-training. A god is a being in service to the whole of life who seeks to understand and then express its true eternal nature without the overlay of old images, negations, and definitions. Become your own heretic vigorously open to inner revelation.

Today, in your heart, feel yourself turning right side up. Allow the Divine Presence of beauty and creativity to be the image of you that you receive into your heart today. This is what you are here to learn to do well. This is the beginning of being fully human. Be still and know.

We Will Get There

"I want you to know tonight that we as a
people will get to the promised land."
—Dr. Martin Luther King, Jr.

Over these past fifty years, Americans have been finding their way through the wilderness of loss, deceit, ideals unfulfilled, violence, prideful pursuit, racial, political, and cultural divides, fear, and inequality. Our brothers and sisters around the globe have navigated similar waters. Yet, still somehow, the winds of resilience, awakening, and healing blow at our back.

As I write these words, this ongoing reclamation journey of our collective soul looks into our future that is reshaping itself and sees brand new possibility and promise. Yes, it is the birth of a new life within a world of souls longing to be free at last from fear's futility. The fulfillment of this soulful longing begins today with us all and it could very well require long-term commitment and uphill climbs.

Any promised land is never the end, only the entry point into a groundbreaking field of new endeavors. It is the chalice of new life and bold creative imagination that is unshackled from the slavery of old worn-out ideas, anxieties, and helplessness. This promised land calls out to us every day of our lives.

As this genesis unfurls, let's also reclaim our collective spiritual roots and send them down deep into our souls. These are our roots: we live in a spiritual universe governed by spiritual laws, all of which arise out of the profound unchanging presence, power, and creative magnificence of Divine Light—the Mother-Father of all—the great soul-satisfying Light that interconnects and sustains every living thing.

And, I say, we will get there. We will come to know our deep connectedness to the Divine Presence and each other in a way that will leave no doubt that we truly are one in this Divine Light.

Speak today a noble declaration from your deep heart for the peoples of our world, a declaration of our relatedness and oneness. Give thanks that we are awakening more and more to this ageless truth. Hallelujah!

Honoring a Birthday

"I can never be what I ought to be until you are what you ought to be. And you can never be what you ought to be until I am what I ought to be.

This is a revolutionary statement that would overturn the most basic, unspoken value of modern culture: competition. We so closely hold competition as the valid organizing principle of life that we have made it the sacred cow of business, economics, foreign policy, sports—even education. It is probably an underlying reason for our tremendous fear of communism, which in its primitive form downgrades competition, especially competition for wealth, though its modern forms show little trace of that awareness (was it Galbraith who said that in capitalism it's man against man, while in communism it's exactly the other way around?).

Because I was not at home in (Martin Luther)King's Christian vocabulary, and because I was dazzled by the courage of his achievements, it took me a while to discover that Martin Luther King, Jr. (whose official birthday, like my real one, is today), was one of the wisest humans that lived among us in the modern world. Perhaps if he had been allowed to live we would be following his advice to 'rapidly begin the shift from a thing-oriented civilization to a person-oriented civilization.' And perhaps the best way to honor his legacy would be to begin it now."[2]

Set aside today as a day to honor and hold sacred the relationships and individuals of your life especially those that inspire you to be who and what you truly ought to be. Namaste.

January 16

Unlatch the Gate

"For what is prayer but the expansion of
yourself into the living ether?"
—Kahlil Gibran

Images of horses being released from a corral to run free in open space still appear in my memory. That rush of release from containment to freedom is exhilarating to witness. Like most all inhabitants of earth whether on foot, in water, or through the air, we are born to be free. Freedom is inherent to life not learned.

We have unlimited stored up power and energy. The splitting of an atom tells this story. Prayer is opening wide the gates of this storehouse and letting what is inside of us stretch way out and breathe our fullness into the world. It alters the landscape of our lives and those around us like a warm January chinook wind sweeping over a frozen land transforming winter into spring.

We are the universe in miniature. Through our full recognition of ourselves as Spirit incarnate we permanently unlatch the gate of containment. When we breathe and expand into the space between ourselves and the horizon by day and a distant star by night, we are setting ourselves free to be prayer in living form.

Prayer then becomes not something you do but that which you are.

January 17

Turn Your Compass

"Love is the only power. Love is the only way. Love,
love, our love. Watch our circle grow."
—Rabbi David Zeller

Not long ago I made one of my very infrequent stops at my Facebook page. The first thing I noticed was a message posted from a significant person in my life who I had been out of touch with for more than ten years. I responded and expressed my happiness in receiving his message. He told me he was now living in Denver far from his former home. It just so happened I was going to be in Denver the next day for that one evening. We were able to meet in person and renew our friendship. The cosmic tumblers all lined up.

Connections are the juice of life. I so appreciated that my friend turned his compass in my direction. Whenever this takes place we are expanding our circle of love. Synchronicities then naturally occur. Stuck places loosen. The membrane which separates us from the world around us opens up more. The painful wounds of past transgressions are soothed.

Who could you turn your inner compass toward today? How about someone you don't know or someone you haven't reached out to in a long time? Let your circle grow even if it's only in your heart. When you extend love, there is no end to what it can create through you.

JANUARY 18

Heated Prayers

"If you love someone, set them free."
—Richard Bach

The first time I entered a sweat lodge I was ushered in by a respected leader of the Crow Nation. He had prepared the lodge and the hot stones placed in its womb. I came at my wife's encouragement.

Prayers took place before I entered. It was strongly suggested I get out of the lodge, if I began to feel overheated. Naked, I entered and found my place on the ground next to the circle of hot stones. Several others took their place inside as well including the ceremony leader. The opening to the lodge was closed. The cleansing began.

The heat became more intense and the humidity rose as water was poured over the hot stones. I realized what was in store. Feelings of danger and fear showed up. I was determined to stay amid my fears, knowing that the door out was only a few feet away.

Finally, after a long while in the sweltering sweaty darkness, I stated my prayers of release. Divine Presence helped me release that which was no longer mine. After a few more moments of precious silence, I very slowly stood up, stepped around the circle of stones, and lifted the hides over the opening to the outside. I staggered into the cold air. I certainly felt physically cleansed through and through like a squeezed sponge. I also felt I needed to be there for reasons I wasn't yet clear about.

Several months later my wife informed me that our marriage was a very unhappy one for her. She was ready to leave and leave she did. So often, there are signs of what is to come and what we will need to release. Since then, I have often prayed for Divine Presence to assist me in releasing that which is no longer mine to hold or keep.

We all need spiritual, emotional, and sometimes community assistance especially when the releasing has a great deal of heated energy associated with it. It is a fact that releasing happens more dynamically when we are moving, walking, sweating, jogging, or dancing. Movement is a powerful antidote to denial or clinging. The energy generated greatly assists in releasing who or what is no longer ours to keep. This could very well be an old identity that needs to be cleansed right out of us.

May you be so moved.

January 19

Remembrance

"There is a magnificent gallery of spiritual art within us."

I'm writing this to you from a room with a view of tree-covered hills many miles away. This vista gives perspective and moves me toward feeling the presence of my true spirit.

Each hour is a turn of the wheel of life and fertile with potential sparkling moments of remembrance. Remembrance is aroused when our viewpoint inwardly stretches us to reach for something grander than our conditioned nearsightedness. Remembrance is the gift of reconnecting with what we already know yet had forgotten. It's like looking into the night sky in the same direction as last week, but noticing the appearance of a grand constellation we'd forgotten about that the turning of time reveals.

How much do we know in our heart of hearts and yet forget? There is a magnificent gallery of spiritual art within us. Life conditioning can lure us away from this great hall.

Who would you be if you lived in remembrance of who and what you truly are rather than being lost in forgetfulness? Let this question rest in your heart. Search for a vista wherever you can find it—the top of a hill, an upper floor window of a tall building, the balcony of a concert hall, a photo of nature's vast display, or wherever your imagination takes you. Wherever it is, allow this larger perspective to be a mirror of remembrance of the grand nature of what is in this universe that is also in you.

May remembrance be a way of life for you from this moment forward.

January 20

One True Voice

"Maybe once we stop labeling ourselves,
then maybe everyone else will."
—Octavia Spencer

A woman I met recently who is now one of my housemates shared with me some of her life story. She was born from an unwed mother in a small Bavarian village in Germany at the end of World War II. From early on, she was often shunned by her peers. For a long time, she didn't know why. No one would talk to her about it. Finally, years later, she discovered that she was being shunned for two reasons. One, she had been labeled "illegitimate." Secondly, she found out for the first time that her absent biological father was Jewish. Sadly, both were strikes against her in her village.

At the age of fourteen, she immigrated to the United States. She again faced the wrath of labelers who called her a Nazi and stupid because, even though she had learned English in Germany, she was often confused by the idioms used by the locals.

She eventually extricated herself from this mean-spirited world and found her way into the emerging alternative culture of the 1960's. In this culture, she was seen as an equal and accepted for who she was. In this environment, as she described it, she began to actually hear her voice for the first time. She had been so affected by rejection and labeling that she often would not speak. If she did, it was as if she couldn't bear to hear herself. I hear her now with a voice strong and clear.

I hear her life as a noble and powerful story. One of the things I noticed when she told me her story was that she did it without making someone else wrong. It was a matter of finding her voice and her truth and saying these things out loud. She is a woman of strength and courage.

May we all become deaf to the loud vexations from the world around us and begin to hear the original voice within us that has always been and shall always be the only authentic one.

JANUARY 21

Shining Stars

"The best introduction to astronomy is to think of the nightly heavens as a little lot of stars belonging to one's own homestead."
—George Eliot

In the dark of night, camping out near 12,000 feet elevation high in the Colorado Rockies, is like a slow dance with the stars. The perception is that they are so close, yet the closest grouping of stars beyond our solar system is approximately 24,000 billion miles away.

We still feel like we have a relationship with these points of distant light. What we see with our eyes registers with a familiarity as if we are gazing into the eyes of a loved one. The infinite becomes intimate. Our hearts beat a bit faster, yet our deep sense of the moment brings an inner calm. One could say that it is as if we are peering into ourselves, only magnified on an enormously grand scale. This is the study of inner astronomy—our relationship with the endless universe and our understanding of how we fit into this heavenly star-scape.

Pause tonight and, from your heart, send your light, your energy, way out into the night sky. Feel the expansion. Then, see and feel the light coming back from your stellar relations. Feel your whole body in shining oneness with it all. It's a wonder, an ecstasy, a divine design you can't ignore.

JANUARY 22

A River Runs Through Us

"The river is everywhere."
—Hermann Hesse

Life is like an endless river with a strong current. It will flow where it needs to go. As beings who live together in this current, we may fight against it and feel we need to fight against each other for our place. Or, we learn to trust our symbiotic relationship with each other and the current that is our life support. We let go and open to its powerful energy supplying all that we could ever want or need.

In the midst of unexpected events that frighten or sadden us, we may feel like we are in this strong current without the strength or know-how to carry on. Yet, it so often happens that these events draw us into our true relationship with one another and we band together even if we're strangers.

Many including myself huddled in a parking lot around a young man who had just been mortally wounded in a drive-by shooting. Trembling in shock and disbelief, we were anxiously waiting for an ambulance to arrive.

I and several others knelt next to him holding his head and hands as he strained for each agonizing breath that were his final ones in this life. In looking around, I noticed, as if conducted by an invisible presence, how everyone stood quietly in a circle, saying prayers, muffling cries, and offering love and support for whoever needed it. It is our nature to reach out and love and support one another. This is what we are here for.

Take a wider look. See with the wisdom of your heart. You are exactly where you need to be. Accept it. Flow with it. Be helpful to others and ask for help as well.

We are the hearts. We are the hands. We are the voices for this great river as it carries us onward. This is what is true.

JANUARY 23

Acceptance

"Healing is not a science but the intuitive art of wooing nature."
—W. H. Auden

For those of us with persistent spiritual yearnings, we could describe healing as the art of wooing the Divine Presence. Every day we enter the arena of healing and participate in the refinements of regeneration. At our cellular level, microscopic bits of light are continually creating new worlds. Some of us are more conscious and curious participants than others in this endless transformation.

Our capacity to heal is enormous. Each of us is a healer. You question this? It has been clearly proven and settled that the deep-seated movement through us of emotion, energy, and heart-infused intention is potentially more transformative than a surgeon's scalpel.

Healing occurs when we let go. When hearing this, there is often a fertile pause in most of us. How do we let go? Best-selling author Anita Moorjani, an ICU, near-death cancer patient who quite suddenly was cancer-free and remains so years later, gave us a hint about letting go. "When I was willing to let go of what I wanted, I received what was truly mine."

It's as if there is a private waiting room that each of us needs to pass through before we nakedly accept our pure uncomplicated selves. In this room, it's just us and Divine Presence. Our part is to ask for assistance in accepting ourselves just as we are, no exceptions. We let the power and energy of unconditional acceptance take over. Shedding and release then begin quite naturally.

Acceptance. Accept that you are here for a noble and beautiful purpose. This is what is truly yours. The deep heart of you knows this. From this great anchor of unconditional love, gaze into and through your eyes and say with all your heart, "I accept and receive this day only what truly belongs to me. Oh Divine Presence, the rest is yours. Thank you for this healing."

JANUARY 24

Soul Force

"That old law about 'an eye for an eye' leaves everybody blind. The time is always right to do the right thing."
—Dr. Martin Luther King, Jr.

Very few of us advocate for violence to resolve conflict or our own inner pain. Even when at our core we stand for peaceful coexistence, certain provocations cause us to discard peaceful methods and resort to violent, vengeful means. We each seem to have our own breaking point. Policy makers have their own line of no return.

Once violence begins, it sets forth a wave of consequences and decisions that create more and more violence and suffering. Violent thoughts and actions create more violence.

Jesus said, "My peace I give to you, not as the world gives...." This lasting peace is not the absence of war or what has been called "negative peace." It is much more like what Gandhi called "satyagraha" which paraphrased means "soul force." It is not passive resistance. It is an oath to stand for our shared humanity. Even when faced with violence in our midst or in our hearts, we remember and choose to look into the face of violence and stand for the light in every person and situation.

There are countless historical examples of the power of this practice. You likely have examples in your own life of making the shift from a desire to act in vengeance to feeling our common humanity. It may have been your ex-spouse or former employer or military commander or parent or a violent perpetrator.

This is the right use of power—the soul committing a courageous act of divine proportions. It is a pledge between you and the Divine Presence to willingly free your hellbent, frightened ego from the grip of fear and anger.

Begin today to get this in your whole being, not just in your intellect. Return to your true source of power inside your deep heart which in spite of fear, simply chooses to not allow fear and vengeance to dictate your response. Several deep slow breaths into your heart literally redirects your energy in a new direction. This is the beginning of the ebb into peace, but "not as the world gives."

January 25

The Thread

"There's a thread you follow...it is hard for others to see....While you hold it you can't get lost. You don't ever let go of the thread."
—William Stafford

Wherever you are right now, if time and circumstance allows, set aside at least five minutes for yourself. If the present doesn't allow for this, then choose a time later today.

Sit or stand very comfortably and quietly, close your eyes and breathe deeply. Focus on your dantian center slightly below your navel by gently resting your hands there. This helps to stabilize your emotions as well as invigorate you. Now, in your inner awareness, see or feel a vortex of loving energy swirling around you. Like a powerful magnet, feel this vortex siphoning away all your concerns, doubts, and fears that distract you from this moment. Everything that is unnecessary to be here now is sent on its way.

It's just you being with yourself. That's it. Relax and stay in this awareness for several minutes and keep your attention on that spot just below your navel as you breathe slowly and deeply.

While in this quiet state, raise your attention to the area around your heart. Gently connect with the meandering path of your time on earth, you and only you making your way through all your experiences. Only you know what you've been through and all that you have felt and been led to do.

The thread of your one-of-a-kind life experience continues to pull you gently forward. Feel this thread gently tugging at you. It is very strong and pliable. Relax, let go, trust. You are well-cared-for. This has always been the case. Take a few more moments to be still, breathing effortlessly.

When you're ready, slowly open your eyes. Remain in the awareness of this loving energy enfolding you throughout your day like a beautiful song.

January 26

The Mind in the Heart

"When the heart speaks, the mind finds it indecent to object."
—Milan Kundera

Great art or music cracks or blows us open to feel deeply and be inspired. It taps into our shared vulnerabilities and yearnings to experience what was previously unknown.

Creative artists are great explorers longing to crack a great egg. The creative process becomes their way to gaze directly into their own vulnerabilities and apparent limitations and keep going. Eventually, the egg cracks open and the unseen and unknown emerges into expression.

There is a vast universe inside all of us. We can't possibly sum up all the creative expression that has taken place in this world over the past ten thousand years. Like the universe, avenues of expression are infinite. Truly, there is no end to who and what we are.

To begin to draw the juice from the new fruits that are ready to ripen in your life, clear your mind. This is done by imagining and feeling your mind dropping into your heart. Visualize and feel the two becoming one.

Now breathe slowly and deeply with your awareness centered in your heart. This mind which is in your heart naturally creates the optimum field for the emergence of love and wisdom through you. Doing this simple mind-in-the-heart meditation is a powerful primer for new creative expression.

JANUARY 27

Celebrate Now

"What wait until you're gone?"

Have you ever considered how you'd like to be remembered?

A colleague sent me an audio copy of a memorial service. It was no ordinary service. The deceased, who was a well-known minister and colleague, had decided to have his service before he left this plane of existence. He was in attendance! I listened as one by one, friends, colleagues, and family members came forward to speak to him before the packed house of celebrants. He was able to receive the love directly. He was then able to say what he wanted to all those present and thank them from his heart. It was an authentic celebration of his life. Shortly after this amazing occasion, this wayshower passed on.

My sense is that his convictions were strong and deep. He wanted to bring with him these final impressions of love and joy as a springboard into life's amazing mystery.

Years later I shared this idea with someone else whose passing was near. Right away he said yes to it. A hall full of well-wishers gathered along with the guest of honor to share stories, laugh, cry, and celebrate his life together. Unforgettable.

This is such a poignant teaching about life. Rather than save the celebration until after you've shed the physical body, do it now. Each day, celebrate the life that expresses as you even if it's in some very small way. Yes, celebrate your life at least a little bit each day.

January 28

Be a Stargazer

"Insuperable barriers arise in the material world, only to vanish once you look at them from the realm of the Stargazer."
—Martha Beck

In the book Steering by Starlight by Martha Beck, she introduces the metaphor of finding and following our own North Star. This inner North Star becomes the guiding light for navigating all of our most important life choices. It represents living our right life, the life that fills the cup of who we are.

This way of steering our way through life creates a real and powerful magic, not magical thinking, but a life lived in the field of all possibilities. As Beck puts it, living in this way allows "your life to flow into zones of astonishment that you could never invent."

This North Star stands as a beacon guiding us toward our life's truest expression. It shows up as a deep and clear knowing that we are now connecting with our most natural divine groove.

What do you want to experience and express in your life that awakens your joy, gratitude, and wonder? Whatever this may be, and you know what it is, as Martha reminds us, begin at the end. Spend at least five minutes each day allowing yourself to simply experience the feeling of the pure joy and fulfillment of having already received what you truly want. Gaze into the wonders of your heaven within. Let yourself go into this feeling.

This simple practice allows the mystical, magical god in you to create delightful manifestations which pop through into your present moment. The wonders of you never cease.

January 29

A Larger Story

"Cast your eyes on the ocean, cast your soul to the sea."
—Loreena McKennitt

Typically we read books and listen to stories or speakers seeking to find beliefs and values which reinforce our own. This may thicken the walls of the comfort zone we inhabit. The more we seek to encase ourselves in the narrowness of sameness, the more dogmatic and crystallized we are likely to become. We find ourselves isolated within a smaller and smaller story.

This way of life is prone to inflame fears of what doesn't fit our self-designed mold. This grinding dogmatism douses our romantic relationship with Divine Presence. We even age more quickly. What are we attempting to protect ourselves from?

Whether it is science, spirituality, religion, or a personal path of seeking, all endeavors that engage with universal truth are born out of a yearning to follow the arc of Divine Presence and discover our true nature and source. Our deep hearts call us to listen for this larger story. Engaging with this expanded reality is where the unexpected comes into play more consistently and begins to remove the film from our eyes, the dross from our minds, and the constrictions which arise from our fear-induced reactions.

Each day is the platform for casting your nets farther out to sea and bringing the infinitely unknown into your lap. This is downright practical, because it brings all manner of previously untouched resources into play. Your molecules can be rearranged, your hopes can be ignited, your visions can stream from inspiration, your fears can be wrung dry. It's as if heaven enters your days.

In quiet reflection today, hold firmly in your deep awareness this vision: "Divine Presence is infinite and disguised as me. All fears are merely tiny drops in a vast sea of consciousness within me. I let go and cast all that I am into this great sea out of which my beautiful new story is born."

January 30

Listening From

"Listening is a magnetic and strange thing, a creative force."
—Brenda Ueland

Dressed for the bitter January cold with ice crystals sparkling in the air, my wife and I clicked on our cross-country skis on this sunlit morning. We headed west via a groomed trail into the forests that led into the eastern edges of Yellowstone National Park. There had been a heavy snowfall the night before. Deep snow had nestled like oversized pillows everywhere.

Not far up the trail we crossed the boundary into the Park. Several miles into the Park in a shallow snow-covered ravine with direct sunlight bathing the western rim, we stopped to catch our breath. I leaned in and listened. It was densely quiet. We did our best to breathe without making a sound and not break this long sacred pause. Not a sound was forthcoming. I felt like I was wondrously stuck in a pregnant moment between two notes in the final climactic measure of a majestic symphony. Eventually, we schussed on down the trail in this cathedral of silence. I now realize that this experience helped to ensure that I would become a devotee of listening and the silence of wild places.

Listening as a conscious heart-centered practice has taught me about how to "listen from" rather than "listen for." In other words, what state of presence am I listening from? A centered, loving, judgment-free state of presence provides the ideal receptacle for someone truly needing to be heard. All of us benefit from truly being heard in this way. The kernel of what's inside of us needing to come out does so because of the magnetic power of a sensitive and loving listener. As famed writer Brenda Ueland expresses it, "You know, I have come to think listening is love, that's what it really is."

Be drawn to the jewel of heart-centered listening whether you are the listener or the one waiting to be heard. It is like being bathed in the healing silence of the Great Mother of All. Be still and listen.

January 31

We Shall Overcome

"Thank God Almighty, free at last!"
—Dr. Martin Luther King, Jr.

I once again reflect on my experience as an American who grew up in the state of Texas where segregation and racism were a way of life. The color of your skin was largely the measuring stick for the content of your character and the opportunities afforded you.

At the opening of a bright, shiny new Sears store in Fort Worth in 1960, my family arrived with thousands of other locals. While browsing with my dad, we found our way to the water fountains. There were two and they were clearly marked: "Whites only" and "Colored Only." I turned to my dad and asked why there were different water fountains for blacks and whites. I still clearly remember the ashen look on his face and his murmured response, "That's just the way it is." Words could not express what he knew was unjustifiable blatant prejudice. The violence of silence haunted this country.

Many of us know that the collective road we've traveled since the days of segregation and institutionalized discrimination has been long and great changes have taken place in our country. Yet, racism still has a foothold and the violence of prejudice is still tearing apart families and communities and nations.

Be attuned this day to how you may be swiftly judging another based on appearance or skin color or lifestyle. Remember how it feels when the tables are turned and judgment is directed at you. In either situation, you are diminished as well as the other.

Return to your heart. Connect to your life from this core wisdom. In your heart, you know how to free yourself from the ghosts of cruelty and how to love the other as yourself. Sing with me: "Deep in my heart, I do believe. We shall overcome some day."

FEBRUARY 1

A Wise Fool

"I want to know if you will risk looking like a fool for love,
for your dream, for the adventure of being alive."
—Oriah Mountain Dreamer

What is a fool? It is one who lacks good sense or judgment. I qualify. I find that fools tend to congregate together and explore possibilities and feelings and visions which are inherently risky. We fools have an idea about what good sense and judgment are yet we are pulled toward our deeper longings.

The women of my life to whom I have opened my heart, have set the stage for my fool to take charge. Several promised me nothing, but I threw myself into their presence and loved them like a fool anyway, only to have them tell me to go away and stay away. Another promised me she would stand by me. Later, for reasons she strongly felt were right, she told me to go away and stay away. All of these had the fiery sting of betrayal, as if every cell of my being was slowly melting and pressing me through the sieve of my smoldering pain.

Life then turned me toward my second wife who I was devoted to for many years. I simply couldn't give my whole heart to her. She did all she could to change that and so did I. Eventually I went away and stayed away. She was the one feeling foolish, broken, and betrayed. Her dream was shattered. I watched and felt her brokenness and feelings of betrayal from a distance. Having been walloped myself by such things, I felt a deep empathic sadness running through me. This also gave me a window into the heart and soul of my first wife who left me behind.

All of these betrayals and foolhardy deep dives have not doused my longing to love with all my heart. As of this writing, I am once again in the midst of loving someone. She shares in this love with me. I find that I am doing less bargaining with her and with the future than I have in past relationships. I show up to open my heart to the wisdom which knows and teaches what love is truly and what love is not. It still feels risky, but I proceed now as a wise fool.

FEBRUARY 2

Be a Living Mandala

"I was seeing in a sacred manner the shape of all
things in the Spirit. And I saw that it was holy."
—Black Elk

There is a unique expression of art which I recently witnessed that is created by Tibetan Buddhist monks. It involves countless grains of brightly colored sand painstakingly laid into place on a flat platform over a period of days. Comprised of geometric shapes and a multitude of ancient spiritual symbols, this sand-mandala is used as a tool for reconsecrating the earth and its inhabitants.

I attended the closing ceremony along with several hundred others. Almost immediately upon the completion of this gorgeous masterpiece, the monks, adorned in their traditional garnet and orange robes and hats, performed a series of ancient chants and prayers, and then set about deconstructing their handiwork. This accentuated the reality of life's impermanence. The sands were meticulously swept up and placed in an urn. To fulfill the function of healing, half was given in small bags to the celebrants in attendance as a blessing to take home with them, while the remainder was carried by the monks to a nearby river. There, like an offering to the gods, it was ritually deposited. It is believed that the river waters then carry a healing blessing to the ocean, and from there, this blessing would be spread throughout the world for planetary healing.

Consider what you cherish, what is truly yours to keep. Ultimately, these are expressions such as love, caring, wonder, respect, passion, and beauty. These soulful moments are what lasts and stand as the true eternal mark of a life well-lived. The sands of time generally sweep the rest away.

Today, mold a grateful heart of cherished moments. When you choose to let this be your habit, you become a living mandala of blessing and healing for your loved ones and community. Be the example.

FEBRUARY 3

Only Love

"Real love never dies."

Many including me were jam-packed into a Glacier Park Lodge employee dorm room to hear a young woman tell her story. She shared the harrowing details of her experience while camping in the back country of the Park four summers before with several friends. They had taken a day off from work as Park employees and decided to enjoy a bit of the backcountry of this beautiful place. In the near darkness of the very early morning, she was suddenly having to flee from her sleeping bag and scale a nearby tree in her attempt to escape the ravages of an unusually aggressive grizzly bear who had attacked their camp. One of her companions was mauled and died. This tragic event was retold in the best-selling book The Night of the Grizzlies as well as in several documentary films.

Accidents and tragedies like this one are part of being in this world. Family members and friends who remain find their own uncharted way to keep on living through such things. You, me, or ones we know have had to do just that. This can be far more devastating than losing a loved one who we know is about to die. That is difficult enough. Sudden tragic loss is like nothing else in life. No metaphor, spiritual teaching, or anecdotal tale captures the reality of what it's really like.

So, those of us who stand nearby, we rise, grieve, and band together. We bring not our heads, but our hearts to these times with our loved ones and friends who face such things. Life is often about the power real love brings to be able to stare into dark places and still create impossibly difficult openings into something new.

Only real love gives rise to the beginning of healing. I felt it in that dorm room of young people that day long ago and many times since. Pause for a few moments this day and while centered in your heart, repeat silently or in a whisper, "Real love always prevails."

FEBRUARY 4

Personal Story Power

"That which distinguishes me is where my wealth lies."
—Bo Eason

For some of us who have placed a great deal of emphasis on living a conscious and meaningful spiritual life, we have often been told, "Get out of your story. Staying stuck in your stories and dramas about your past leaves you at the effect of your past. The goal must be to overcome the episodes and stories of your life and free yourselves from their dramatic effects." I understand this. Yes, being free from past mistakes and hurts is important.

What if we could embody the whole of our story and rather than being deflated or discouraged, we experienced being empowered and enlivened? I have said many times that all things in life work together for a greater good for those who have the heart to embrace it all...yes, ALL things. Bringing the fullness of our hearts to all that we are and have experienced, sews all things together into a wildly beautiful, but not perfect, patchwork quilt.

Take a close look at the scenes and episodes of being you. Allow this message board to awaken you to how all the different experiences of your life add up to a powerful revelation and message worth sharing.

Beginning today, reimagine your life's story. Rather than rejecting pieces and parts of your life, hold all of the experiences of your past and present in your heart. From this heart-centered presence, consider the whole of what you have passed through. Sense the heroic nature of your one-of-a-kind path. This reframe can truly uplift and transform your life. From this day forward, awaken to the empowering story of being you.

FEBRUARY 5

Making Music With Your Life

"Grace is our natural state."
—A Course in Miracles

Each of us seems to have a hollow place inside where ashes of incompletion lay. I liken it to a person who clearly knows in her heart that she has the potential to become an accomplished musician and is gifted a new instrument by a loving supporter. She admires her instrument as a fine piece of craftsmanship with elegant resonance and tone. Yet, she chooses to never become a musician and learn how to turn her instrument's sounds into music that elevates her spirit.

Her instrument becomes one more amongst millions which lie in wait in their cases, propped up in the corner of a room or stored atop a shelf in a closet. If these abandoned instruments could emote, they would feel like that hollow place inside, potential gone to waste.

Even with this, it still remains that there is something we are destined to do with elegance and grace, our most natural groove. We've all been there—in the zone. If it was for a moment or a minute or a month, we felt like a finely tuned instrument making great music. All sense of insecurity or reluctance vanished. We were transported and set down in a green field of fearlessness and faithfulness. Creation was alive and lit up and so were we. All the dust of our lives settled into place. We felt light as a feather and, at the same time, firmly on the ground.

Even if long-held feelings remain encased in darkness, there is a magical divine design in you which still knows how to open and make music with what's inside. May grace come to meet you in that hollow place and bring courage to your heart and healing where needed. Ask and you shall receive.

FEBRUARY 6

Flowing Waters

"For whatever we lose (like a you or a me), it's
always our self we find in the sea."
—E. E. Cummings

Flowing waters sustain us. Waters flow into our homes and are essential to our sustenance and cleanliness. Waters fall from the sky to the earth, supplying streams and rivers flowing to the sea. Let the waters flow. Waters we drink flow into our bodies and hydrate, feed, rejuvenate, and cool us. The sound and energy of flowing water, if we stop to listen and breathe deeply, loosens the fibers of tension that bind us. It also diffuses healthy negative ions into the air we breathe, generating a long list of health benefits. Skillful dancers mesmerize us with their water-like embodiment of fluidity. Let the waters flow.

Tears flow in times of sadness and joy. When feelings move through us like water, they don't stay lodged inside. If feelings don't move for long periods, as we know, eventually all hell breaks loose.

We are water—75-80% as babies, 50-65% as adults. We are designed to flow.

I understand why I and many like me are irresistibly drawn to be in or near moving waters. We are returning home to our fluid nature. Waters know what to do with the hardened edges of us. We are ever so gently opened and softened allowing us to be a fish again in the waters of our lives. Any frozenness or resistance inside breaks apart almost automatically.

Author Norman Maclean famously penned these words: "Eventually, all things merge into one, and a river runs through it." It is as if flowing waters are the liquid of this great oneness, circulating in various forms through every dimension of existence. Breathe into this marvelous wonder today and smile a knowing smile. You are water, forever flowing free.

FEBRUARY 7

Humor Me

"Laughter is the shortest distance between two people."
—Victor Borge

I was speaking with a close friend who had experienced a series of mishaps that were very bizarre and stressful. Fortunately, no one was injured. After listening to his plight for a good while, quite suddenly the table turned, and within seconds, we both began to grasp the humor in these strange series of events. Simultaneously, we began to laugh, and quickly, much of the nail-biting and gnashing of teeth became knee-slapping relief. Once the hilarity subsided, we were able to really connect.

We can discover humor in the most unlikely of moments. It's there for the taking. Now, without further adieu, how about I provide you with a moment of laughter.

A mangy looking guy goes into a diner and orders a cup of coffee. The server says, "No way. I don't think you can pay for it." The guy says, "You're right. I don't have any money, but if I show you something you haven't seen before, will you give me a cup of coffee?" The server says, "Only if what you show me isn't risqué." "Deal!" says the guy and he reaches into his coat pocket and pulls out a hamster. He puts the hamster on the floor. It runs across the room, up the piano, jumps on the keyboard, and starts playing a tune. And the hamster is really good. The server says, "You're right! I've never seen anything like that before. That hamster is truly good on the piano."

The server gives the guy a cup of coffee. He savors it for a while and calls the server over. "How 'bout one of those omelets?" "Money or another miracle, or else no omelet," says the server. The guy reaches into his coat again and this time pulls out a frog. He puts the frog on the table, and the frog starts to sing. Heads are turning everywhere. The frog has a marvelous voice and great pitch. A fine singer.

A stranger from the other end of the diner runs over to the guy and offers him $300 for the frog. The guy says, "It's a deal." He takes the three hundred and gives the stranger the frog. The stranger runs out of the diner. The server says to the guy, "Are you some kind of nut? You sold a singing frog for $300? It must have been worth millions. You must be crazy." "Not so," says the guy. "The hamster is also a ventriloquist."

Contrasts

"The deeper that sorrow carves into your
being, the more joy you can contain."
—Kahlil Gibran

That real inner sense of connection to my own deep spirituality began when the young woman who would become my wife gave me a copy of Kahlil Gibran's The Prophet. Gibran accomplished in a few weeks what twenty years of attending church was unable to do. He reached my deep heart. His uncommon way of reflecting on our human contrasts opened me to plunge more fully into my own. I was able to feel a more loving acceptance of myself and a beauty inside of me that I never knew was there. He touched my soul and I began to awaken to a level of awareness beyond the veil of who I had believed myself to be.

For two seasons I played the part of Bob Cratchit in a local community theater production of Charles Dickens' A Christmas Carol. One of Cratchit's lines that I would say with fervor was "I'm rich!" In spite of being portrayed by Dickens as dirt-poor, even humiliated at times, Cratchit felt rich in love and family. This stark contrast is what makes him such an endearing and powerful character.

Our capacity to bear the truth of life from both sides of the mountain is what makes us so amazing. We can feel depths of sorrow and suffering and turn right around and rise in elevation to feel joy and ecstasy.

On my final Sunday with them, one of the spiritual communities I served, presented to me a beautiful stained-glass collage of many hearts connected together. As I held it for the first time and felt the joy of my love for these people and my appreciation for this gift, I fumbled it. It fell and hit the carpeted floor. When I picked it up, right away I noticed there was one small crack. Immediately I thought, "Oh know!" Then, I had a light-hearted aha. I realized that my exquisite gift was now an honest reflection of life. Lasting love and compassion form out of the imperfections, pains, and cracks we share.

Take several slow deep breaths into your heart. Make room now in your larger awareness for all that you are and all that you have been through and felt in your life. You are like a great sphere of energy forever expanding and contracting. In the center of this energy, feel the Divine Presence. It stands as the enduring balance point, holding in wisdom and love the amazing contrasts of you. Give great thanks.

FEBRUARY 9

Healing Morn

My eyes are filled with a newborn light
as the ripening Sun takes cosmic flight.
The azure sky swallows all its rays
and autumn leaves softly glow and amaze.

Raw passion performing in nature's way,
hawks soaring above long-shadows'-play.
My mind clamors for its morning rush,
but quickly quiets with an uplifting hush.

True wonder convenes within my soul
all edges and words that've opened me whole,
and cast into furrows plowed ever so deep
true love's fertile soil now ready to keep.

So I listen closely with a graceful ear
to reach and capture a sound so clear.
Wrapped in stillness I feel a hovering wind
which invites my heart to open again.

My dear brave soul ascends one more step
along the path of life that love has kept.
Bright light streaks through my window pane.
Oh glorious Sun, rise in me again.

February 10

My Brother

"We all have the same needs."
—Marshall Rosenberg

As part of a weekend intensive, I was in a group of twelve naked men sitting on the floor. We all were meeting for the first time. Ages ranged from about 18-70. We were directed by a facilitator to openly talk about our sexual experiences. My nervous system and feelings of vulnerability instantly went into overdrive.

What poured out from our hearts in the next two hours touched a deeply sensitive nerve. The shame, guilt, sadness, pain, anger, and tears couldn't be bottled up anymore. I was startled to discover what had been hidden away in the recesses of my dark closet that I had been holding onto for so long. No one in our group had ever been with other men in this way.

While feeling repeatedly staggered and distraught by what was being revealed, I was also profoundly moved. I felt the leading edge of a great healing for all of us who had bared our bodies and souls.

As Rosenberg teaches, I was seeing that you and I have the same basic needs: to love and be loved, to let out what's inside of us and not be judged and demeaned, to forgive and be forgiven, to feel safe and supported, to feel connected with others. That day I clearly got it that you and I are more the same than we are different. The word "brother" took on a powerful new dimension for me.

The Undercurrent

"God is a great underground river that no one
can damn up and no one can stop."
—Meister Eckhart

Our consciousness, like a hyperactive octopus, reaches into every aspect of our lives and leaves its mark on our experience.

An essential element in creating quality states of consciousness is surrender. Surrender isn't passive resignation. It is yielding to the flow of life. Surrender is being fully receptive to the present moment and not reacting to events or circumstances with fearful resistance. In this empowered state, we see much more clearly what needs to be done. We are able to take effective action.

We become, as Jesus expressed, "like the lilies of the field. They neither toil nor spin." Through it all, the things in the natural world live from what Eckhart Tolle describes as an undercurrent of stillness and presence. Whatever is taking place around them is allowed to be. It therefore becomes our practice to develop the awareness to discern and feel this undercurrent of stillness in us. This is the source from which everything useful and creative arises.

Realize that you are this undercurrent of stillness, this peace that passes all understanding, moving through all things without disturbance. This inner positioning is the source of creative action and free of constraint. When you connect with this field of conscious presence in you, you are living from the center of your universe, from the seat of your soul.

Take time this day to stop, breathe deeply, and sense the undercurrent of stillness which is present in your heart. Give yourself this gift today even if for only a few minutes. Create your experience from this great, undisturbed, underground river. There is likely a miracle waiting to happen.

FEBRUARY 12

Arrows

"We belong to eternity."
—John Lissauer, Mary Fahl

There are moments in our lives that feel like the end of the road. There is nothing beyond them except the space to consider our ultimate destiny.

One such moment recently took place as I was standing shakily on the speaker's platform of my mother's beautiful new church sanctuary and feeling and speaking tenderly about what she meant to me now that she was gone. Another such moment was watching my fragile father grin broadly while reeling in what would likely be his last caught fish from his sacred Lake San Cristobal in Colorado.

Life is not so much about places as it is about moments in time with others and ourselves, moments that filter out all that is unnecessary, old, and tired, leaving only a spirit, an essence that is deeply felt, tangibly divine.

At times, arrows fly that are destined to pierce our hearts, to lay us wide-open to why we are truly here. I say, for everyone's sake, let them fly. This is my prayer for us all.

FEBRUARY 13

Silence is Golden

"Go placidly amid the noise and haste, and remember
what peace there may be in silence."
—Max Ehrmann

Music opens an auditory channel to Divine Presence. The intervals of notes and silence form a resonance that vibrates through us like a tuning fork. The playing of certain musical compositions returns us to our natural balance and serenity, our deeper home.

Does your life have the quality of a beautiful musical composition? If the experience of harmony and serenity are elusive for you, then like all superb musical compositions, you need to enfold silence in between intervals of sound.

Sounds without silent moments can become noise and lead to noisy lives. Listening to others becomes difficult. Sensing the still small voice of spiritual guidance and clarity is drowned out by the many voices inside our heads and out in the world.

There is an urgency drawing us toward intervals of silence. Like listening to recitations of beautiful poetry which flow with a rhythm of words and silence, we are designed to listen with our inner ears to our souls. There we discover refrains of wisdom and peace echoing back to our conscious awareness. Unlearn the practice of endless noise. Give the gift of silence to yourself.

Use this day as a testing ground for listening with inward attention on your breath and heartbeat. Keep it there even when you are hearing with your ears what others are saying to you. Keep your vocal expressions to a minimum. Feel the gift of silence flow around and through you. Develop your connection to the still small voice within. Let this music play.

FEBRUARY 14

Be Love

"Love is the cure, for your pain will keep giving birth
to more pain until your eyes constantly exhale love
as effortlessly as your body yields its scent."
—Rumi

Who doesn't love to be in love? Most of us could be a primary character in a lengthy novel about love.

We could tell our stories about what it's been like to swim in love's waters. For most of us, that story evolves to a point in which we remove ourselves from its watery depths and feel it still clinging to our skin. We've been in. We've been out. We've been soaking wet at times, somewhat damp other times, and then, absolutely bone dry.

All the while, love itself remains. It's our movements and choices that determine love's presence or not in our self-made realities.

But, you and I know, as Rumi pointed out, being in and out of what feels like love, is not the same as being love. Being in love leads to being out of it at some point. When we are out of it, we're usually in some strata of pain because we are separated from our heart-of-hearts— love itself. We have learned through cultural and personal experience how to exile ourselves from what love is. It's no wonder that we are so often captured and moved by any story, myth, or poem which speaks to the yearning to return home.

So, give **heartfelt** attention today to Rumi's words: "your eyes constantly exhale love as effortlessly as your body yields its scent." For you, what does love feel like, sound like, look like, taste like, and smell like? Effortlessly allow love to be you.

February 15

Blankets of Love

"It's that place in between that we fear. It's Linus when his blanket is in the dryer. There's nothing to hold on to."
—Marilyn Ferguson

As we pass into adulthood, the glue and familiarity of family or community continues on as a real human need. We long to feel comfort, connection, understanding, like-mindedness, love, learning, and compassion encircling us.

I have been a participant and leader in a spiritual movement for over thirty years. The time came when my spirit awakened me to the reality that I had allowed this blanket of comfort and familiarity to gain too tight a hold on me. I caught wind that over the years I also had left behind several essential aspects of myself in order to fit in and feel the comfort of belonging and connection. I'm regathering those pieces now and savoring the possibilities of getting closer to myself again.

There are times to be held in the arms of family and community and times to go apart for awhile and look into yourself again. It may be for an hour, a day, or a year or more. To leave the old familiar field fallow for a time and plow a new field of self, is essential at least every seven years in order to grease the wheel of wisdom and evolution. Seeking and sowing familiarity along with moving toward the new and unfamiliar are both powerful ingredients of a life well lived. You are designed to embrace both.

Set aside all concerns of the world for a few moments. As you rest in the silence, imagine and feel your favorite blanket enfolding you. Take several minutes and let yourself be held in this blanket of love and support. Now, centered in your heart, see and feel yourself moving in the direction of your longings and aspirations. Feel this movement along with your blankets of love and support.

Wherever you are, wherever you go, take the strength of this love and support with you as you stretch toward what inspires you.

February 16

Miss Patience

Today, on my mother's birthday, I offer you an excerpt from a letter written to her by her father in 1938 when she was twelve. My mother's father and mother had been estranged from the time she was an infant. After infancy, my mother saw her father in person only once. His many letters to her constituted almost the whole of their relationship. I believe they expressed what my mom so beautifully modeled and gave, especially later in life, and what we all long to experience and express.

"My precious little girl...

Did you know you are most precious to me? Not only to me, but to that nice mother of yours, too. You are very precious to us both, simply because you are you. Both of us wanted you to be born; both of us waited, anxious and as patient as we could be for your coming to this earth. When you arrived, we decided to name you 'Patience,' because both of us had learned just what patience really meant, and we were then experiencing the just rewards for our patience. You were that reward, and we both know our reward is superb. That's what we think of our precious little girl—our Miss Patience. May you so live that we will always hold you as our most precious possession. The same advice is good for us—may we also so live, as to be worthy of such a dear girl, and of the priceless love we both know she bears toward us. Keep all of that in mind, my darling, as you journey each day through life, knowing all the while your sweet mother and I are ever mindful of the same thing."

February 17

Leave of Presence

"I think about that 'empty' space a lot. That emptiness is what
allows for something to actually evolve in a natural way. I've
had to learn that over the years because one of the traps...is to
always want to be creating, always wanting to produce."
—Meredith Monk

Like many of us in American culture, I know what it's like to feel as if the drumbeat of doing never stops. A very close loved one, is also a doer. When she is not actively doing something, her mind is thinking or having judgments about what she could or should be doing and generating feelings about those thoughts or judgments. Stopping this persistent onslaught doesn't usually end at bedtime. Even in the sleeping position with lights out, these thoughts and feelings persist and essential sleep is compromised. There is no time to empty. Agitation, numbness, worry, depletion of energy, and near exhaustion are some of the prime occupants of her life or anyone on this treadmill.

I, too, have been vulnerable to this parasite at times. Several years ago, nearing a personal crash, I had to take a three month leave-of-absence from work. Like my loved one, over a long period of time, I gradually had taken what I call a leave-of-presence. My ability to have the presence of heart and mind to create balance and sanity had left me.

During that time off, I emptied my energy system of many of the effects of this leave of presence. I took extensive time to rest, write, listen, walk, heal, reflect, and explore. Balance comes when we take to heart the mantra of radical self-care and include in the flow of everyday life these essential energy boosters. They can be bite-size.

Start today to bring presence into your life. Stop and take a leave-of-absence from mentally processing or physically doing. Have three bite-size moments of emptying, about one minute each. Get still and quiet. Breathe slowly with your conscious attention only on your heart-space. This simple practice will move you toward your natural balance point.

FEBRUARY 18

Evergreen

"Life is enduring."

Amid a smattering of rain, I enjoyed a long walk with a friend. As we ascended a hill southwest of Eugene, it was obvious that this hillside had been clear-cut several decades before. There was a healthy stand of new trees making their way to ever-increasing heights.

I took notice of one evergreen tree near the hilltop, much taller than all the others, standing alone and looking out over the countryside like a watchtower. This lone tree had somehow survived the clear-cut. My friend and I took a moment to pay homage to this testimony of endurance, strength, and inspiration.

My imagination kicked in and I mused, "If this tree could speak, what stories it could tell and what lessons it could teach!" There was a time when it found itself alone on the heels of destruction. It kept living and growing, and eventually abundance emerged everywhere.

There are clearly times in which we experience the descending blows of human life. Yet, the vibration of life remains and grows and amazes and stands as a living testimony to faith and endurance. This quality of knowing and vision awaits us all in the watchtower of our souls.

May the wider view come and take your heart. May you truly feel that even in the midst of emotional clear-cutting, your roots are enduring. You may turn a blind eye to this at times. Yet, I still say, "There is a tower of strength and love in you."

I still see that one tree standing strong and tall—a watchtower, evergreen.

FEBRUARY 19

Heal Thyself

"We merely need to open our eyes and realize what
is already here, who we already are—as soon as
we stop pretending we're small or unholy."
—Bo Lozoff

It is true that at times we live at the mercy of the compulsion to protect ourselves. These compulsions usually develop out of painful childhood and adolescent experiences. We adapt and learn how to show these compulsions to the world rather than who we truly are. They eventually become dominant shadow aspects of our personality. They are such things as self-deprecation, martyrdom, greed, arrogance, and being obsessively controlling.

Each one of these flaws or personas create strategies to keep their dominance going. This childish way of acting out or protecting ourselves from recreating painful experiences is our shadow at work.

Hiding inside ourselves in these ways creates a pained existence of its own. In Hinduism, this is called maya or illusion—creating a false reality and pretending that it is authentic. Even with this vortex at work, we can still free ourselves from this prison of our own making.

Becoming heart-connected and heart-directed is a way of attuning to yourself and the world around you and frees you from the prisons of your own making. This cools your brain and nervous system which have conditioned you to focus on trying to avoid old hurts.

Take one of your compulsions and give it a heart-power treatment. After several minutes of heart-centered breathing, become aware of one of your compulsions. Drop that compulsion and any associated feelings into your heart-space. It's like being dipped in healing waters. Feel the compulsion dissolve into this powerful loving energy.

FEBRUARY 20

Powerless

"Lean on me when you're not strong."
—Bill Withers

My family and I entered an elevator in a South Dakota forest about twenty-five miles from Wyoming. Yes, an elevator. It is the entrance to Jewel Cave National Monument. Known for its stunning crystalline colors, this spelunker's dream is an almost endless network of caverns and crawl spaces.

The elevator dropped us deep underground into the large main cavern. Several minutes into the guided tour, all were forewarned that the lights would be turned off and to prepare for complete blackness. When the lights went out, my two young children instinctively grabbed onto me and held on during the minute or so of blindness. I remember how solid I felt and how glad I was to be able to ease my children's fears.

On occasion, I am so strongly aware of the powerful remnants within us of being a child. There are times when the lights go out and our world feels like a dark place. All we really want is to be able to grab hold of someone who loves us and feel the strength and comfort of being safe and protected.

For me, serving in adult roles and teaching about living emotionally and spiritually healthy adult lives for so long has had its adulterating effects. Admitting that I still have childlike needs doesn't come easily. Similar to the first step of A.A., there are times when we simply need to admit we feel powerless. In this case we feel powerless over adulthood and need to ask for help, love, and support without having to apologize.

May your strengths and needs embrace each other within your heart and teach you how to ask for support and draw to you those you can trust and lean on.

February 21

Soul Mates

"I love you for putting your hand into my heaped up heart and passing over all the frivolous and weak things that you cannot help seeing there, and for drawing out into the light all the beautiful and radiant things that no one else has looked quite far enough to find."
—Roy Croft

These words so gracefully speak for themselves. What could we add?—possibly a simple, elegant pause. Let's pause and make note of all those in our lives who have been willing to look past our faults and have chosen to focus on the radiant things about us.

In my heart and imagination, I'm going to bring together into one space as many of them as I can recall including animal companions. You could do the same. Some are still on the earth plane, others are not.

This is what I imagine and feel taking place. I see us coming together in the center of this great room, close enough to be able to touch one another. Through a great skylight, a warm and radiant light shines upon everyone. I see us joining hands (dogs would simply do what dogs do) and feeling the powerful, joyful bond of eternal love which sees and expresses only the truth of who we are. There is a deep silence of immeasurable gratitude...soul mates together.

In time, the light and the love are all that remain.

February 22

True Voice Activist

> "The singer has everything within him. The
> notes come out from his very life."
> —Rabindranath Tagore

Many times I have been aware that I am unable to find my true voice that John 1:23 describes as "the voice crying in the wilderness." It remains remote. Rather, I have been able to create sounds and words that I and others hear. It doesn't make for very effective communication. I suspect you can relate.

Communicating from the heart is creating open access to our inner wilderness and feeling and speaking forth from this connection to ourselves. When we speak or communicate from this wilderness, it literally creates a different vibration. We have discovered once again our true voice that speaks not to entertain or impress or hear the sound of our voice, but it speaks from an intimate depth within us. Like a great wilderness area in the natural world, this true voice can't be controlled or corralled or altered by our fears of it. How many times have you heard it said, or you've said it yourself, "I'm afraid of what might come out of me?" Fear or convention gets ahold of us and silences and blocks the voice of our deep heart.

Come to an agreement with yourself today. Be your own heart monitor, an activist for your true voice. Listen from your heart. Speak from your heart. That's it. Try it on. Don't let your fear stop you even when it shows up in some loud way.

Start with one day. This is a way of loving yourself and learning more about what you can truly contribute to your family and community.

FEBRUARY 23

Be an Empty Vessel

"Thirty spokes are joined together in a wheel, but it is
the center hole that allows the wheel to function.
We mold clay into a pot, but it is the emptiness
inside that makes the vessel useful.
We fashion wood for a house, but it is the
emptiness inside that makes it livable.
We work with the substantial, but the emptiness is what we use."
—Lao Tzu

So often in nurturing relationships I find that the most transformative approach is to "be empty"— no agenda, no blame, no urgency, no controlling. Allow the connectedness that is being created in the moment to generate the direction and purpose of being together.

I'm seeing that words are needed less and presence is needed more, especially in these times of greater emotional and collective intensity. The power of silence empties the mind. Whatever arises from that silence has the fragrance of genuine connectedness and heart.

So, if you feel the discomfort of silence in moments with others, let it ride. Trust it. The focus shifts from "what do I need to say?" to simple attention to the silence and the space of present moment awareness. You now experience those around you with a different set of ears and eyes.

From this arises synchronicity, spontaneity, honesty, and love. As Lao Tzu says, use the emptiness which is the container for Spirit to create healing and wondrous surprise.

FEBRUARY 24

The Truth Made Visible

"Healing and change are one and the same thing."
—Carolyn Myss

Molecularly speaking or in consciousness, we know we are not the same individuals that we were in our past. You and I are a form of consciousness made visible, moving through space and time with particular identifiable markers (DNA). We experience a powerful enduring essence that allows us to navigate the ever-changing creative impulses of life.

In other words, we are expressions of dynamic light and energy in living human form, not solid objects. As you notice your breath circulating in and out, acknowledge this eternal truth of what you are. Let this truth inform your heart and mind. Whatever experience you are having, it can change with one conscious connected breath. This truth shall endure forever.

Taking this message into life leads to this understanding: If we choose to be conscious, heart-connected participants in what is taking place within and around us, we alter the molecules and emotions of our experience. What we see through our inner lens and energize through our hearts is what we get. In this invisible realm of consciousness and creation, there are no limits. Therefore, there are no limits to what is created or made whole through us. This is a certainty.

FEBRUARY 25

Ears to Hear

"In the beauty of the ending day there is
always something to believe in."
—Julie Flanders

There is something we are meant to be, some innate intent that hums loudly inside of us. Far too much time is spent tuning it out due to being overrun by the inoculation of voices, time demands, messages, and devices. Of all the things we could decide to mute, we choose to silence the message about why we have taken birth. It may be something we aren't ready to hear. We can become deaf to its message.

A wise one once said, "Whoever has ears to hear, let them hear." Often the purpose of reading sacred passages that inspire us or listening to words from teachers of ageless wisdom is to tune our inner hearts to our purpose and destiny—to return home. This message may not come in words, but in a feeling. It may not come as a voice, but as a knowing.

The following simple meditation is powerful daily medicine: (Feel the natural pauses and spaces in between each part. The spaces can be as long as you need them to be.)

"Breathing deeply, collect all your thoughts, feelings, and needs together and consciously place them in your heart, your deep heart. Continue breathing slowly with your full attention and energy there. In this sacred awareness, ask the question, 'Why have I taken birth?' Breathing more deeply into your heart, listen closely. Repeat the question several times if needed. Receive what comes into your whole being. Feel gratitude for the insight and clarity that you receive."

Make note and keep your heart open to receive what comes to you not only now, but in the hours and days to come.

FEBRUARY 26

Prodigal Shift

"Sometimes I wrestle with my demons.
Sometimes we just snuggle."
—Unknown

The word demon is derived from the Greek word daimon meaning "deity, divine power, lesser god, guiding spirit, one's guiding genius, lot or fortune." (Online Etymology Dictionary) Well then, bring on those demons!

Demons, wisely understood and felt, wake us up and call our attention to what remains covered up inside. It's usually what has gone unexpressed or uncreated in us.

Anger is one of these demons. It usually gets a very bad rap. We can't seem to channel it without hurting or scaring ourselves and others and feeling shame or guilt. So, we try to suppress it. This has it's own side effects—depression and resignation among other things. Eventually, it boils over which leads to more side effects. We contract. On and on it goes. If anger goes unexpressed or is expressed in hurtful ways, it hides a deeper truth.

Eventually, on our own or with the encouragement and safe container of a professional or friend or healer or community, we feel the anger and give it voice without it hurting someone. In a ceremony designed to give men a safe and controlled environment to feel their demons, I was asked to stand face-to-face with my twenty-three-year-old son Zach. He was feeling anger and grief regarding some painful events in his life related to me. I could feel the searing pain in his anger. With strong support and coaching from the facilitators, he finally let it all out. This freed him to feel and express what was underneath it—his love for me and his deep sadness for the loss of his life as it once had been. In the end, we cried together and held each other like never before. We lived through this prodigal shift. Something that was lost had been found.

There is a guiding wisdom even from these demons that points toward a wider view of life. Rather than viewing difficult and disturbing events and feelings as if you're stuck inside them, from a supportive container, give voice to these darker energies and find your way out. You discover that the truth has been hidden very nearby. Even darkness can lead to love.

February 27

Remove the Mask

"A mask is what we wear to hide from ourselves."
—Khang Kijarro Nguyen

When being interviewed for seminary acceptance, I eagerly wanted to show up and have the answers to whatever questions were asked by the interviewers. One particular basic question stumped me. I had no idea how to answer it. Be that as it may, I stumbled my way through an answer. My masquerade was an obvious blunder.

Months later, after I had started my seminary training, my faculty advisor, who was also one of the selection committee interviewers, in my first consult with her, said to me point-blank, "When someone asks you a question and you don't know the answer, simply say, 'I don't know. I'll take the time to learn more about this topic.' You will never be all things to all people or have all the answers. You made a fool of yourself."

I had been so fearful of revealing that I lacked the requisite knowledge and understanding of important topics, I was willing to create the illusion of knowing in hopes that my listeners would buy it. My mask didn't work. It couldn't hide the truth. The very thing I feared came upon me. I made a fool of myself.

I believed my vulnerabilities would keep me from my deepest aspirations. This is a common mistake many of us fall into. In my anxiety of not having it all together, I was willing to trash one of my best qualities, authenticity, in order to appear mistake-free.

I clearly learned from this mis-take. When responding to a question with "I don't know," we let the world see our human vulnerabilities which paints a real portrait without surreal tricks. We reveal a comfort with ourselves as we are, an attractive quality in a leader and wayshower. Go ahead and remove your mask.

FEBRUARY 28

One Hour, One Day at a Time

"May the winds of change blow you where you long to go."

There has been enough change and loss in my life this past year to fill a lifetime. At times I have felt this life-sucking vortex of energy overpowering me and rendering me near lifeless. Even in the midst of this, I have been able to find something inside of me. What it is I'm not certain. I keep writing and feeling the pulse of life touching my heart somehow, some way.

The presence of an eagle is with me. I scour for food, food for my soul. I fly in my imagination, going places that bring a brighter light and expand my horizons just enough to carry me forward to the next hour. May the presence of an eagle be with you today.

I'm sitting in beautiful sunshine which is a precious experience in Western Oregon winters. Let the light shine through you today. All of us have found our way through loss and painstaking change. We are pioneers moving through uncharted waters and culling the depths of who we are in order to gather together in our hearts the various essential pieces of ourselves and keep going.

So, stop and listen closely. Feel your heart beating...beating. Breathe your deepest breath. Remember and acknowledge that there is that in you which is greater than that which is in this world. Divine Presence is with you, as you. I join with you in this oneness of Divine Presence today. Blessed be.

Sailing Through it All

"We are vessels designed to be filled with inspiration."

When we set sail toward creating something new, and old inner voices and uncomfortable feelings and stories pop up, how do we respond? I use a simple practice I learned from heart-intelligence coach Christian Pankhurst. It begins with identifying and feeling the feeling associated with the inner voice or story. It could be fear, sadness, loneliness, inadequacy, etc. Then, given that feeling, identify what you really want. This could be something like greater courage, or feeling clarity about your direction, or deeply connecting with a loved one. Once you've identified what you want, let your awareness of it settle into your deep heart.

While staying consciously connected to your deep heart, breathe slowly, and allow yourself to feel what it is like to already be experiencing what you truly want. Stay with that feeling and inspiration and enjoy it for a few moments. Then, decide what simple action step you are willing to take that would support what you want. Consider this in your heart and make note of what comes to you.

Allow your connection to what inspires you to fill your sails. This will supply you with the wisdom and energy necessary to move through your resistance and bring life to your new creation.

MARCH 1

Flapping Our Lips

"Newborns reminded her of tiny buddhas."
—Jodi Picoult

I have loved singing most of my life. Just this week I received my first voice lesson from a professional voice coach. What vocal exercise do you think she wanted me to try? She said, "I want you to put your lips together and after a deep breath through your nose, exhale slowly through your mouth while your lips make a flapping and vibrating sound like babies do." You know what I'm talking about. It's similar to the sound you make when you are exasperated about something or the sound horses make with their mouths.

She demonstrated and asked me to give it a go. There I was ready to elevate my voice and singing skills by blubbering with my lips. My first attempt was weak. I got a bit better the next few times. There was something a bit unnerving about regressing into baby sounds in front of a woman I had known for fifteen minutes. Then, she said that this would be my vocal practice for the week. Supposedly, it helps to strengthen the muscles of my mouth and jaw. So, I've been practicing blubbering my way up and down musical scales and casting spit around.

One thing it has done is change my state. I'm passing this on as a possibility whether you're wanting to strengthen your facial muscles or not. We all could benefit from focusing on making blubbering vibrato sounds. At times it would probably be better for us than other ways we flap our lips.

MARCH 2

A Worthy Cause

"Stand on your story, not in your story."
—Lisa Nichols

I resigned my last leadership role in ministry partly because it was evident that I was succeeding in one area of my life, but other areas had broken down over several years. The connective tissue of the community I was serving was getting stronger. There were small victories in many areas. Things were moving in a good direction. But, inside of me I was coming apart. Incredible time and energy was being poured into my work and financial challenges continued for the community. My health was a concern.

Most importantly, I was increasingly aware that I had outgrown the role I was playing and the spiritual philosophy I was teaching. My integrity was compromised. I couldn't possibly bring my best. My long time marriage had been a consistent struggle to keep alive and fulfilling. It was at a breaking point and so was my life. It was as if the love in me had drained away.

Achieving one victory at the expense of almost everything else is no victory at all. I very reluctantly decided to bring this long cycle of my life to a close—my career in ministry and my marriage. Both endings were painful and frightening. I was leaving behind so much of who I had been for a future that was completely unknown. There was a string of good and loving individuals who were affected and some were confused and hurt especially my wife. But, one thing was solid and clear. I had come to that moment of my life in which I had to be responsive to me, to what my deep heart was telling me. It was time to catch up with my own soul and come to know myself again. Fifteen months later, I am even more clear that I did exactly what was needed for me and for those I loved and served.

We all have met moments like this—big feelings, big fears, big decisions, big changes. Because these crossroads feel so enormous and overwhelming, as I did several times, we back away out of fear. We stay the old course. There is a cost of allowing fear to control our lives. It usually involves various scenarios creating hamster-wheel high stress and painful compromises. The most familiar path is not always the best path. That's a fact.

Neglect can be subtle to see, especially if you have been neglecting yourself and what you love? A life that represents and feeds your whole self is a worthy cause. Serving and giving generously of your time, love, and support certainly has its place. Overdone, it becomes a treadmill of sacrificing and compromising. By all means, love generously and fully, but be sure to include yourself in this circle. Without loving and caring for you, you die slowly. You deserve better. That's the truth.

March 3

Let the World Deal With It

"I am not what others think of me."

My father contracted polio as a small child. The result was a malformed left leg and foot which he has lived with his entire life. He walked with a decided limp. As a child, when I would walk with him in public, passersby would often turn and stare, wondering what might be wrong with him. I never ever noticed my father being concerned or bothered by other people taking notice that he was physically challenged. I was bothered. His condition became the inspiration for living the life of his choosing.

In visiting my father yesterday, I reflected on his example as I pushed him along in his wheelchair under the sunny Colorado sky as others walked by and noticed him lilting to one side. He's clinging to life and unable to walk or speak. I felt a love for him that seemed to have vacated my heart for decades. I was remembering what he had lived with for eighty-six years—all the stares and misdirected judgments that others had laid at his feet. In spite of this, he so often had a broad grin and an appreciation for where he had come from and what he had gone through. He lived the life he had dreamed of.

I kissed his cheek and thanked him for his priceless example of how to live. Unable to speak, he eked out a wry smile.

Most of us fall short of who we have come here to be, because we have become overly concerned about what others might think of us. Live the life you are called to live. Let the world deal with it. The qualities which distinguish you are your wealth.

March 4

Do a Timeout

"I put away childish things."
—St. Paul

You have to do a timeout. When this bit of news is directed at either of my son's daughters they have a huge upset, as if doing a timeout is actually punishment. Ha! Yes, getting quiet, spending time alone, watching through the window as the snow falls, and drawing a picture of the family pet are all certain to be some form of torture. Their screams of resistance would have one think so.

I find that so many grown children still do the same thing. See if this describes you or someone you know and love. They are stressed to the max and almost always over-thinking about what has to be done. They are overworked, overmedicated, and sleep-deprived. When someone dares to suggest that they do a timeout and stop putting the active meter into the red zone and consider taking time and space for themselves or getting help or support, it's as if inside they are screaming, "Oh, no! I can't do that! I'd be banished from the action. Nothing would ever get done. I wouldn't know what to do with myself!"

The loudest voice inside of us often gets the most attention. This sounds so much like the loud voice of a small child not wanting to feel punished by doing a timeout. When we, as busy people, living busy lives, continue on and on to listen to and be led by this inner tyrant of hyperactivity, we are, in fact, punishing ourselves and doing a slow burn. We literally get inflamed. The side effects of this are huge. The physical and emotional effects of inflammation are being revealed by science. Some of us go all the way to burnout. I have. We are attempting to earn some kind of gold badge of recognition and worth.

What a telling admission: "I wouldn't know what to do with myself." That's the whole point in this life. You are here to learn what to do with yourself, how to be with yourself, how to value and love yourself, and truly create the room inside to love and feel the value of others. The voice for sanity within your heart is always there as a thunderous whisper. It's not the loudest, but clearly is the wisest. Listen to your heart.

MARCH 5

I Am Everywhere

"Split a piece of wood and I am there. Lift
a stone and you will find me."
—Jesus

There are very ancient rock formations up a side canyon of the Colorado River near the Utah border that are almost black in color. They are two billion years old. While there, I spoke to them and respectfully touched them. I felt my deep past in that moment. We are all made of the same stuff, fired from a single source, linked in spirit to our countless ancient ancestors everywhere present across the multiverse.

There is a magical forest of live oak trees on Cumberland Island, Georgia. It's as if ecstatic tree music is playing there that humans faintly hear. Endless trees spawn countless twisting branches which undulate and bend up toward the sky and, reaching too far, eventually arch downward and almost kiss the ground. Each branch longs to express itself and stretch to its limits and beyond, always moving in harmony with its surrounding arbor-mates. While there, I got the feeling that there has to be a choreographer. Nothing seemed out of place including me. It's a beautiful cooperation.

The breath of our Source is incomprehensibly sustaining and still breathing fully through all things, as was the case when the master teacher uttered the words above, geologically speaking, only a short time ago.

There is one life, one presence, one spirit, ancient and new, forever with you. As you breathe slowly and deeply, feel your heart open and allow yourself to receive this truth today. Feel a renewing strength growing in you now.

March 6

Pull Up Anchor

"I am the only one who can tell the story of
my life and say what it means."
—Dorothy Allison

I gather together what is left of my possessions and haul them into a 10' x 10' storage unit. Most of my old household belongings, photos, and keepsakes are discarded and left behind. A few I keep and hold dear. Less and less does my past define me and determine the story of who I am. I appreciate being here.

We can slip into spending too much time and attention looking at past events and defining ourselves based on the meaning we've given them. The best personal example I can come up with is: "My mother didn't display affection toward me when I was a child and teen, therefore, I am not lovable." Is this actually true? No. Yet, for the longest time, I allowed this story to be the stage from which I acted out my life.

Is it possible to look at events of the past without attaching meaning to them and final judgment on ourselves? Of course. You and I get to define today who we are and what stories we create about ourselves. This is the transition inside from seeing ourselves as someone trapped in a script imagined in the mind of a confused child to someone choosing to be a wise caretaker of our sacred identity. It's the commitment to shift from being powerless to being powerful.

Tell your story. Bring your heart to it, the kind of heartfelt truth that has a roar. The past and its stories shape and teach you, but need not define you. You are always much more than the story of your life. Pull up your rusty anchors from old familiar harbors. Let your story and all its episodes arrange what you feel and think so that you sail across the waters of your past from a new vantage point of your most amazing life.

MARCH 7

Love Your Enemies

"I love you without knowing how, or when, or from where."
—Pablo Neruda

A minister gave a talk on forgiving our enemies. He said to everyone present, "Let's all forgive our enemies. Let's do it now. A prayerful silence enveloped the room. He then said, "Is there anyone who has still not forgiven their enemies? There was a pause. Then, an old woman in the back raised her hand. The minister responded, "How come you haven't forgiven all your enemies?" She replied, "I have no enemies." "Wonderful. Please tell us about how it is that you have no enemies," said the minister. She proudly answered, "I outlived the bitches!"

Being fortunate enough to outlive others is one way to arrive at having no enemies. This is certainly not the transformational approach. It has been said many times in many ways that the beginning of the resolution of the enemy question is to recognize it is within ourselves. Noted Jungian psychoanalyst John Sanford writes, "We carry the enemy in our hearts. We hate the enemy because it contradicts us."

Staring through a glass divider at the local jail, I listened to a broken man feeling powerless to change his experience. He murmured, "I can't get out of my own way." His deep disgust with himself was palpable. He clearly embodied his own worst enemy.

This shadow, the unknowing of what is really creating your experience, is maddening. However, your heart knows. It knows that you are not right with yourself. You can't outlive what is inside of you that you haven't yet faced.

Where there is an inner enemy, an inner critical voice, there is always a great love. This presence of love will outlive all of us. Bring your inner enemies face to face with this love. What you have rejected or hated within you is simply crying out for love. From your heart, ask that this love flow into ALL the dark spaces inside of you. This is a great beginning to getting out of your own way.

MARCH 8

Get Some Sky

"Pain has a way of clipping our wings and
keeping us from being able to fly."
—Wm. Paul Young

After many consecutive days of rainy, cloudy weather in Western Oregon, the sun made an appearance. It was confirmed that the sky behind the clouds was still there. I noticed when standing at my window looking toward the blue sky in the distance that there were two hawks circling and soaring. They continued to go higher with each circle of their upward-moving spiral. Eventually I lost sight of them.

They seemed to be expressing their pent-up nature to soar after being grounded for such a long time. I imagine their instincts knew that this time of year the clouds and rain would likely return very soon, so don't hold back. Stretch those wings and get some sky while it's there.

Feeling the exhilaration of stretching out beyond, maybe even far beyond our auras of pain and suppression is a ramp to joy. What is being suppressed within us does not serve us or those we love and cherish. That which remains unexpressed and unmoved is not our friend. There is a time for everything even that which is crying to come out.

March 9

Music is Everywhere

"The hills fill my heart with the sound of music.
My heart wants to sing every song it hears."
—Oscar Hammerstein

My eldest sister Diane left this earthly plane in 2003. She was an accomplished pianist and organist among many musical gifts. In our household, the piano was often sounding into the ethers. Diane was a devoted student and practiced tirelessly. Much of the time, she would play in phrases and repeat them again and again, feeling her way into the essence of each composition. Eventually, the whole piece would come together.

My favorite piece that she learned and played often was Frederic Chopin's breathtaking Etude, Opus 10, #3 in E major. It always urges my heart to open. It is pure beauty. Chopin noted that this piece was the most intimate piece he had ever composed, stating that, "In all my life I have never again been able to find such a beautiful melody." I so deeply appreciated Diane's love for great music combined with her tenacious effort to learn and perfect her art. Her piano expressions are still very much with me today.

The ancient Greek muses (from which the word music is derived), were goddesses who presided over the arts and sciences and were believed to inspire all artists, especially poets, philosophers, and musicians. My sister was my very first muse and her music is in my soul to stay. All you muses of the musical arts, I love you. You are my bliss buddies.

To you my precious readers: remember, music is always with you. It truly is a gift from the goddesses and gods in our collective family. Let the joy of music take your heart today and heal you in whatever way is needed.

March 10

Detours

"I have lived on the lip of insanity, wanting to know reasons,
knocking on a door. It opens. I've been knocking from the inside."
—Rumi

Most all of us relate to the feeling of life happening to us. S..t happens. Powerlessness can set in. Truth is, it's not so much about the experiences we are having, but rather the conclusions we make about our experiences. These conclusions then serve as the lens through which we generate a whole set of related feelings and thoughts. Our conclusions about what has happened to us creates its own inner ecosystem which flows into everything else and may be life-giving or toxic.

There is a very wise saying: "What you think of me is none of my business." As a minister for many years, one of the hazardous tendencies was making others' opinions about something I said or did my business. From time to time, this put me on Rumi's lip of insanity. I wanted to know the reasons why. I would literally become others' opinions of me which would hinder my ability to be myself. I allowed it. It was like choosing to head down a long detour and at some point feeling lost. This flaw in me became a powerful teacher.

For any of us flailing around and getting lost, eventually we find our way back. Hopefully, we learn how to remain true and loving to ourselves. Ultimately, what matters are the conclusions about ourselves that we carry on the inside.

It matters knowing who you are in your heart, what you want to contribute to the world, and what your core values are, along with simply not giving power to the criticisms of others. This is authentic self-esteem.

The Whole Mountain

> "Spiritual friendship...companionship...intimacy...
> is the whole of the spiritual life."
> —Buddha

It has been a year since I left behind my twenty-six years in ministry. Numerous friendships and community connections have receded into the background. Most of this year has been spent alone. I'm learning about the other side of the mountain—friendship, companionship, and intimacy with me. I've ventured there on occasion, but prior to this year, never for an extended length of time.

This mountain does have two sides. Its strength and beauty comes from experiencing and feeling the whole of it. There are those of us who have spent most of our lives in service to and in companionship with others and know much less about ourselves. And, vice versa, there are those of us who have spent much of our lives as a lone soul and less time with others.

Each have their beauty and their place and time. One without the balance of the other is like a bird with a clipped wing. It can't fly. It can hop around, but is much more vulnerable to prey. It's unlike a bird.

Buddha taught that living the spiritual life requires a willingness to complete the circle of what it is to be a spiritual being having a human experience. We all feel the imbalance when we spend far too much time and attention on one side of our lives.

I challenge you to find your way to the other side of your mountain. The path that spirals around the whole mountain several times is the only path to the top where we can truly appreciate the full view and wow factor of being human. Love and know your neighbor and love and know yourself. This is the whole of the spiritual life.

MARCH 12

One Heart

"We all see the same sun and we all breathe the same
air and we all feel the earth beneath our feet."
—Unknown

Often while in pain, whether it be physical or emotional, there are those of us who isolate from the rest of the world. We lose our sense of place in the community and disconnect from others. I have been prone to this.

I returned from Colorado a few days ago after being with my son and his two young daughters. He is moving through a difficult divorce and remains the primary caretaker for his two girls.

For the first several months of this experience he largely isolated, not wanting to "trouble" family and friends with his painful tribulations. His emotional suffering and stress led to shut down. As a result, his suffering worsened. Gradually, friends and family rallied and called him out of his isolation. He began to allow others into his space even with his pain. Letting others in was the catalyst for letting out what was trapped inside of him.

This is compassion—letting others in. Essential to compassion for yourself is to pick up your end of the golden thread of oneness and allow others to come into your space and love you, support you, and connect with you. We often do not want to allow others to witness our pain. We may have a particular inbred message which holds onto the distorted belief that letting others see us in pain would be an embarrassment or a show of weakness or vulnerability. Such nonsense.

There is nothing more deeply divine than to know each other in the fullness of our humanity. This way of life elevates us onto the path of feeling the healing power of remembering that we all arise from the same Divine Source, the same beating heart of oneness.

March 13

I Want to Live

"I want to live. I want to grow. I want to see. I want to know. I want to share what I can give. I want to be. I want to live."
—John Denver

My close friend Bill was having disturbing health issues. After a number of tests and doctor exams, it was revealed that he had a very large tumor that had wrapped itself around his brain stem. A neurosurgeon told him it was inoperable. This meant that he would be powerless to do anything about his declining health and the debilitating and increasing side effects of the tumor. He would only have a few months of life left at best and the quality of that remaining time would be poor. Bill called to tell me the devastating news. I attempted to console him.

It was several hours later that Bill called me back. He told me that the neurosurgeon had called him back with a different scenario. Evidently, the surgeon hadn't completely given up and decided to send Bill's x-rays to a colleague. The two of them discussed the possibilities by phone. They concluded it was possible that a surgical procedure might work. It would be life-threatening. There was a 50-50 chance he would not survive the surgery. If he did survive, there was a high probability that he would experience paralysis or other significant nerve damage. So, in the span of an hour or two, Bill went from a death sentence to a ray of hope.

Even with the high risks, Bill agreed to the surgery. For the most part, it was a success. He experienced permanent nerve damage to the left side of his face. He spent several very challenging years in rehab. But, he was able to move forward into the future and walk, talk, see with one eye, hear with one ear, and express himself wisely and well.

Here in 2014, seventeen years after his surgery, Bill is doing remarkably well. He lives with an altered appearance as well as other side effects of major brain surgery. He remains one of the brightest, most insightful individuals I know and clearly the most courageous and inspiring.

Such heart, such a noble and dazzling spirit, is inherent in everyone of us. Pay tribute today to those in your life who, against all odds, found the unspeakable courage to live. Life is an astounding creation.

March 14

Beyond Belief

"This is beyond belief!"

It is common to be asked, "What do you believe?" I don't know about you, but knowledge, information, and creation is so rapidly changing that whatever I think I may believe is running out of breath trying to keep up.

When we have an experience that is extraordinary and amazing, we often spit out the phrase, "That was beyond belief!" When does someone ever ask you, "What's beyond belief in you?" Do you ever recall anyone asking you that? I don't.

What is beyond belief is the realm of all things possible where we feel the awe and wonder beyond words. Life beyond belief is about being who and what we are without the weight of being cast in a mold of belief and being willing to explore the questions beyond the edges of our known selves. Beyond belief is an urgency to be courageous, truthful, and vulnerable, constantly challenging the veracity of the stories that have defined who we are. Reaching for what is beyond belief takes to heart that love is real, but refrains from defining it, yet is always opening wider to its undiscovered dimensions.

Pause and turn your attention in this moment to whatever creates in you a feeling of awe and wonder: nature, new technologies, unconditional love, acts of courage, art—whatever creates this feeling in you now. It is this quality of experience that could stand to spread out into your life and move the needle on your beyond-belief-meter.

Tightly-held beliefs can be detrimental to your health. That which is beyond belief is a powerful friend.

MARCH 15

For or Against

"We do not need different individuals in power, so much as we need a different kind of power in individuals."
—Michael Nagler

I read another article today on a new movement against something. In valiant attempts to make a difference in the great concerns of our day, movements have formed to establish "The War on..." or "XYZ Against...." When we create organizations and ideas that are fundamentally fighting and warring against some kind of enemy, be it injustice or drunk driving or drugs or poverty or cancer or wars or, the latest, alzheimer's disease, my life experience has taught me that what I strongly resist persists and, ironically, it often grows.

Any one of these movements would be considered sincere and mostly well-intentioned. But, does it work to resolve and change the illnesses of our world through going to battle with them? I'll let you be the judge.

Let me bring this point home to our daily lives. Let's say you are addicted to alcohol. It's slowly destroying what has been most important to you especially your relationships with your loved ones. We know that if you become hell-bent on fighting it, you'll lose. It is a near 100% certainty that using your willpower and intellect to stop it will not work. No matter how much effort and gnashing of teeth you throw at it, you will end up spinning your wheels.

In A.A., the first step to success is to stop fighting it and admit that this approach renders you powerless. This gets you started down a path of sorting out what will work, who you are, and what truly inspires you to act wisely and bravely on your behalf.

So, I leave this for you to simmer on today. If you are a danger to yourself and others, reach out and get the help, support, and protection you need now. Otherwise, I ask you to please consider these questions. What do you stand for? What taps your deepest wells of inspiration and common spiritual sense? These questions can form the tourniquet to begin to stop the bleeding caused by fighting against so many things so much of the time. It's exhausting, expensive, and, at best, marginally effective.

Align with ageless spiritual wisdom and the laws of nature and the universe by acting upon what you stand for and treasure rather than what you are fighting against. Let this serve as the genesis of energizing you to take inspired action that brings lasting change.

MARCH 16

Out of the Nest

"To be fully alive, fully human, and completely awake
is to be continually thrown out of the nest."
—Pema Chodron

While walking along a downtown street among tall buildings, a tiny young bird dropped from the sky onto the sidewalk in front of me. I reached down and picked it up. It was about the size of the palm of my hand. At first, it lay motionless and appeared to not have survived the fall. Not knowing quite what to do, I did what came naturally. I very gently stroked and caressed it between my hands and spoke words of healing love.

After several minutes, it twitched ever so slightly while still lying awkwardly on its side. I continued stroking it and speaking to it with love and reassurance. I couldn't give up on the possibility of life somehow popping forth.

To my surprise, the bird wiggled several times. Then, it halfway leaned into a near-standing pose in my hand and, just like that, flew off into a nearby tree. I was elated. I stood by for several more minutes to make sure it wasn't going to fall to the ground again. To my delight, it stayed perched in the tree.

When we fall, it is our hope that there is someone there to pick us up and hold and caress us for a while as well as whisper to us that everything is going to be alright. We are grateful when a caring heart stays present with us while we feel the shock of what hit us.

Life at times pushes us out of our nest even when we aren't ready. All we can do is fall. This is a test of our metal and willingness to face our fear and be reshaped. I am deeply humbled by all the ways others have been there to tend to me even when I was broken inside and felt lifeless.

Feel the warmth inside for those who have already been there for you when you have fallen and cascaded into fear. Your time will come to return the love. I know that there is more than enough to go around.

MARCH 17

Opening the Gates

"Nothing is enough if fed by scarcity."

I was married with a toddler and another child on the way. I was selling insurance or attempting to anyway. I loathed what I was doing and the results reflected it. After making only one sale over four months, we had run out of money, and I was excavating the bowels of my VW floorboards for stray coins. In my terror and resignation, my pride finally crash landed. At my wife's insistence, I applied for food stamps.

This was a new beginning in which I knew that I could "no longer afford" to be doing something simply for the money. I was having a spiritual and emotional heart attack. Within twenty-four hours, it became clear that the course of my life needed to change. I didn't know where my deep heart was leading. Somehow I was aware that I needed to trust what I was feeling and the guidance I was receiving. I did.

Within a few months, my life was on much more solid footing and heading along a new path. That deep dark well of scarcity was being capped. The feeling of scarcity will grind anyone down. Everyone reading this understands what I mean.

Notice I used the word loath in describing what I felt about my insurance-selling days. It was only a year or so after the VW excavation that I began to make the connection between loathing and my experience of scarcity.

What we carry in our hearts, when weighted down by such deeply destructive feelings, is like placing our lives under siege and being trapped inside a starving village with no escape route. Once the feeling we hold in our hearts truly connects with our soul's aspiration, the inner thieves of scarcity leave, and the gates of our lives open to the natural abundance everywhere present.

Wake up today to any way you may be loathing something or someone. There is likely a direct link with the scarcity that is showing up in some aspect of your life. If this is going on, reconnect in your heart with your soul's aspiration which is completely removed from any feeling or habit of loathing.

Return home to what you are truly called to be and do. Abundance is likely to follow.

MARCH 18

The Way of the Heart

"Oh give these clay feet wings to fly to touch the face
of the stars. Breathe life into this feeble heart."
—Loreena McKennitt

There are moments of truth in everyone's life that invite us to lean into something even if it terrifies us. So, I'm leaning. I'm leaning into the depth and breadth of the heart. To me, the heart is that which sources life's beautiful possibilities even when the whole world seems to be falling over an abyss. This kind of divine enormity that shows up in human form is awe inspiring. Maybe I'm simply too tame. This kind of wild and powerful mastery screws with me. It leaves me staring into my own life and feeling a longing to connect with this kind of resourcefulness.

I know that the way of the heart is not bound by worldly fears and structures. It is sublime and primordial and echoes up from a deep well of remembrance and reminds us: "All things are possible." It is a deep well of creativity, beauty, humility, generosity, love, and courage. This way of being is like having a wisdom teacher in our pocket, showing us how to get out of our own way and be the way of love and wisdom rather than be in the way of love.

Thank you for joining with me as we take each other by the hand and walk into this wilderness together this year. I'd much rather have my tribe go along with me. The way of the heart is before us. Divine Presence be with us.

March 19

Collapsing the Old

"I give you this to take with you: Nothing remains as it was. If you know this, you can begin again, with pure joy in the uprooting."
—Judith Minty

A black hole in deep space begins with the death of a star collapsing in on itself. Where the star used to be, gravity becomes infinitely powerful and everything that approaches this vortex gets sucked in, even light. Theoretically, matter then contracts into a single point, infinitely dense, infinitely small. Even time comes to an end. This reality startlingly resembles the conditions for a big bang, a massive explosion of energy which marks the beginning of a new universe.

This is how energy moves in us. When we allow the death, sometimes gradual, of our life as it has been, we begin to experience more and more the overwhelm of too-muchness. Our sense is that our hopes and dreams are collapsing. We feel the weight of this collapse. The greater the sense of collapse, the more powerful the pull toward self-destruction. The feeling is one of being sucked into something that is out of our control—a black hole. We feel heavy, contracted.

Then, as many of us know, we "hit bottom." From that point of utter hopelessness, there emerges the paradox of enormous latent power to create a new life.

This is a powerful, beautiful truth. The ongoing movement of creation is unstoppable even when we are tumbling into what feels like a black hole. Only by surrendering to the death of old patterns and identities do we create the conditions for a new beginning.

Quietly give attention in this moment to what is needing to collapse in you. It is time for something about you to die so that you may live. This death is the starting point for a burst of new creation through you. Feel this new creation swiftly approaching you like the light from a nearby star. It is infinitely powerful, infinitely new.

MARCH 20
True Help

"Listen to the heart deep within."
—Paul Levine

We're with someone struggling and in pain and like an uncontrollable reflex we scramble to try and fix the problem. How quickly we forget what it is to be helpful. We assume that we're supposed to come up with solutions.

Much of the time, the most helpful thing to do is just listen with the heart. I recognize that most of the time when I'm letting loose with something upsetting inside, the last thing I want from the listener is to be treated like a fixer-upper. I simply want to get what is inside of me out and to nestle into another's nonjudgmental presence.

We all have the deep need to get out of our heads and fall into the softness of life from time to time. Let today be one of those days for you.

MARCH 21

The Squeezed Juice

"Love...with all your heart...."
—Jesus

The Dalai Lama says, "The highest perfection of altruism, the ultimate altruism, is Bodhicitta complemented by wisdom. Bodhicitta, the aspiration to bring about the welfare of all sentient beings and to attain Buddhahood for their sake, is really the distilled essence, the squeezed juice of all the Buddha's teachings."

Jesus confronted us with these words, "Love your enemies and pray for those who persecute you, so that you may be children of your Father in heaven; for his sun rises on the evil and the good, and he sends rain on the righteous and on the unrighteous." (Mt. 5: 44-45)

Whether the path is one of a Buddhist serving the welfare of all or being a follower of Jesus fulfilling the call to flow love to everyone no matter what they've done, we all know that there are those among us who more clearly master the calling to serve and love.

My friend Jesse from Savannah, despite being physically devastated by the merciless effects of diabetes and in her last moments of life, openheartedly said to me, "I love you." Her words went directly into my heart.

Have we come here to love and serve and be bodhisattvas or devoted disciples of the heart in our own unique way? If you've forgotten or been caught up in life's detours, stop for a few moments and consider "the squeezed juice" of why you are here? The answer for all of us is always in some fashion learning to bend our will, our passions, and our purpose toward love.

Let this be the template for your day and your life.

MARCH 22

Respect or Revenge

"What we do to everything, we do to
ourselves. All is really One."
—Black Elk

Throughout my junior high and high school experience in Texas, I played quarterback on the football team. Quarterbacking often put me in a defenseless position. I was on the receiving end of vicious tackles and body blows.

My last year of high school, I asked my coaches to give me a chance to play defense, to be one of the ones delivering the aggression on others. At first they didn't think that I had it in me to be the aggressor. I proved them wrong. They discovered that I had an underlying aggression that even surprised me. I realized that I had a great deal of pent-up anger at being smacked around as quarterback for so many years. I was very eager to return the punishment to my opponents. In fact, I excelled at throwing myself headlong into others.

However, when I was off the football field, any tendency to harm another was unnatural to me. That contrast was disturbing. One moment I was prepared to deliver blows on others. When off the field, I would seek to be understanding and respectful of another.

Seeking revenge or reciprocity does harm to both the giver and receiver. In the philosophy and art of aikido there is an attitude of respect for all things at all times. Furthermore, aikido teaches that in all situations, whether it is friend or foe, always be ready to harmonize.

This attitude of respect greatly determines the effectiveness of the action we take.

So, what would help you disarm and truly do unto others as you would have them do unto you? The answer to this question could change your life and our world. In Sufism, the golden rule is this: "If you haven't the will to gladden someone's heart, then at least beware lest you hurt someone's heart, for on our path, no sin exists but this."

MARCH 23

Silent Depths

"Speech is the voice of the heart."
—Anna Quindlen

Each of us is drawn to a unique resonance and vibration. The specific manifestations each of us love in this world including the music, people, colors, art, nature, homes, animals, and activities, are simply outer reflections and extensions that match our identity.

Discovering and communicating from our true voice is another way of creating a match. We pop the bubble and come out to be heard. It's raw and barrier breaking. It's a way of truly being ourselves.

To find our true inner voice and then be able to share that with others has significant transformative effects in every area of our daily lives. One simple practice to jumpstart a connection with our true inner voice is born from a fact about all great music. All great music is born from silence.

When preparing to say something of real import no matter the setting, before uttering a word, bring your energy and mental attention to your heart. While breathing with that focus, maintain silence for a few moments. Then allow the words to begin to flow out of that silence even if you have no preconceived notion what you are going to say. Nothing is contrived or rote. This is a trust exercise which could very well be the most critical aspect of the search for your true voice.

It always begins within the silent depths of your own heart. Let it go. Let it flow.

MARCH 24

A Life-Changing Birthday

"She became a living, loving soul."

Nothing alters our personal reality more than the births of our children. My daughter Hillary was born six days after my twenty-second birthday. Her birthday is today.

She was a forceps delivery. Parental mistake number one was giving the pediatrician permission to use forceps. For many years, every time she cried, got emotionally upset, or felt tired, a big red spot would appear next to her right eye. The forceps had damaged those facial tissues. Parenting is an experiment with consequences.

Love is also an experiment with consequences. Nothing compares to the love a parent feels for a child. A fourteen-year-old child may be hurling objects and penetrating verbal daggers at a parent, but that deep core parental love for the child remains as does the child's love for the parent.

Hillary was an amazing gift of grace to raise. There was rarely a glitch in her loving and considerate behavior. There have been occasions when throwing things at me would have been fitting, but she didn't. Even words of disdain never came my way, at least not within earshot. Thank you Hillary! I am grateful for all the ways you expressed your love for me even with all my imperfections.

Great love sometimes has great pain squeezed out of it, but the love rests solidly in that sacred sanctuary of the heart. Earthquakes are powerless to alter the real and seemingly mythical power of love that flows between a child and parent.

There's a reason why Jesus described the Divine Presence as "Abba" meaning "Daddy." I suppose that he felt an unbreakable bond of love and affection with this Divine Presence that only a child and parent could understand. God was no longer an authoritarian commander-in-chief, but rather an unconditional loving presence. I rest in this sweet love for my daughter Hillary, a beautiful soul.

May this same sweet love move through you today and back to those you cherish..

MARCH 25

Divine Presence

"You have a unique divine signature."

Healing is taking place everywhere all the time. Consider in your life all the ways healing takes place, or expressed in another way, notice all the ways the inherent wholeness in the universe is putting things back together again.

Whether it is a skin wound, or a passage through emotional turmoil, or true forgiveness in a relationship, or fear turning into love, or cells rejuvenating, or deep breathing transforming stress into relaxation, or a homeless person finding a home, or someone receiving a new hip, or releasing an old worn-out belief about yourself or someone else, or observing tiny seedlings beginning to grow after the earth is scorched by fire, or experiencing a disease morph into health, Divine Presence is always breathing new life into this experience we share.

Tap this awareness, the awareness that is finely tuned to the regenerating nature of divine life everywhere present. Be enfolded in this garment of wholeness formed out of unconditional love. This sends a message to your heart, mind, body, and emotions to recalibrate, to vibrate the fullness of life, the life of Divine Presence. This Divine Presence has a definite signature that becomes the new you in which disease or discord simply cease to exist. The secret is being able to feel this presence, this awareness, this Divine Presence within and around you.

Meditate on these things. Preface your quiet time with whatever mantram or phrase or sacred scripture that elicits this feeling in you. Then, let your quiet time spill over into the rest of your life so that this vibration of Divine Presence is with you always.

MARCH 26

Spiral of Abundance

"One heart beats for all...All hearts beat for one."
—J. V. Hart

There is an abundance of life in the universe. Abundance by nature generates more of itself. Even if you aren't spiritually oriented, you get it. It is like love. The more you feel it and share it, the more love grows inside you and returns to you. There is a cosmic harvest waiting to happen all the time. There is a source-field from which arises infinite dimensions of creation. We are always in the midst of this field creating something. Always.

Ageless spiritual wisdom and physicists now confirm that our thoughts and emotions are clearly interconnected and creative. If we amplify and generate judgments, fears, projections, and chaotic emotions, then more and more we become aligned with these energies. The same holds true with constructive thoughts and emotions generating love, kindness, resourcefulness, cooperation, and joy. At the level of consciousness, we are certainly in this field of abundant activity together.

Knowing this, we can still fall prey to abandoning our hearts and participating in a flood of agonizing foolishness. Or, we can learn ways to stay in our hearts and be a player in mobilizing the inspiration to experience and pass on the gift of unlimited abundance.

In the silence of your heart, hold the image of a spiral. Arising from the center, see endless bands of creative energy turning and rippling out into the present moments being experienced throughout the universe.

Feel and visualize this wavelike movement of abundance. One heart is beating through all of life. In this same awareness of the spiral of life, see and feel all expressions and cycles of life moving together toward one and the same point of common good in the center. All hearts are beating as one.

MARCH 27

What is a Friend?

"I will tell you. It is a person with whom you dare to be yourself. Your soul can be naked with him (her). He seems to ask of you to put on nothing, only to be what you are. He does not want you to be better or worse. When you are with him, you feel as a prisoner feels who has been declared innocent. You do not have to be on your guard. You can say what you think, so long as it is genuinely you. He understands those contradictions in your nature that lead others to misjudge you. With him you breathe freely. You can avow your little vanities and envies and hates and vicious sparks, your meannesses and absurdities and, in opening them up to him, they are lost, dissolved on the white ocean of his loyalty. He understands. You do not have to be careful. You can abuse him, neglect him, tolerate him. Best of all, you can keep still with him. It makes no matter. He likes you. He is like fire that purges to the bone. He understands. He understands. You can weep with him, sin with him, laugh with him, pray with him. Through it all— and underneath—he sees, knows and loves you. A friend? Just one, I repeat, with whom you dare to be yourself."
—C. Raymond Beran

A friend presented the gift of these words to me in a lovely frame. It has been with me ever since. I keep it in a conspicuous spot in my office as an ever-present reminder of unconditional love. May something in it speak to you and remind you of friends past and present as well as prepare you for friends yet to come

Take time out this week and remember to touch your gratitude for every expression of friendship that has come your way in this life, from two-legged ones, four-legged ones, and the universe.

MARCH 28
The Breath of God

"When we're holding big parts of ourselves back, it's hard to be
loose and natural. And when we're holding something as big
as the breath back, it's impossible to be free...we've rendered
the soul homeless. It can't breathe, exist, or move disconnected
from the body. The body is the womb of the soul."
—Gabrielle Roth

As an ongoing practice, conscious, slow, deep breathing has become a cornerstone of my life and sense of well-being. It's like sturdy tracks to a train. Without them, the train, like life, struggles to fulfill its purpose and go where it needs to go with confidence through all kinds of conditions. Derailing may occur.

Practicing conscious deep breathing as a way of life changes us. It slows down the fast-paced agitations of our minds as well as relaxes our bodies. Slow, conscious, deep breathing provides greater energy, keener brain function and ease of movement.

Going further with this, breath has ancient mystical roots. When responding to a woman's question about the nature of worship, Jesus answered in his native language of Aramaic, "Alaha ruhau." (John 4:24) This has been traditionally translated into "God is spirit." In the Aramaic language, the word ruhau meant spirit or breath. "God is breath" evokes a powerful connectivity with the breath we breathe every second of every day. This recognition and connection with breath is like a form of worship.

Give it a try. With your inner voice, breathe in "God is"(or the Divine Presence is or I am) and breathe out "breath." Breathing then becomes more than supplying oxygen to your body and dumping carbon dioxide. It is the means, like meditation, of generating an ongoing illumination of your spirit, as well as the divine spirit in others and the world around you. You experience everything energized with the breath of Divine Presence.

March 29

Healing What Hurts

"What are you if the people who are supposed to
love you can leave you like you're nothing?"
—Elizabeth Scott

When I discovered that someone dear to me had violated a sacred trust, it crushed me inside. I distinctly remember telling myself something like, "I can't allow my feelings to spill out or be thrown out at this person because my life and the lives of those depending on me would descend into chaos."

I created a defense physiology. I armored myself to protect me and others from the pain, fear, and anger I felt. Along with that, I did everything I could to resolve my insecurities about this relationship. I worked three jobs, about seventy-five hours a week. I continued my evening college coursework in spite of having so little time to actually study.

What could I do to convince this person that I was worthy of her love? I gave it my all, but this was a design doomed to failure.

A number of years later, I chose to go for what I truly wanted to do with my life. In the beginning, it was met with support. Eventually, it was not. My fear of abandonment, which took over my inner world years before, was realized. She no longer wanted me in her life.

From that moment forward, my life became about healing this wound and unwinding the fear and pain that had sent me into defense and overcompensating for not feeling loved. I needed ministering to. As I later realized, I jumped through numerous hoops to become a minister in order to not only minister to and empower others, but to be ministered to myself.

This is often why you and I choose to serve in the ways we do. There is an unmet need or healing that awaits us. Our chosen path gives us the opportunity to wake up to what is really taking place inside. We can discover a divine kind of order in it all, if we have the willingness and courage to have all things brought to the light of wisdom and understanding. Pain and fear can be transformed into strength and love. I know this to be true.

MARCH 30

Choice Point

"Sometimes the dreams that come true are the
dreams you never even knew you had."
—Alice Sebold

While working in Glacier National Park, Montana, I made a side trip to neighboring Waterton Lakes Park in Alberta, Canada with my parents who were visiting from Texas. On our way to Canada, we decided that we wanted to make a stop in the village of Waterton. We arrived there midday in the bright sun and took in the breathtaking views of surrounding mountain peaks and pristine Waterton Lake. We noticed a lovely Swiss-style hotel on a high spot overlooking the lake and decided to turn onto the long drive leading to its hilltop perch.

As we were getting out of our vehicle in the hotel parking lot, to our surprise, a helicopter descended and landed on an open grassy area nearby. Several men in coat and tie exited. Another man in casual attire exited behind them. They walked toward the hotel and we entered the lobby just behind them.

When I got close enough to get a good look at the one dressed in a casual western shirt and tie, I immediately recognized he was Canadian Prime Minister Pierre Trudeau. After asking around, we were told that Trudeau was simply making a quick appearance and social stop in Waterton to meet and greet some of the locals and tourists—a bit of political goodwill.

Trudeau stood on a spot at the far side of the lobby where a microphone was ready. He said a few words and offered to greet and meet anyone who wanted to come forward. The three of us immediately went to stand in line. When it came our time, I shook the Prime Minister's hand and introduced myself along with my parents and told him we were from Texas. I still remember his firm handshake and warm smile of greeting. He thanked us for coming to his country.

My father, who couldn't resist such a grand opportunity to lay a story on a head of state, in his friendly Texas drawl, proceeded to twist some yarn about this being his first time in Canada and that the Prime Minister seemed like a good man. Trudeau politely thanked him. This was my conservative Republican father out-of-the-blue speaking to the liberal poster boy Trudeau and chalking one up for human cooperation. My mom snapped a photo of the two shaking hands and grinning widely like long lost brothers. It was unforgettable how this moment fell into our laps.

Walking away from the hotel only minutes later, we watched as the helicopter lifted off with the Prime Minister aboard, leaving behind the fortunate few who just happened to be in the right place at the right time. We marveled at how all the small choices we had made that day had led to this moment of connection with the political leader of Canada.

What awaits us each day is a mystery. When we move our choice point, or viewpoint, or trajectory of understanding one degree, it often leads to radically different outcomes. Surprising opportunities are freed up to come into the circles of our lives.

It is some kind of unwritten principle of creation—stay open and allow yourself to be led. Then prepare to be favorably surprised.

MARCH 31

A Twist in Perception

"There is a crack in everything God has made."
—Ralph Waldo Emerson

Surging up through a large crack in the earth's surface high up in Oregon's Cascade Mountains, a great flow of water emerges from underground to form the headwaters of the McKenzie River. Having passed through layers of volcanic rock which serve as a perfect filter, this water is some of the purest on earth.

It meanders about ninety miles downhill mostly through dense forests of towering evergreens and then disappears into the Willamette River. From there the Willamette River flows northward through a wide Oregon valley into the great Columbia River at Portland which flows northwestward wide and deep. Eventually, these waters empty into the cold waters of the Northern Pacific Ocean just past the picturesque city of Astoria.

This synchronized relationship has been ongoing for thousands of years, at least eight thousand of those years as home to native peoples. Natural bounty and beauty have been a mainstay here. These sacred waters are nourishment for body, soul, and spirit.

We all have cracks caused by insecurities or painful events. These cracks in us lend themselves to becoming larger openings out of which emerge an ever-renewing flow of wisdom and energy to shape our lives in new ways. Rather than being our adversaries, let's allow our imperfections to be the catalysts to open us to the rich surprises which lay underneath.

This twist in perception provides the perfect filter through which your life's purpose is clarified. A higher power is revealed.

Feel your way into your heart today. Make conscious note of one of the cracks in you. Standing back from it as if viewing a work of art in progress, look closely with an open heart. What do you see? What are you ready to discover and express that lies underneath the surface? Hold this awareness with love.

APRIL 1

Do a Lucinda

"There is great heart in this world."

In September 2005, thousands of members of our human family were devastated. They lived in the lower ninth ward of New Orleans. Soon after, I found myself volunteering in a relief shelter serving food to homeless hurricane Katrina survivors who had been bussed 500 miles to Fort Worth, Texas.

There was one particular woman I'll never forget. Her name was Lucinda. She had become separated from her three children in the chaos of the hurricane's aftermath. She didn't know where they had been taken. Nothing was left. All her things from her former life had been left to rot in the storm waters. With nothing and no place to go, she was put on a bus bound for Texas. For the week or two that I served meals, each time I served Lucinda, she would always show a caring smile and say, "Thank you. You're beautiful."

Eventually, one day I went and sat next to Lucinda in the shelter dining area. She opened up and told me her story. Diabetic and heavily overweight, she described scraping a life together as a single mom of three children. Then came the retelling of the terror and hurricane force winds and rising waters in her home and the frightening separation from her children who had been staying with a friend when the hurricane hit.

She then did a graceful pirouette and asked me about my life and if I was happy. She was genuinely asking **me**, this guy she had just met who was well cared for, how I was doing?! Oh my! When I got up to leave, once again came the words, "Thank you. You're beautiful."

I don't know what eventually happened to her or her children. Tears well up every time I remember Lucinda's beautiful spirit. Even in the midst of devastation, the spirit within certain souls is astonishing. May this spirit rise up in powerful and truly helpful ways for anyone among us who is experiencing great loss.

The next time someone helps you or serves you, rather than taking that overture for granted—do a Lucinda—and say, "Thank you. You're beautiful." Or, simply do a Lucinda because you want to make a contribution to the greater good for all. Thank you. You're beautiful.

APRIL 2

What If?

"And forget not that the earth delights to feel your bare
feet and the winds long to play with your hair."
—Kahlil Gibran

A former traveling musician and acquaintance of mine had a momentous event take place in his family. His mother won a $336 million powerball jackpot. She purchased the winning powerball ticket at her local convenience store while my friend was buying some rainbow sherbet.

Well, I have rather snobbishly declared that I don't waste my time and money on buying lottery tickets. I even made an ethical stand against supporting lotteries because they become another form of gambling and contribute to the destruction of lives and families. Of course, there is a brighter side to this issue. Monies get poured back into communities, providing much needed services and improvements.

I am aware that many of us, including me, have a strong work ethic. At age eight, I began working for my father in the summer, making and pedaling snow cones in the Texas heat. I married young and had two children by age twenty-four. Most any bent toward play took a back seat to work and discovering what I was here to do and be. To allow myself to do something for pure fun and enjoyment has not come easily.

Play is the choice to lighten up, loosen up, and laugh it up. In balance with all things, what if we were to play more? What if?

What I know is, if you or I choose not to play except when pushed and shoved into it, our health and heart suffer. Playfulness contributes to our quality of life and opens us to love more freely and show up with greater aliveness. There may even be a jackpot waiting. Let's play!

Spiral of Inspiration

"The mountain air is beautiful in the sunset...and the birds flocking
together return home. In all these things there is real meaning,
yet when I want to express it, I become lost in no-words."
—Tao Yuanming

For many years I have led group meditations. Often, these meditations would take place immediately before giving a talk on a spiritual theme. During the meditation, if I was able to open to the inner deep quiet, I almost always felt better prepared to speak and draw on the wisdom beyond words. I found this to be true as well when preparing to write or sing. Some way to open to and receive inspiration is needed.

Our almost unlimited access to great ideas and endless information doesn't change the truth that authentic and meaningful living, loving, and communicating can't be forced. Inspiration is required and can't be manufactured or faked.

True inspiration is about feeling our connectedness to the universe and its infinite, immeasurable, dazzling qualities. Divine Presence is not something we control. We draw from it in order to celebrate being human. An inspired human, who truly lives to serve the greater good in this world, is as divine as unconditional love.

We eat and sleep to survive. We live to be inspired and to inspire others. Our sources of inspiration have no end and lie in wait for our hearts and minds to open and receive. And so it goes.

APRIL 4

Simple Presence

"Better by far to see the simplicity of raw silk's
beauty and the uncarved block."
—Tao Te Ching

So many of us have indulged in the complexities of modern culture and felt the unnerving anxiety of this way of life. Countless times, after sitting with those overwhelmed by some complexity, rather than add to the complexity, I would do my best to have my response be simple. The intent is to significantly slow down the wheels of anxiety.

For example, I may ask if I can place my hand on that person's shoulder. Or, I make certain I sustain eye contact. Or, I give an understanding nod. Connect in some simple direct way. This helps to bring any mental activity to a slow simmer. We breathe into the bond that we begin to feel. Then, the moment opens to simple presence. (SP)

Further along in verse forty-eight of the Tao Te Ching, it is written, "To attain knowledge, add things every day. To attain wisdom, remove things every day." Being in SP with another removes our minds' need to weave problematic mental and emotional webs which entangle us in unnecessary troubles and hide us from deeper wisdom.

Begin by practicing SP with yourself today. Start with the raw elements. Let connected breathing be your anchor. Be more conscious of each inhale and exhale as they flow one into the other, continuing on through every breath. Simple is powerful.

April 5

Let There Be Light

"Then God said, 'Let there be light,'
and there was light."
—Genesis 1:3

I stood in the interior of the world famous Chartres Cathedral in France gazing at the sunlight sifting through the stained glass windows known the world over for their clear and deep cobalt-blue color. Chartres Cathedral has the largest collection of preserved medieval stained glass windows in the world and receives more than two million visitors a year.

Despite its renown, Chartres became known as one of the dirtiest monuments in France. Centuries of pollution, candle smoke, corrosion, and grime had obscured the radiant colors of its famous windows and severely darkened most interior surfaces.

Thanks to a public outcry by the many who loved this great work of art, contractors have now completed the first phase of a mammoth restoration. Many of the gorgeous windows have been cleaned and repaired revealing their former radiance. The interior is undergoing a thorough cleaning and refinishing to restore this sacred space to its original beauty. Restoration continues.

There are those of us wanting to restore ourselves to former glories. It seems to me that what we are really going for is to have our light shine through as brightly as possible. The age of the body will show and eventually succumb to the years. But, the radiance of our light is not determined by where we are on our personal timeline. Our luminosity is as bright or dim as the cellular love and appreciation we feel and express each day of our lives. It is an interior restoration of the original light established in life from the beginning.

Take some time today to do some restoration. As you breathe into your heart, see and feel the warmth and brightening glow of light within you. Hold that glow for a few seconds. When you exhale, do so slowly. Feel the old grimy energies, which have trapped the light inside of you, breaking up and flowing out of you into the earth. Allow your breathing-action to cleanse and brighten you. Let there be light in you.

April 6

On Fire

> "We would rather be ruined than changed. We would rather die in our dread than climb the cross of the moment and let our illusions die."
> —W. H. Auden

These words of Auden are sobering yet point toward a truth. Change has often been understood as the one thing in the human experience that is certain. If it is biological, or circumstantial, or economic, or opinion, or atmospheric, yes, change is a certainty.

When it comes to truly changing ourselves especially long held beliefs and patterns, it tends to be a different matter. Change is not certain when it comes to these things. That presence and spirit in our lives that animates and inspires us to change may be elusive for some and not for others.

Auden was onto something when he stated that at times we simply need to let our illusions die. One of my personal illusions is that I have no sustainable identity and livelihood outside of being a minister. It is this illusion that has from time to time generated an immobilizing feeling in me. I am compelled, as are so many others, to shatter the hold of such illusions.

This is where the element of fire is so important. It is the burning energy we feel to not be frozen by such illusions, but to stand solidly in the fire of our passion to no longer be powerless to change.

I recall a drill in football which was called "stand your ground." I would be instructed by a coach to create a circle about eight feet in diameter. In full protective football gear, I would stand in the center of the circle. One at a time, a teammate on the circle's perimeter would charge at me and try to knock me out of the circle. After about ten to fifteen seconds, the coach would blow his whistle. Then, another would charge at me. On it went. I had to scratch and claw and feel my inner fire in order to do whatever was necessary to stand my ground and not be moved outside of my circle no matter what force was being applied.

It is this inner fire that is the fuel to burn through any lethargy or fear of purposeful and fulfilling change. It is one of the great gifts of the human experience and our soul's evolution. Find your fire. Call on Divine Presence to fuel your life and assist in burning through what no longer serves you.

APRIL 7

Ending Hostile Takeovers

"What I mean by being centered is experiencing being at
the center of my cosmic web, being aware of my position.
This is really the only place any of us ever are, and it's
important to feel our centrality at the core of it."
—Anita Moorjani

Waking up at 3:30 a.m., it's as if something or someone popped the top off my restless mind. Those annoying gremlins of inanity insanity grabbed the steering wheel of my thoughts and wouldn't let go. They shamelessly paraded me through all the things left undone and needing attention as well as the things from the past that I could or should have done differently as well as things that others have done to me that were hurtful or judgmental. This scenario is widespread in the daily lives of many of us.

How do we unseat these mental parasites? Anita Moorjani, whose near-death experience has been widely discussed, returned here from the other side and offered the following piece of powerful wisdom. Somehow, we must consciously get centered in our lives. Feel the centrality of being firmly in the center of the turning of our wheel. Get clear that this is our rightful place.

This only happens when you move your centerpoint from your brain-mind to your heart. All the forces of heaven and earth then rally to come to your support. This includes the gremlins of the mind. Living from the heart through the consistent practice of heart-centered technologies, greatly eases the tightly strung tensions of obsession overflowing from your mind and causes your heart and brain to become more consistently synchronized. When this occurs, hostile gremlin takeovers are highly unlikely.

When rising in the morning and just prior to bedtime, bring your full attention to your heart. While breathing slowly, feel in your heart the energy of these words: "I am centered in the heart of my life. I relax into deeply knowing that this is where I belong and where I choose to stay."

APRIL 8

Growing Younger

"I think the life cycle is all backwards. You
should die first, get it out of the way."
—George Carlin

There is a photo of me at age seven squinting in the bright sunshine while proudly displaying my white Easter jacket and bow tie. This photo reminds me of the circle of life weaving and spiraling into the future, constantly changing form and appearance. The spiral turns, wisdom evolves, the body ages. Squinting into the sunlight of a new day, we continue to catch glimpses of the wonder and mystery of the spiral of life through birth, death, and rebirth.

The late comedian George Carlin did an infamous comic bit on reversing the life cycle, starting at death and ending with birth. It is hysterical. In his zaniness, Carlin helps to truly shift our perception of the birth-death-rebirth cycles. Life is perpetually calling to us in a powerful way even as we physically age and pass through numerous inner and outer changes.

Author Frank Whitney put it this way: "The early morning dawn discloses to us a new world. In our heart-of-hearts there is a soul cry: 'I too would like to be born again with the morning dawn. I would like to begin again.'" The mystic heart in all of us is attuned to new life superseding the old, new ideas replacing useless and crystallized ideas.

Yes, Carlin, is correct. There is a divine activity in our hearts and souls forever longing to turn chronological time on its ear. The spirit of new life has a potency to wake us up, to ignite the heart and soul to love again, to dance again, to sing again, to celebrate again, to be in wonder again. Receive the unending gift of life today.

Take five minutes to meditate in your heart on the unending spiral of life turning and turning and recreating you now. Give your heart and mind to this truth today and feel the presence of your seven-year-old returning to greet you.

April 9

An Original

"If you're not prepared to be wrong, you'll never
come up with anything original."
—Sir Ken Robinson

Much of the time, creating something original is confounding. For many of us, we still chase after the elusive creative magic. Maybe this is the block. We are chasing after it rather than letting it capture us.

In my spiritual training, I have learned to embrace this piece of wisdom: "It is not I, but it is the Divine Presence in me that does the work." This can be said in many different ways and applied in a wide variety of creative avenues: healing, singing, writing, speaking, performing, loving, pottery making, etc. The above piece of wisdom suggests that each of us has access to a creative muse or genius which transcends everyday consciousness and awaits our undivided trust and attention. We can plug into it. Yet, it remains a bit of a mystery how this transference of energy and creativity occurs.

When strongly feeling the flow of creating, the fear of doing something wrong is put to rest for a while. The voices of perfection and nitpicking are given something else to do. Creating actually is the art of simply being, minus the artifacts of trying to make something happen. It is allowing the cosmos to express itself through us, as us. We become a whisper of Divine Presence making an original impression.

Let that be your prayer today. Invite this endlessness of creativity to come to you and make its home in you. Like an adult asking a child to come closer for an embrace, say with your heart, "Come, come, come. Oh creative spirit...come."

April 10

Heart Appeal

"Dehumanizing is bad medicine."

Once I was in the middle of leading a Sunday service and a man sitting in the back row was speaking out loud for all to hear. Eventually, I had to stop the service and say to everyone there, "Excuse me for a moment." I went to the back row and sat down next to this man I had never seen before. I addressed him like a human being rather than some devilish character. We talked for a few moments and he agreed to continue the conversation outside.

After a few minutes speaking with him outside, it was clear he was disturbed. He needed someone to listen to him as well as guide him about getting the help he needed. We parted amicably and he left. I returned to the service and kept right on with what I had been doing.

When confronted with difficult people in difficult moments, I am reminded of Mahatma Gandhi's teaching of satyagraha which literally means "holding to the truth." Here are Gandhi's words: "It is never the intention of the satyagrahi to embarrass the wrongdoer. The appeal is never to his fear; it is, it must be, always to his heart....He (the satyagrahi) acts naturally and from conviction....Satyagraha is gentle, it never wounds. It must not be the result of anger or malice. It is never fussy, never impatient, never vociferous."

The secret to all this as I see it, is to stand in your strength and stay in your heart. Moving through life in this way establishes a steady inner fulcrum to help with staying balanced when all the world around you has gone mad.

April 11

Pure Delight

"The delight we inspire in others...returns
to us more radiant than ever."

I spent a weekend in and around the hamlet of Manzanita on the Oregon coast. I officiated a wedding ceremony on the beach with the couple and family and friends huddled close together as the cool ocean breezes chilled the evening air. The celebration was thirty-six hours long—pre-wedding, the wedding, several wonderful meals together, walks on the sun-drenched beach, etc. It was pure delight.

Yes, pure delight. This is usually not listed among the "Ten Essential Practices for Enlightenment." However, I just changed my list and deleted "worldly detachment" and added "pure delight." I experienced pure delight for almost the entire weekend. A spiritual leprechaun was cajoling my soul to get with the delight program! Even the vow-of-poverty man, Saint Francis, boldly declared, "Where there is sadness, let me sow joy." Let's get sowing.

Too often, it has been said or inferred that leading a committed spiritual life is a "hero's journey." I value this metaphor to a point. Contemplating the hero's journey gets one salivating about overcoming inner obstacles and slaying the dragons of past mistakes and conjures up images of austerity, hours of prayer and meditation, and a studied, wise, courageous, activist approach to all things. Dionysian festivities and pure delight are not on this kind of spiritual agenda.

How about exquisite food, exquisite silence, exquisite walks in the sun, exquisite music, exquisite reading, exquisite flowers, exquisite relating, exquisite scenery, exquisite time with loved ones? Pure delight is not a sin. The sin (error) is not having more experiences of pure delight.

Well then, let there be delight!

April 12

Aura of Love

"It's love's illusions I recall."
—Joni Mitchell

Gazing into the faces of my children while they were blissfully sleeping, always brought my racing mind to a halt. Love would fall over me. On the tail of this love were tiny whispers of assurance ushering me into an inner chamber in which all seemed right with my world.

I knew they were much closer to the heart of Divine Presence than I. Illusions of love had yet to take hold of their hearts. They were still cleanly bringing love from the other side of the veil.

Illusions of love have so many faces and voices. In the grip of these illusions, we grasp, cling, and judge. Let's just say that these are our human attempts to find and feel what's become misplaced and masked over the years.

Love is love. At times, it's as if a very warm wind blows into our hearts and opens us to feel what's been hidden away. The heart and soul of an unadulterated child stands before us in our deep memory. Most all of us come into this world bearing the truth of what love is and what it is not.

I have a studio photo of me when I was two years old. I'm smiling broadly and looking off away from the camera. For many years, I have kept this aura of me close by, because every time I look upon that face I feel a brush with heaven.

Take to heart today that every moment is pregnant with the truth of you, with a love that has no end—no illusions, no tricks, just love without conditions. Ask with each breath that this love come back to you. Namaste.

April 13

Forgiveness is the Key

"Forgiveness is the key to happiness. Here is the answer
to your search for peace. Here is the key to meaning in
a world that seems to make no sense. Here is the way to
safety in apparent dangers that appear to threaten you
at every turn, and bring uncertainty to all your hopes of
ever finding quietness and peace. Here are all questions
answered; here the end of all uncertainty ensured at last.
The unforgiving mind is full of fear, and offers love no room
to be itself; no place where it can spread its wings in peace
and soar above the turmoil of the world. The unforgiving
mind is sad, without the hope of respite and release from pain.
It suffers and abides in misery, peering about in darkness,
seeing not, yet certain of the danger lurking there."[3]
—A Course in Miracles, Workbook, Lesson 121

Life is what we make of it, an endless array of choices. Forgiveness is one of those choices. It is always available.

Forgiveness is about loosening the grip of fear. This loosening opens the way for the power of our true and caring spirit to reclaim our lives. It is a purposeful movement of our hearts. At times, it feels as if it is not something we can do ourselves. We therefore call upon a greater power, a higher authority within us. We place our hearts in the heart of Divine Presence. This is forgiveness.

Surrender your story of judgment and justification for remaining unwilling to release the source of your bitterness. The perceived alienation between the human and divine in you will then be over. You will be transformed and returned to your rightful place in the center of your heart. You will then be free to fulfill your divine purpose—to love and create with all your heart, soul, mind, and strength. Therein lies your happiness.

APRIL 14

The Perfect Storm

"I live to feel this lightning in the perfect
storm where earth and heaven meet."
—David Wilcox

There are times in life when we simply don't like ourselves. A friction smolders when who we long to be stares into the heart of who we have become. This gap between the two may at times feel like a chasm, a chasm too deep and wide to dare cross. We stand on the edge of this persistent discomfort and struggle to mount a comeback and be the person we truly have come here to be.

My experience reveals that being in integrity with who we have come here to be requires great courage. We can't bypass the courage requirement. We walk all the way through.

One heart-directed practice generates significant strides. It is the practice of feeling the vulnerabilities of fear and doubt as they arise in the midst of approaching life-altering choices. You breathe into your heart and call the Divine Presence to flow into these vulnerabilities. It is like great arms enfolding you and shaking you to your core.

This is the power of divine love, the perfect storm where earth and heaven meet in your very being. Abide there for awhile. Feel this power creating in you the capacity to shed the old hardened skins of conditioning. What is revealed is a more divine likeness which you have waited to see and feel once again.

APRIL 15

Our Human Bond

A woman along with her young son visited Gandhi and asked him to get her little boy to stop eating sugar because it was harmful. Gandhi quickly replied, "Please come back next week." She left confused but then returned with her son about a week later. "Please don't eat the sugar. It's not good for you," Gandhi told the young boy. He then joked with the boy for a few minutes, gave him a hug, and sent him on his way. As the boy scurried off, his mother stayed behind and asked, "Bapu, why didn't you say this last week when we came? Why did you make us come back again?" With a smile Gandhi replied, "I too was eating sugar."

Gandhi was clear that it was essential that he remain connected to his humanity and the humanity in others. He lived this principle no matter one's status or station, even toward his adversaries and those who remained aloof from the people in their exalted places of government or wealth. This eventually led his circle of friendships to include the whole of India and many around the world.

Authentic human connection was the basis for the satyagraha movement in India. Gandhi's willingness to take a stand for our common humanity, whether someone was a devoted follower or staunch adversary, empowered a transformation for millions. He understood that healing our inhumanity was the key to awakening love in every human heart.

Take notice of how you may still be allowing your fear-and judgment-driven inhumanity to block you from experiencing the humanity in another. I hear this inhumanity expressed frequently. When confronted with dislike or discomfort of another, one can easily retreat into name-calling and criticism. We even do this to ourselves.

You've often heard it said, "Where's our humanity?" Well, it's never far away. Look again within your heart.

April 16

A Lonely Voice

"I can hear the echo in a maze of words...a
lonely voice behind a door."
—Emil Adler, Julie Flanders

With the level of activity, busyness, and connectedness, especially in western cultures, I ache when hearing that loneliness is a chronic condition. It has been said that we humans are hardwired for connection. Unfortunately, being around people at home or work, or being socially active, or emailing, texting, or social media messaging appear to be minor factors in being able to avert the feeling of loneliness.

I have often spoken in front of large groups. Even with all that attention, strangely at times I have felt alone and disconnected. I was not connecting with the love or sense of purpose inside of me and therefore not connecting with my listeners. My mind would be active and busy and words would be flowing out, but my heart would be unable to open and receive the love and energy available in the moment. Many of us can relate to this experience even in everyday conversation.

Loneliness often arises out of the experience of not finding meaning in life. Meaning is born of love. Loving another in a heartfelt way adds meaning and value to our lives. Love what we do and meaning follows us. Love what we read or create and our deep heart opens the door to feeling connected to life. Love the beauty of nature's amazement and a sense of fullness pours through us. Love ourselves as beings of value and we discover our place in the world and find little need to hide in our inner isolation through staying busy.

Love and meaning open the doors you hide behind. Start over. Look directly into your eyes today or the eyes of another or let your eyes fall on something beautiful. Stay there for at least ten seconds, preferably much longer. Feel the heart of being connected. Doors will open. Love will rise again.

APRIL 17

I'll Do it Myself

"Give, and it will be given to you. Good measure, pressed down, shaken together, running over, will be put into your lap. For with the measure you use, it will be measured back to you."

—Jesus

A good number of us grew up in a family environment in which our own basic needs for love, caring, and encouragement were not met. Our parents were so absorbed in meeting their own needs that they were unable to do what we expected and deserved. We thought, "If my parents aren't going to freely love and care for me, I'll do it myself. I'll just have to figure out how to get my own needs met."

This was a blow to us, but we managed to get through those years. As we matured and entered into relationships, we struggled with knowing how to stop focusing on our own needs and truly be present with the other in support of their needs. This is a narcissistic trait playing itself out. Addictions often arise.

Look honestly and gently at your life. It is natural and essential for each of us to learn to love and take care of ourselves. However, if this "care and love" creates a wall in us which amputates the empathy to walk in another's shoes for awhile or the ability to love without having to get something in return, we are simply reenacting the disconnection and fear we experienced as an uncared for child.

We are designed to be connected with each other in loving ways. Love is unlimited in its expression throughout all aspects of life. All of us are lovable and loving at heart. Childhood experiences are a melting pot of love and all that is unlike love. In the sorting out, we can choose to claim the gold of love in us at any time.

Reaching out to others without the need to get something back is a practice that truly begins to break down the wall of fear of being left alone and unwanted. As Jesus' words so powerfully emphasize, you will discover an abundance of love overflowing into your lap. Let your walls begin to come down.

APRIL 18

Love is God

"I believe that the human heart...is the best temple."
—Sir Arthur Conan Doyle

The physical heart is an amazing life-sustaining organ whose constancy and energy is awe-inspiring. That heart-centered constancy and energy which sustains and unifies all our physical systems into a marvel of creation, evolved out of a cosmic, life-generating, coherent, powerful, infinite energy. In the ageless wisdom that stretches across various spiritual traditions, this unified field of energy and what it generates could be summed up by three words: Love is God.

The wisdom of the heart, by design, draws from ageless wisdom and distills this cosmic love and energy into usable forms. This allows each of us to readily access this love and transform our daily experience from being an inner battle to being an awe-inspiring healing revelation of how to act, create, and live in ways that de-stress and rebirth us. We then make decisions and communicate in ways that truly help to heal ourselves and our world of the ills of profound fear, helplessness, incoherence, and narcissistic indulgences. We become the frequency and vibration of the infinite love that is Divine Presence.

Throughout your day, carry with you in your whole body and breath that the power of infinite love is your source and inspiration.

See and feel its constancy and circulating energy like a river's source ceaselessly flowing up from underground. It is always with you wherever you are.

April 19

My Beloved's Hand

"Set me as a seal upon your heart."
—Song of Songs 8:6a

While holding my beloved's hand, I could feel a great surge of energy electrifying my whole body. I felt like a tuning fork sounding a perfect note.

Sexual energy has very potent transformative spiritual dimensions. When allowing it to flow, it disarms our defenses. This amazing power has become lost in the many crevasses of society's distorted messages about sexuality.

If you peak around the corner from the shadows of the shaming mainstream mantras about sexuality, you'll discover an ageless wisdom still alive and breathing. Out of this wisdom oozes the following: Sexuality and spirituality are two halves of one whole. Two bodies and two souls who feel a sincere love for one another are primed to sexually join and experience the divine. Heaven and earth, the spiritual and physical, through sexual union, give birth to a new person. Through deep-hearted sexual expression, we discover what it means to love one another and truly make love. It is as if two become one, a divine incarnation.

Arising from ageless sources, this heart-wise message is a big "yes" for many of us. Our collective healing comes when we bring these beautiful truths to our children, families, and communities. A healthy vibrant sexuality births a transformative spirituality and vice-versa. When we are with others, touching, interplaying, and interacting, all is a field in which we have the opportunity to co-create love, to give birth to God particles. Let's bring sexuality into this sacred field and acknowledge that it belongs there, rather than being separated, excluded, demonized, and dehumanized.

Be still. Bring your full attention to your breath. Slowly let your attention center in your heart. Now, with one hand gently placed on your genitals, and the other hand over your heart, send this message from your heart to your sexual organs: "May true love always flow forth from me in sacred and playful ways creating heaven on earth. And so it is."

APRIL 20

Homecoming

"And the Colorado Rocky Mountain high. I've seen it
rainin' fire in the sky. You can talk to God and listen
to the casual reply. Rocky Mountain high."
—John Denver

Starting when I was seven years old, I couldn't wait until early July rolled around every summer. My family and I would pack into our car and head west out of the intense, mind-numbing "heatmidity" of North Central Texas. We would make our way to the northern New Mexico mountains where days were comfortably warm and nights were cool and ripe for campfires. The air and sky were pristine and the waters were clean, clear, and ice-cold. The rippling sounds of stream waters, ever-present pine scent, high altitude air, and views of mountain peaks, left me blissfully happy. My body and spirit felt at home there. I dreaded the return trip to Texas.

I've had a near lifelong love affair with the Rocky Mountains from Taos, New Mexico, to Lake City, Colorado, to the Grand Tetons of Wyoming, to Glacier National Park, Montana. Wherever I've lived, I have always taken these grand places with me in my heart. These one hundred thousand or so square miles feel like my sacred ground.

Both my sisters loved these spaces too and made Colorado their home long ago. Eventually, my mom and dad were moved to Colorado to live near one of my sisters. It seemed fitting, knowing how they initiated us into our high altitude love affair.

Each of us have places we call home. They open a space inside for feeling the sacred. Today, in your heart-space, return home to that feeling. Go to a place close at hand or a place in your imagination which brings you home. It is a feeling, a way of breathing and knowing that being you, just as you are, right where you are, is exquisite and complete. There are beautiful mirrors of this homecoming all around you.

April 21

Being Fully Human

"Keep on walking. Keep on..."
—J.D. Martin

Giving our whole heart to another or to a cause or a new endeavor creates the breeding ground for courage and fear to mix it up. For several years, I would weekly sit in a twelve-step group circle and feel this friction at every meeting. Years later, I was feeling big love for someone and when I took the time to gaze into her eyes and truly feel all that was rising to the surface, that same friction was present. To rise up and give my heart to recreating a new life in the aftermath of a downfall or broken relationship has been an incredibly juicy place for me.

All around the world on this day, billions of us feel fear, the kind of fear ignited by voices inside our heads. This is the busiest, most consequential crossroad in our world—where the fearful voices inside our heads coupled with the resulting apprehensive feelings meet up with the human need to act and move forward with courage and inspiration. This has been called the fiery clash between fear and love, illusion and truth, darkness and light. It's biblical for sure.

We all long to have courage get the upper hand and the fearful voices inside our heads to lose influence and recede. We don't aspire to reduce our life energy to something bucket-sized and submerged in some kind of scary Tolkienesque middle-earth place. We deeply feel our longing to be fully human which occurs as we experience the divine center and expansive circumference of our soul and spirit beyond the reach of fear's poisonous side effects.

Today, make the inner journey in your heart-of-hearts to your favorite power-spot on the planet, a place where you readily access and feel great courage coursing through you. In this place, you are relaxed, supple, and connected to Divine Presence. Grounded here, fear weakens. You are safe. Feel and see your life energy expanding far beyond your physical body. Return here as often as you like.

APRIL 22

A Love Affair

"I feel the earth underneath my feet and all is well."

It's Earth Day. As Americans, we have been gifted a glorious land. Rare in beauty and filled with spaces of unmatched grandeur, the planet Earth expresses itself as a marvel from sea to shining sea in North America. Over millennia, art, architecture, literature, and music have been created to celebrate this most enchanting orb of unimaginable divine presence. Our relationship to Earth is a bond of oneness we cannot deny.

We are its keeper and it is ours. Air, earth, fire, and water continue to be reimagined in countless forms and gilded craftsmanship that testify to the limitless powers of manifestation. This Great Mother is our Mother and we choose to take care of Her in the same way that we are asked to care for our own soul. Earth and all her elements are sacred—"on earth as it is in heaven."

As Aramaic language scholar and spiritual teacher Neil Douglas-Klotz expresses, "*Arha* (an Aramaic word) means 'earth'; in fact, it may be the original source of that word. In sound-meaning, it evokes the sigh of the human species whenever it feels the support of the earth underneath and remembers to treat it as another living being, rather than an object to be exploited."

Join with me this day in sighing with a feeling of great love for this living being we call Earth and the beloved Divine Presence that it embodies. From this Presence we have arisen and it is this love we celebrate at this time, a love so splendid that we are gifted this living space of splendor to inhabit.

APRIL 23

Earth Love

"What can we give the Earth that we haven't given in the past...a way to live here on Earth...make it last and last and last."
—David Roth

It is the time of year when many of us become more attuned to our link in the social-ecological-spiritual chain. It's springtime. Nature's energy is blossoming everywhere. What do each of us offer on the altar of Earth's magnificence?

I offer up these five "green vows" suggested by Joanna Macy to inspire and guide us along our earth journey:

"I vow to myself and each of you:

- To commit myself daily to the healing of our world and the welfare of all beings.
- To live on earth more lightly and less violently in the food, products, and energy I consume.
- To draw strength and guidance from the living Earth, the ancestors, the future beings, and all my brothers and sisters of all species.

- To support each other in our work for the world and to ask for help when I feel the need.
- To pursue a daily spiritual practice that clarifies my mind, strengthens my heart, and supports me in observing these vows."[4]

The earth's bounty continues to pour into our lives each day. Let's ensure this continues far into the distant future. Actions speak much louder than words.

APRIL 24

Your Place Under the Sun

"Your centerpoint is ever-present. Seek and you shall find."

Our love-affair with the natural world inspires us to be **all** that we can be. There is an all-ness about each of us that is framed by reflections everywhere in nature and in each one of us. It's in every set of eyes, in every night sky, in every rush of sun rising.

Soil is what we make of it. We tend and feed the soil of our souls with our hands, our visions, and our intentions. Creation's homing instincts center us in Divine Presence. We get it now. The longing toward home, seen and felt in our world as homesteads, gathering circles, kisses of affection, poetry, knowing looks, warm hearths, and spiritual homilies, always points to this Divine Presence in and around us. It is our cornerstone, our lamp of truth, our fire of creation, a boundless love. Yes, it is the center of the universe, the source of all life, reverberating in our hearts.

Take your place under the sun. Feel yourself in this center where Divine Presence and all its sources of love, wisdom, and support stand ready to claim you as their own.

APRIL 25

Respectfully Yours

"Keep what is yours and leave the rest."

During a high school basketball game, my coach put in a substitute for me and sat me on the bench next to him. He looked me straight in the eye and said, "I'm not going to play you if you aren't going to give your best effort. It's obvious you're not. Sit here and think about it awhile." Even though I was irked, I respected him and, after a short time of sitting there, I knew he was right. As one of the key players on the team, I began to focus on how it felt to be letting my teammates down because of not giving my best. I then started imagining how I would give it my all once he put me back in the game. He left me on the bench for a long time.

When he finally put me back in the game, I did give it my all and redeemed myself. When the game was over, I still recall how happy I felt and how the coach acknowledged my efforts. I don't even remember if we won the game.

Since then, I've recalled that particular episode many times. It seemed to stand out. Why? The coach was honest with me without trying to guilt or shame me. I felt he had earned the right to coach me, because I knew he cared about me as a person and wanted the best for me in life. It was about love.

Most of us have received feedback or guidance throughout our lives whether from an employer, colleague, parent, casual observer, spouse, or teacher. Some of those who coach us have earned that right. Listen to them. Others haven't. Take what they offer with a grain of salt and move on. Some give feedback adorned with love and respect. Others give it carelessly, projecting their inner shadows on us without respect for our person.

Whatever comes toward you, keep that which arises from love and respect. Be clear. The rest doesn't belong to you.

APRIL 26

Wonder of Wonders

"My heart...said my cells had lost their memory for how to multiply
in a more connective, healthy way and, as a result, were engaging in
a thoughtless 'cancering.' They had somehow become disconnected
from their coordinator of healthy energy—the heart. My cancer
seemed to be the result of cells that had become heartless."
—Paul Pearsall, Ph.D.

While taking long walks in nature I often feel energized, centered,
and creative. Many of us experience this whether it is a nature walk,
pouring love out to another, or experiencing our favorite music, book,
activity, or food. There are reasons why we do the things we love. We
reconnect. Our heart, mind, and body calibrate into an integrated
whole because we are in love. The heart sends messages cellularly to
the rest of the body and energetically to others close by that all is well.
This creates well-being.

When we are not connected with what or who we love, we literally
become disrupted down to the cellular level. In this confusion,
anomalies occur. Illness or lack of well-being result. We can't reason
our way out of these cellular predicaments.

As Paul Pearsall states, the heart is the coordinator of healthy
energy. Its value far exceeds its extraordinary function as a mechanical
pump. Its wisdom is our central sun, our deep tap root, tuning us to
our optimum vibration like a fine musical instrument. We westerners
are beginning to get this.

Breathe love into your chest. Love what your heart is and what it
provides. It's a wonder of wonders.

April 27

Lotus Flower

"I yearn to let go of yearning."

We yearn for love and affection. We yearn for acceptance. We yearn for looks of encouragement and uplifting words in uncertain moments. We yearn to make our mark on the world, to manifest success. We yearn for our loved ones to be well and happy. To yearn is to "have an intense feeling of longing for something, typically something that we have lost or been separated from." I've come to know that there is a subtle dimension to my everyday life that is playing out this search and it likely will continue on throughout my life. Yet, I know there is something more than what I yearn for.

The larger world we live in and the inner world we create tend to play out their consciousness games on the outer edges of truth and sanity. The force of these yearnings for what's missing or lost keeps us hanging onto each day of life and to each other. The unending spin of being in this pattern is dizzying and demanding. I resist writing about it.

I've often given voice to the metaphor of peeling away the layers of an onion as reference to uncovering what we yearn to have and who we yearn to be. It's becoming a bit unnerving to realize how many layers have been peeled away in my life. There seems to be no end in sight. It's as if this never-ending shedding is the only way to reveal what is hidden, what is missing, what is at the core of being a soul having a human experience. Not so.

I'm in a place of seeing our lives as the revelation of a lotus flower. Like the lotus, we emerge from muddy waters. This image reminds us that there is always a depth and beauty to who we are that even multiple layers and the stirrings and agonies of life can't hide—always.

Within this sacred identity, there is no clinging, no yearning. May all your yearnings lead you to this depth of wisdom and the clear spiritual vision of what you are. Set this sacred intention in your deep heart today.

APRIL 28

Tell a New Story

"We all want to look back at the story of our
lives and know that it made sense."
—Michael Margolis

What's your story? I challenge you to explore what is compelling about the story of your life. I don't mean all the ways that you may have been spurned, spoiled, or rejected, or fallen short of your dreams. Rather, tell me what has turned you inside out yet you kept going. What ways have you deeply loved and been altered by it? What ways have you stared straight into fear and still found the resolve to keep going? There is a story of you waiting to be greatly valued and uplifted.

The human experience is a daring and noble endeavor. You have taken it on. You may have been less than graceful or prepared or willing or appreciated yet you have experienced and created a one-of-a-kind groove in our collective story.

If you feel stuck in a story that seems to invariably overtake you and leave you regretting, resenting, or retreating, then allow those vulnerabilities to serve as the ground from which you begin to feel and envision a new story. This new story portrays you as truly feeling alive, deeply understanding, and connected to the powerful spirit in you, the great heart in you that has brought you through to where you are now.

Begin today. See your life's story through new eyes, through your heart which knows that you actually have traveled far along the hero's path. Call yourself back to this truth.

Come to Your Senses

*"Have you ever had the experience of stopping so completely,
of being in your body so completely…and that is-ness
grabs you by all your senses, all your memories, by your
very genes, by your loves, and welcomes you home."*
—Jon Kabat-Zinn

My beloved and I are facing a separation in several weeks. We'll be living a great distance apart. We don't know how long this could last… several weeks or months or years. When she expresses her genuine feelings of sadness, fear, or anger, I tend to retreat inside myself and awkwardly strategize about what I should do to help her. Intimacy drifts away, because I struggle to be present in the moment completely. I can't seem to befriend either of us. If I express the feelings moving through me the best way I know how, I feel her contracting. No presence…no connection.

Being heart connected opens the door to being in my body completely and slowing down completely so that this "is-ness" can take center stage. My beloved is not trying to harm me. She is only feeling what's inside of her and letting it out. This is-ness or presence occurs when my heart-space remains open, and I take my beloved into my heart and receive her just the way she is without trying to change her.

The path to this wise and loving response is to practice stopping completely, and through focused breathing and attention in your deep heart, feel being in your body, connecting with your senses in the moment. For electricity to flow safely and efficiently, it is essential that there be a wire that is grounded to the earth. For the healing, loving energy of life to flow fully without harm, it is best to be connected to your heart which will keep you open and present to the moment whatever it brings.

APRIL 30

More Than a Statistic

"That which does not kill us makes us stronger."
—Friedrich Neitzsche

Many of us are contributors to certain statistics. I have gone through two divorces. When I married my first wife at age twenty, I was certain I would always be married to her—one life, one marriage. I believed it was part of my hardwiring. Divorce was inconceivable to me. To my knowledge, only one relative in my large extended family had ever been divorced. My parents had been married for sixty-eight years until my mother died in 2013.

My first marriage came crashing down after fifteen years. Rates of divorce rise for second marriages. Recently, that marriage became a painful statistic after twenty-two years.

Is it true that that which doesn't kill us makes us stronger? It may or may not be. I do know that I have been broken into pieces on several occasions. It's like standing over what once was your favorite priceless family heirloom that had been entrusted to you. It is now shattered into small pieces on the floor. After you feel whatever you need to feel, you eventually pick up the pieces and throw them away. It would be futile and painstaking to try and put it back together again. We may try simply because we refuse to accept it's gone.

Strength can increase when we face the stress and pain of brokenness and accept that this healing time is going to be fertile, raw, scary, and messy. Ironically, these are the ideal conditions for something new to be born. We are like clay again with some old shards mixed in. We have been given the hands and the heart by the Divine Presence to shape what remains. We find there is more within us than we realize. The well-used analogies of a bird being kicked out of its nest or a baby learning to walk certainly fit.

Almost every day of our lives we have passed through some form of adversity from rubbing against an old hurt, to questioning our abilities, to receiving undo criticism. We are far more than a statistic.

Using the words of Marianne Williamson, I say to all of you, "You are powerful beyond measure." Take this into your heart today. Quietly, gently, humbly let this enfold you.

May 1

Forward Movement

> "You thought you had the choice to stay still
> or move forward, but you didn't."
> —Ann Brashares

What keeps us moving forward? Life itself is at times enough. At other times, our energy is on life support and we reach through life's thin veil and ask for help. If we don't, we fall. Falling has its own benefits, like a child learning to stand on its own two feet.

When to lean into others for help and when not to is often a question for me and for many I have hugged in their time of unknowing. There is no rule of thumb on this. I do know that it is not an either or question.

Truly learning to be all that we are in this life requires at times the gumption and bravery to go on, to move ahead without falling into the arms of a helper. We absolutely need to find and feel our own inner strength and resolve.

Other times seem to require that we let go and ask for help in getting up and taking the next step. We need to toss aside not only the urge to do it our way, but also the reluctance to have others see us in our time of struggle. We surrender our hardened hearts to the community of divinely human love and let it be our strength and guide.

Ultimately, may you be compelled to reach inside yourself, put one foot in front of the other, and move ahead. May each step and breath be framed with these words: "The power of divine love expressing through me is my inspiration and guide." With this firmly anchored within you, whatever you decide to do, you'll be in good company.

MAY 2

Solid as a Rock

"Blessed are the peacemakers."
—Jesus

There are times when emotional upset feels like a maddening and complex knot. Hence the expression, "I am tied up in knots." These knots remind me of a childhood experience. My dad would hold between his hands what appeared to be a very complex mishmash of string woven together. Then he would ask me to pull on one strand and suddenly the entire web of intertwined string would magically disentangle. It really wasn't as daunting as it seemed. It was an illusion.

Inner peace is a tangent of time in which we can almost feel and hear a soft and subtle hum calling us to get quiet inside. This hum emerges as emotional and mental knots unwind and take leave. The obsessive machinations of the tempestuous mind dissolve. We've entered into the cave of the heart, the I of the storm, beyond the spin of the mind's illusions. Our hearts are the only option for peace.

For most of us, the calm of inner peace is highly sought after yet elusive. We know intuitively that we are much better at anything when we are inwardly rooted in peace. It occurs when these roots are in the heart of our being. Rather than commanding center stage doing a master illusionist act, the mind goes backstage in accordance with the heart's directive. It now serves as a supporting actor for the heart which is in the leading role.

Heart-centered presence generates a formidable peace that passes all mental understanding. Like a great mountain, this deep peace stands solid and unmoving.

Return to your heart. Breathe into it. You'll soften and feel more disentangled and at ease in silence. Listen to it. It will teach you a sane and harmonizing rhythm and pace that is not dictated by the world around you. This is only the beginning.

MAY 3

The Ball is Turning

"Want a better world than the one you are
in now? Listen to your heart."
—David-Uriel Ibarra

I heard this analogy today from teacher and intuitive Becky Walsh. We all are on a ball. This ball is stuck in an out-of-balance holding pattern with the "powerful" few on the top and the disempowered masses on the bottom.

The truth is, we can't change much of anything especially this imbalance of power if we aren't willing to feel and express our own power. We can't make the world a better place without this move— period. Owning our power and sharing it with others starts to create the same empowering movement in those with whom we share it. This movement causes the ball of imbalance to turn so that the power in our world becomes more equally expressed among a larger and larger group of people.

Empowerment. It's not a thing or an act. It's a frequency we carry, one in which we truly feel in our hearts that we are in what The HeartMath Institute calls "coherence." There has been a paradigm shift in recent years. We now know that our hearts are in communication with our brains every moment of every day. Science has made it conclusive. The electrical and magnetic fields of the heart are far, far stronger than those of the brain. Our true power to alter ourselves and the physical reality around us lies in utilizing our hearts. So-called miracles occur because of the heart's synchronizing effect on our whole being.

It is not inconsequential when you focus your attention and breath in your heart even for a minute. Many times during the reading of this book I suggest you do just that. It opens you to feel and be more empowered because your heart and brain are in sync more often. The fearful controlling brain becomes less dominant. Your frequency changes. Your personal power ball turns toward greater balance. For you and all of us, this movement makes a difference.

MAY 4

To Multitask or not to Multitask

"Dream of all the masterpieces you'd be thrilled
to create, but work on just one at a time."
—Rob Brezny

Let's admit that there is a collective current moving through much of the world that has accelerated. It is what we so whimsically call multitasking. We're not sure whether we should put it on a resume. We're not clear whether it is even desirable or admirable to be known as a competent multi-tasker. In the absence of sanity, some would declare that there is no choice in the matter. We either need to multitask or be overwhelmed by the backlog of things to do. Multitasking is a necessary evil. I can't get on that horse and ride it.

Why? When attempting to multitask I am not present to what I am doing. It is as if my body is there, but my attention took a leave of presence. The more natural rhythm of one thing at a time also takes leave.

Multitasking reminds me of a circus juggler who is not only tossing balls, bowling pins, and flaming torches in the air at the same time, she is also riding a horse in a standing up on the saddle and facing backwards. It's very entertaining, but we clearly know not to try this ourselves.

If each of us began to live the maxim of one thing at a time and when that one thing is completed, we move on to the next, we likely would start to feel what we largely avoid feeling by being preoccupied with attempting to split our attention into multiple pieces. In addition to not being continually distracted from the moment, we would begin to experience the moment as it is and regain what passes us by when lost in this dogmatic cultural conformity. This is an appeal to balance and doing things well, as well as being able to be more present to the ones we love including ourselves.

Slow down, way down. Practice doing one thing at a time. Let your attention and love flow into it. In your thoughts, attend to the one thing you are doing now. That's all. When finished, move on to what's next.

MAY 5

Waiting for a Miracle?

"Back outside my window, quiet as can be, all that
time making up my mind if angels wait for me."
—David Wilcox

What do we do when difficult people or difficult predicaments show up in life—attack, retreat, go into fear? Or, wait for a miracle? What's the miracle we're hoping for—that the "difficult person" or "difficult circumstance" will disappear? Or, that an angel clothed as a human being will rescue us, heal us, enlighten us, or inspire us?

From time to time, I will find myself facing these kind of difficult moments. Yet, waiting for a disappearance or miracle hasn't proven to free me or teach me or help me.

All of our relationships and all of our life circumstances and experiences are grist for the mill. It is the passage through them and any difficulty along with it, that we discover and create the spiritual muscles and sinews that strengthen the heart, quiet the angst, and refine the vision to realize what is true and what is illusion.

When facing a personal trial, it helps me to remember the beautiful words of Rumi: "Out beyond ideas of wrongdoing and rightdoing is a field. I'll meet you there." This connects us to the larger truth of the oneness that bridges any sense of separation with someone. It is a potent poetic wake up call. Then, we bring something more empowered and enlightened to these passages through difficulty.

Miracles are the natural outcomes of making the inner decision to migrate in your heart to Rumi's field. Even while being in this judgment-free space, we can still stand firm in our convictions, but we do so centered in our hearts, not in our need to be right. Give it a go.

May 6

Impressions of Light

"I see more clearly now."

Light, the glow of the universe that manifests in spectacular varieties, flows in, through, and all around us. Jacques Lusseyran, blinded at age eight, became a leader in the French resistance in World War II at age sixteen.

In his writings, he invites each of us to realize that the light we see with our visual perception is merely a facsimile of the true radiant luminosity of eternal light within us. Read his stunning autobiography And There was Light. His experiences of the inner light leave you at times in a state of breathless curiosity. You, too, want to be able to see the light within.

Master inventor Nikolas Tesla discovered that, "All matter comes from a primary substance, the luminiferous ether." Light is a universal phenomenon that allows us to experience glistening water, kaleidoscopes of color and shade, trees waving in the wind, the glint in someone's eye, stars and planets in the night sky, or words on a screen. Then, there is the inner world of dreams and cellular light that manifests radiant well-being. The list goes on: auras, lasers, photography, solar technologies, hands-on healing...all the ways light takes shape and form. Light is in the center of our being and in all creation.

We've only just begun to comprehend and benefit from the spiritual technology of light. Jesus' light that shines and the Buddha's path to enlightenment are examples. So much remains unknown, a vast mystery. Yet, you and I, along with the great mystics and sages, continue to explore all aspects of sight. One moment at a time, in our consciousness, the unknown emerges into the light of understanding.

Breathe into your heart and cease all outer activity for a moment. Now, ask the light which inhabits every cell of your body to illuminate you and provide the inner vision you need to live with loving power and clarity of purpose.

MAY 7

A Second Chance

"Resentment is taking poison and
expecting someone else to die."
—Unknown

Resentment is an unpleasant thing. It is deadening. It demands that certain conditions be met by someone else or we continue to harbor feelings against that person and slowly cook. Sometimes we hold resentment against ourselves. Others don't really want to hang out with us. We don't like hanging out with ourselves when resentment clings to us. It stinks.

It even gets linked to diseases such as cancer. There is an entire field of study called psychoneuroimmunology which examines the relationship between psychological processes and our nervous and immune systems.

A relatively young woman I counseled prior to her receiving a heart transplant, talked about personal resentments she held toward herself as a mother. I couldn't look past the potential connection between what she was holding and feeling about herself and the death of her heart.

I sense this is one reason why we hang out with animals. Rarely do they hold resentment. They don't have the capacity to do it. They get scared or angry or hurt but only for a brief time. Then, they return to their everyday behavior and attitude of friend, companion, and playful spirit. They don't take the poison. It does makes me wonder how evolved we really are.

Be aware today of the toll resentment has on you and how it could be creating various pipelines that flow undesirable stuff your way. While breathing slowly and deeply into your heart, if any resentment persists, bring this feeling into your awareness. Then, given this feeling, what is it in your heart that you truly want to experience right now that doesn't rely on another person's actions? Let yourself feel this feeling. In this revelation lies the peace that you seek and a second chance to restore yourself to the sanity of love.

MAY 8

Ancient Secret

"There is nothing hidden that won't be revealed, and there is
nothing secret that won't become known and come to light."
—Jesus

Occasionally, I wonder what it would be like to have ancestors from hundreds of years ago experience how we live and the world we've created today. Given all the magnificent advances in science, engineering, culture, and technology, they might think we have become gods.

With that said, there are some things which have remained largely the same since the time of our ancient ancestors. The ageless wisdom shared by almost all cultures and spiritual traditions revealed long ago who we truly are, our unlimited capacities, and our love for creation and one another. These things are described simply as Truth, that which remains unchanged and universal even if the words we use to describe them have evolved.

Standing amidst a grove of giant northern California redwoods, some of which are said to be 2,000 years old or older, I can't resist looking up. As the sunlight streaks through from high above, I can't see the treetops. Like gods, they stretch far beyond my human eye. This place feels heavenly. Indigenous peoples of long ago must have believed that these monuments of creation were where the gods lived.

What I felt that one day must have been what ancient peoples must have felt—a deep reverence for these natural cathedrals—an awe-inspiring love.

Wherever there is awe-inspiring love, there is a burning ember of truth. Love abides in the heart of everything whether it is here one day and gone tomorrow or a revelation of the infinite. The ancients knew this. You and I still have something to learn from them.

May 9

Mother of All

"It is a word of love as old as the world."
—Ghislain Van Houtte

The poem "Maman"(French for mom), by Ghislain Van Houtte hung on my wall for many years. Written in French, it begins with this line: *Il est un mot d'mour aussi vieux que le monde.* Translated it means, "It is a word of love as old as the world." Yes, it is. Mom, Mother, ever so ancient, the stronghold of infinite potential, never abandons her roots as the Source of all that is alive. Planted in the soul of the world, She has been the recipient of both blissful adoration and brutal scorn. The Great Mother remains as the ever-present space for creation to perform its magic without fail, an unconditional gift of love.

Another line in this poem says, *"C'est un mot ravissant plus doux qu'une caresse..."* which means, "It is a lovely word more gentle than a caress." You and I come to the altar of life everyday and in some way the ravishing beauty of this universe spills into our lap. Beauty is our daily muse that gives our routines and challenges a lighter lyrical touch. Mother is an energy forever flowing through us, inviting us to soften what is rigid within. Jonas Magram, in his song, "Mother Take Us There," writes, "Oh Mother take us home. Please melt these hearts of stone."

Maman is so many things— the relentless stand for justice, the clarion call for peace, the fierce protector of the vulnerable, the outspoken voice for the partnership way, the path of forgiveness, the rising tide of ways to heal, a source of inspiration, and so much more. There is no end to Maman.

My mother's father would often end his letters to my mother with these words of love, "Give that sweet Mother of yours a kiss for me." Let's all follow suit today.

Give Maman a kiss, an expression of affection for all She is and all She gives, whether it be the mother that gave you birth, or the Mother of all that is alive.

MAY 10

Deeply and Fluidly

"We are the fruits of the wind...and have been
seeded, irrigated, and cultivated by its craft."
—Lyall Watson

The wind is an essential part of the circulatory and respiratory system of planet Earth as much as air is essential for breathing. Wind, air, and breath ensure that all life is sustained.

We can therefore imagine that our breath is also a conduit that opens our awareness to what Jesus described as *ruhau*—spirit, the quantum source of life. This understanding has its roots in ancient yogic teachings and practices. More advanced students of yoga learn how to do breathing practices which then prepare the heart and mind of the practitioner to experience the higher self or spirit.

Most of us have never been taught how to breathe in ways that would increase and improve our energy and calm our body and mind. Conscious, controlled, breathing practices, learned from a good teacher are priceless. Great athletes know this. Accomplished and inspiring speakers are attuned to this. Singers and stage actors, who are skilled in their craft, are aware of this. Individuals who have minimized the toxic effects of stress and fear know this. Students of longevity realize this.

To breathe deeply and fluidly is to live deeply and fluidly. We move through life with greater ease and wisdom becoming more akin to dolphins rather than mule-like beasts of burden. We are the fruits of the ways we breathe.

Give consistent attention to your breathing and begin to breathe more slowly and deeply. It will be like a wind blowing through a smog-filled valley. This is only the beginning of what's possible. The rest is up to you.

MAY 11

Unbroken Circle

"Every creature has a religion. Every foot is a
shrine where a secret candle burns."
—St. Thomas Aquinas

Yesterday evening in the damp cool air, a young man was standing on a street corner holding up a sign which said, "Please. I need gas. Thank you." There was a gas can next to him. He was grimacing from being chilled to the bone.

I pulled into the parking lot next to him. As I got out of my car, his girl friend walked up at that moment and I greeted them both. I bought them a full can of gas, shuttled them to their van a few blocks away, gave them a jump start, and drove away. They were very appreciative and kind and told me that they lived in the van with their dog and had been getting a little bit of work here and there through the help of a friend. I felt for them.

By reaching out and not ignoring the homeless and disenfranchised, not only does it help them with basic needs, but it also creates another important outcome. In some small way, it reaffirms their place, their voice in the human community, a basic need that most all of us have. Frankly, it even inwardly nudges me toward feeling included and reconnected to the larger circle of life.

May the following message be reflected back in concrete ways to all those holding up a sign of need in our world: "I see you, I hear you, and I acknowledge your sacred place in our community." Pass this on to those in your circle wherever you are.

MAY 12

Set-point

> "I was a coward. I used to be haunted by the fear of
> thieves and ghosts and serpents. I did not dare to stir out
> of doors at night. Darkness was a terror to me."
> —Mahatma Gandhi

One of the most powerful individuals of the twentieth century, Mahatma Gandhi, was an inspirational and revolutionary leader in politics, religion, and social justice. It was because of the transformational power of his devotion to God that he was given the title Mahatma, or Great Soul. He continues to be viewed as a Hindu saint. Yet, this Mahatma experienced fear and terror to the point of crippling his ability to function in his community. Through it all, he found his way, and tapped into the collective soul of a nation, which eventually led to their freedom from British rule.

This is a story for the ages. Through his ever-increasing devotion to God, Gandhi discovered a pathway that dramatically altered his emotional set-point for fear. As a boy and young man he was gripped by fear. His fear set-point would trip easily, giving fear a great deal of power. Fear had such sway that he was paranoid and highly self-protective. Gradually, this shifted, and Gandhi's emotional set-point for fear changed. Over time, his capacity to face and live through fear became enormous, because his clear connection to Divine Presence greatly diminished fear's power.

May this true story of someone haunted by fear, who later became the heart and soul of a revolution, awaken you once again to the power of the living spirit within you. Your emotional set-points for fear or shame or anxiety are not fixed in stone! When the truth of the living spirit within and around you is embraced and energized, there are no limits to its transformational effects.

I leave you with this poetic vision from award-winning novelist Frank Herbert: "I will permit it (fear) to pass over me and through me. And when it has gone past I will turn the inner eye to see its path. Where the fear has gone there will be nothing. Only I will remain."

May 13

Nester or Traveler

"My hero's always ten years away."
—Matthew McConaughey

In this world, nothing ever remains the same. We are always connected to the thread that pulls us ahead. Some of us are nesters and settle in for the long haul. Some of us don't stay in any one place for very long. We are travelers and prone to cyclically move on.

Some years ago, I needed to settle an issue I had with myself. I sense some of you will relate to this. For the longest time, I held it against myself that I was one of those who did short cycles of nesting. Five years seemed to be my limit. Something would happen to move me on to what was next. Coming from a family subculture in Texas of longtime nesters, I judged that I had a defect like some kind of contraption with a screw loose that I simply couldn't locate. Years of teaching self-acceptance and love finally took down my wall of judgment. More and more I was able to give myself room to be me.

I'm drawn to Matthew McConaughey's words. It helps to remind all of us that we have something we are reaching and stretching for. No matter whether we are primarily nesters or travelers, we are designed to imagine new and better worlds. It's in our DNA, because we are offspring of an endless multiverse forever expanding. Some would describe it as being created in the image and after the likeness of God.

May mercy always abound, whether nester or traveler, in your ongoing evolution. You play a divine role. Thank you for doing and being your part.

MAY 14
Brushstrokes of Gratitude

"Gratitude is not only the greatest of virtues,
but the parent of all others."
—Cicero

I encourage you to take notice. Divine Presence, your infinite and constant resource, is the wind that bends you toward gratitude. Like water that continually bubbles up from underneath the surface, gratitude is an effervescence that never dies. It is a cause, a life-changing viewpoint. It is a way to participate in the flow of time that stirs up divine energy in your midst.

When in gratitude, the universe cooperates and every single justification for negativity or hurtful behavior is shown to be senseless. Gratitude is a feeling, a pure, unadulterated awareness that brightens life. You discover countless small, previously unnoticed graces

There are times when any one of us may simply not be able to go directly into the fullness or feeling of gratitude and appreciation. When you're in that place, reduce your field of attention to very small points of awareness such as, noticing that you took a conscious and slow deep breath or you petted your dog or you stopped your mind chatter for ten to fifteen seconds to truly hear what someone else is saying. This presence is a start, a brushstroke of easing off the accelerator of habitual, attitudinal sleepwalking.

Start where you can. You know the feeling of gratitude. You can choose to arouse and live in it more often. You can become a master of gratitudinal living. We are spiritual beings, living in a cooperative spiritual universe, governed by spiritual laws, and graced with a kaleidoscope of life-fulfilling gems.

MAY 15

A Road Map

"Decide today what you want to set aside and
what you want to take with you."

For decades, roadside memorials of loved ones have been devotedly maintained by family members. They place flowers and symbols of love and God near the site of their loved one's departure from this world. I drove past a sign that read, "In loving memory of Stephanie. Please drive carefully." Whenever I pass one of these memorials, I pause inside, and send out a message of love and compassion to the family and the one departed.

This particular life experience we are co-creating is what spiritual teacher Joel Goldsmith called "a parenthesis in eternity." View it as a pilgrimage in which we are gathering together that which draws us closer and closer to love's essence. We have all come forth from the beauty and mystery of life eternal and are now on moving walkways heading in one direction. In one moment, each of us is whisked away and redirected down an alternate path through a portal and into the light beyond.

What do we choose to set aside and what do we choose to take with us? I suggest we set aside, one by one, our sources of suffering. Let's take with us our sources of love. Make this decision now.

Set your heart on this creation. When your portal appears and you leave your physical form behind, your sources of suffering will be shed and your sources of love will go with you, providing an inspiring and elegant road map ahead for you and for those you love.

The hallmark of a life well-lived is establishing your cord of connection to your higher purpose and power. Consciously enter into the cave of your heart today and ask your higher power to fulfill your higher purpose through you. May your loved ones follow your example and be a living memorial to your life and love.

MAY 16

Reunion

"Return again, return again, return to the land of your
soul. Return to who you are, return to what you are,
return to where you are born and reborn again."
—Rabbi David Zeller

There is a powerful painting by Howard Pyle entitled "The Mermaid." When I first saw it, I instantly fell in love with it. I have a large print of it framed and mounted on my wall. It portrays a young man on the edge of a rocky shore passionately embracing a beautiful mermaid as she rises up from the ocean waters. It is obvious that they are endeared to each other and reveling in their reunion. You get the feeling that they had carefully planned this loving rendezvous.

We are now realizing that there are natural collective forces calling us to create a powerful partnership of the masculine and feminine energies in our world. It is not simply a trend or fad. It is a natural evolution, a confluence destined to be. A new story of who we are is being born. Powerful feminine energy is now rising into her rightful place and being seated at the throne of this new reality alongside the masculine.

The living cornerstone of our emerging story as divine-humans is the full development of the genius of the heart, that which lies at the intersection of the earthy, body-centered, deep-feeling, feminine polarity, and the omnipresent intelligence and bold initiative of the masculine polarity. The equilateral cross is a powerful symbol of this union.

If you operate predominately in one polarity or the other, destiny is attempting to pull you toward the deep-middle in which your heart and mind cooperate and body and spirit join. Follow that lead. From this deep-middle, your predominant polarity is strengthened and the other polarity is given more room to be developed and appreciated. Not only your relationships, but also your personal life-force, become more passionate and purposeful. You are being reborn.

Recite silently in the first person the words of Rabbi Zeller above. Feel this powerful message in your heart.

May 17

Plug-ins

"To be sensual is to be aware of the subtle…energy of the heart."
—Paul Pearsall, Ph.D.

What we call love is felt when two hearts are synchronized. This occurs from direct eye contact, or affectionate touch, or full body love making. Anecdotal evidence gathered by Paul Pearsall, which is detailed in his book The Heart's Code, suggests that intimate physical contact "may be important in providing energetic nurturing and rhythmic synchronization to the heart from another heart, just as a low-fat diet, regular exercise, and a less stressful life helps protect it." This same evidence also suggests that the loss of sexual activity for an extended period may very well contribute to heart attacks or heart failure.

Making conscious contact with the energy of love is essential to our well being. I would add that it is essential to soul development which involves the more subtle qualities of creativity, intuition, meaning, and purpose. It's as if we live in one large expansive beating heart. When we open to sensually feel and synchronize with all the ways this beating heart expresses, we are happier, stronger, wiser, more energetic, loving, and creative.

It's up to each of us to discover our very own personal plug-ins to these heart rhythms. Nature, music, art, sex, athletics, healthy food, deep friendships, family, creativity, prayer, meditation, poetry, and spiritual study are some of these. It is inspiring and comforting to realize that we've been provided endless ways for our hearts to synchronize with the power of love.

Consciously sync up today. Give your whole self the love it needs. You'll live long and prosper.

MAY 18

Boomeranging

"After you were born you forgot what is true, but
like a boomerang it will come back to you."
—Robert Anderson

As a child I loved throwing just about anything. Throwing a boomerang however was like nothing else. The experience of throwing something into the distance and having it come back to me was a thrill. It felt like a form of magical mastery. It was not about arm speed or power. Boomeranging was about grace, beauty, and proper technique.

I loved my shiny turquoise version. I usually would stand in my backyard facing a tall elm tree about twenty feet in front of me and throw the boomerang to the right of the tree. I'd watch and wait for several seconds as it would skirt around the tree, then curve right to left, while dodging electrical wires and telephone poles. Suddenly, it would reappear spinning by the left side of the tree and directly back to me if everything went according to plan. That didn't happen very often, but when it did, it was pure joy.

Clearly, there is a built-in boomerang dynamic operating in this world. Consciousness works in an elliptical way like the pattern of the Earth revolving around the Sun.

Whatever we throw out into our world finds its way back to us. It's not magic or mystery. Consciousness works just like physical reality, boomeranging its way through the universe of time and space, affecting its environment, and curving its way back to its starting point. It is very freeing to know this. It's something we can play with, now that we know the rules.

Be aware today of what arises from within you that you throw out into your world. These choices create a path of effects that leads back to you. And, of course, there are no trees or electrical lines that get in the way. Use the beauty of this universal law to make your life and your world a much better place to be.

MAY 19

Heart Episodes

"Follow your heart and make it your decision."
—Mia Hamm

Some years ago, because of unusual circumstances in my marriage, I reluctantly chose to leave behind my community, my work, and a life that I loved, and move far away to a place unfamiliar to me. In my first month there, I began having severe chest pains. They continued off and on for several months. I finally went to a cardiologist for an exam. My physical heart and circulatory system were found to be in good health. The doctor called my heart episodes "undiagnosed chest pain." He said that such a thing is common especially in times of high anxiety or depression.

It pained me to leave the community and life I loved. Leaving behind anything or anyone we love can be painful. Our hearts and nervous systems will give us that feedback.

That specific experience later brought to light that certain critical choices I had made in my life were attempts to avoid triggering a loved one's big fears or vulnerabilities. That has been one of my vulnerabilities. I've overridden my inner knowing. These overrides have pained me. I thought I was showing compassion for someone I cared for, but, in truth, I was allowing their deep personal fears to overwhelm me. No one benefits in the long run.

The human experience is a sacred gift and a great undertaking. You and I are learning how to utilize what lies underneath all of existence, the healing wisdom and power of love, and allow it to guide us through every moment and every choice. Sometimes this means that we make choices which lead to loved ones feeling pain we'd rather them not feel. Wanting to save another from their pain is understandable, but it often has harmful side-effects for us self-appointed saviors.

Notice when you may be overriding your heart in favor of attempting to avoid lifting the cap off the painful past of a loved one. It could be harmful to your well-being. Listen to your heart rather than your fear.

MAY 20

A Full House

It's very crowded in this house.
I know everyone who's here.
They're quite familiar.
Each has a voice of their own.
I'd like to pretend I don't know some of them,
But everyone claims I created them and gave them life.
Down the main hallway I enter a large room.
There's Likable who smiles at everyone and says just the right things.

There's Count-onable who never lets anyone down.
There's Forgivable who easily lets go of past stuff.
There's Doable who sees through everything to a solution.
There's Agreeable who never stops looking for ways that we are alike.
There's Playable who loves to skip about
and wear things that don't match.
There's Believable who walks the talk and shines a bit brighter.
There's Imaginable who has great visions
and asks for help to create them.
There are others of a similar ilk in this room.

I move on to the next room.
I feel heavy in here.
There's Controllable who pseudo-innocently
waits to be told what to do.
There's Uncontrollable who acts out everything and wears no clothes.
There's Miserable who feels yucky, angry, and refuses hugs.
There's Unforgivable who feels exiled from the
rest and self-inflicts repeated lashes.
There's Disagreeable who hunts for what it thinks might be wrong.
There's Unlikable who feels isolated and ugly and different.
There's Unimaginable who remains a mystery to everyone.
There are others here, but it's getting so cloudy I can't see.
I leave to explore other rooms where I find many, many, more selves.

I head outside and stand back from the house.
With it in full view, I close my eyes and
open my heart-centered awareness.
With each deep breath, I send love into all its
spaces and to all the selves within it.
I see the house now filled with love and love only.
I feel happiness coming over me.

MAY 21

Lost and Found

"The soul is a candle that will burn away the darkness;
only the glorious duties of love we will have."
—St. John of the Cross

Imagine with me the following: You see an ugly, old, tattered blanket tossed in a dark corner of a seldom-used closet. It's been left alone and ignored for years. But this time, rather than ignore it, you decide to pick it up to discard it. To your amazement, underneath it lies a long-lost card from a loved one who years ago wrote on it the following words: "No matter what, I'll always love you." You can hardly believe your eyes. You feel a surge of emotion.

The old blanket is like a holdover of painful rejection that rises at the thought of someone who left you behind. For a long while, you hide it away in a dark corner of your inner life.

Eventually, on your own, or at the encouragement of a friend or therapist, you reluctantly turn toward this old unresolved feeling. It's suffocating and ugly. Through it all, somehow you begin to feel lighter. The pain lifts.

Then, you are startled to discover what's been hidden underneath it. What you uncover is a deep feeling and awareness of a great love that you buried many, many years before. You feel the same naked loving energy that drew you to this loved one in the beginning.

This time, you feel this love hitched to gratitude rather than pain. You realize your great fortune to have experienced a love such as this and, doubly, to have uncovered it in your deep heart again. You were deftly guided through it all to arrive where you started—in the heart of love. You have lived through a prodigal shift—"he(she) was lost but now is found." (Luke 15:24)

There is a guiding wisdom even from these dark corners of painful transformation that points toward the wider view of the landscapes of our lives. Rather than seeing events as if we're stuck inside a camera looking at our lives through a tiny aperture, we find our way out of the camera and, with new vision, see parts of the whole picture that we have been missing. All roads eventually lead to love.

May 22

Monkey Business

"What are you waiting for?"

In certain parts of India, monkeys roam the streets like dogs and cats. Eventually the numbers grow so large that it becomes necessary to capture many of them and remove them to remote areas. The locals discovered that the best way to capture them is to put a nut in a large narrow-neck glass jar and place each one outside.

Monkeys love nuts. The monkeys reach into the jar, but they can't pull their hand out as long as they hold onto the nut because their hand forms a fist and gets stopped by the narrow neck. If they'd simply let go of the nut, they could easily remove their hand and run away. But, they keep their hands tightly fisted around the nut. Thus, it becomes rather easy to walk up and grab hold of a monkey and carry it away because that large heavy glass jar is attached to the end of its arm.

After a period of mourning the end of my marriage to my children's mother, I wanted some form of justice. I bargained with myself that justice would be served if she expressed remorse to me for what I had judged to be an act of cruelty. I was reaching into the jar of what my mind was convinced was rightfully mine and holding on tightly. I couldn't resist the temptation.

Hooked to this for years, I carried this expectation like a heavy object attached to my heart. I was easily carried off into some tangent of hurt or sadness every time I met up with this expectation in my mind. I sacrificed happiness at the altar of waiting for my idea of justice to be delivered. It never happened.

As my hurt subsided, my wise and compassionate heart took over. Justice naturally emerged, because the heart-effect mercifully helped me to realize that being attached to my reactive mind's idea of justice was punishing **me**. More light continued to pour in and the truth became clear. Letting go in the end came easily.

I ask you to notice from your heart of compassion where you may still be clinging to what you feel you have coming to you. What have you bargained for that you've never received? If you allow your reactive mind to hold onto having its way, you only hold yourself hostage to this monkey business. Reach into your heart of compassion and ask the Divine Presence in you to assist in letting go. Justice for you is then served.

MAY 23

Well-Worn Paths

"Follow it forward expecting to break things—
rules, conventions, precedents, your own vulnerable
heart—but knowing that you'll heal strong."
—Martha Beck

For more than twenty-five years, I needed to create something wise, witty, or inspiring to say on a weekly basis. As a minister, I believed there were unwritten rules as well as longstanding conventions that established the boundaries of appropriate self-expression. Some of the rules were my own and others arose from the philosophical and organizational framework I worked within.

Creating frequently collides with all this. From time to time, I have chosen to throw a stone through these glass ceilings and trust my intuition and personal integrity. I created new precedents even if it didn't match the standards of the world around me. I still test these waters. I know I am far from alone in this regard.

Life has well-worn paths that we get to know all too well. The time comes, whether we feel ready or not, to take leave of these ways that Jesus called the "path of destruction."

If you take time to consistently connect with your heart-space, you will be called to look straight into the truth about your well-worn paths and conventions. It is necessary, unless you attempt to push the pause button on the natural evolution of being you.

Look up. Raise your sights. There is a whole new world within you. Take the first step even if you break something.

May 24

Untangling our Hearts

"It is up to us to listen more than hear,
to look into more than past."
—Nick Trout

Near San Francisco, a female humpback whale became entangled in hundreds of pounds of crab traps and lines and eventually was struggling mightily to be able to access the surface and breathe. A rescue team arrived. They dove in and worked for hours to free her.

Their efforts were successful and she was freed. Once free, she swam in what witnesses described as joyous circles. She then swam up to each rescue diver one at a time and nudged them and pushed them gently around. It was obvious the whale was thanking them. Many of those involved described this as the most beautiful experience of their lives. The diver who cut the rope out of the whale's mouth said that the whale's eyes were following him the whole time. "I will never be the same," he was quoted as saying.

The bonds we have with animals, from the great whales to the mighty hamster, are ancient and deep. Leave it to them to teach us about love, loyalty, celebration, and appreciation. They freely give us their hearts even in the midst of our human insanity.

Today, look directly into the eyes of a loved one, animal or human, for as long as reasonably possible. Feel their heart-space and yours. Silently, allow gratitude and joy to flow. You will never be the same.

MAY 25

Ears of Nature

"How do I listen to others? As if everyone were my
Master, speaking to me his cherished last words."
—Hafiz

We all want to be known, even if it is only by one person. We want to give ourselves to the world and have the world respond and acknowledge our voice, our place. This is in part why nature is such a powerful presence in our lives. We feel like we belong there, because we know that nature has no judgment of us. We are one of her own.

To truly be heard by another creates the feeling of being one of their own. The listener opens to us and communicates with or without words that we belong in their hearts.

Listening without prejudice and from deep within is putting on the ears of nature. This is meditation with your eyes wide-open. May you learn to bring this art to all those you love and serve. It will certainly come back to you.

MAY 26

Familiarity

"I know you from somewhere."

There are rare moments when the spiral of life turns a certain way and the unexpected happens. We meet someone for the first time and there is an almost immediate recognition of one another. It's as if we are coming together again after a very long cycle of being apart. We pick up right where we left off. We may not know where we left off, but it doesn't matter. It is a joy to experience the feeling of being reconnected.

Reflect on this for a moment. There are certain souls to whom it appears you are bound by an invisible golden thread which pulls you back together again, whether you've known each other in this life or not. This spiritual link keeps you in relationship even when you are away from each other.

Familiarity and attraction have elements of mystery about them. Cherish them especially when clear feelings of love enfold your connection with others. You are joined in ways that stretch your worldly sensibilities. It is one of the treasures of living with an open heart.

Take a few precious moments to be still. In your heart, one by one, bring together those with whom you feel you have had a unique and beautiful connection in this life. In the silence of your heart, reaffirm your gratitude for the golden thread that joins you, even with those who have passed on. Feel the love that binds you together always.

MAY 27

Befriending Yourself

"Meditation practice isn't about trying to throw
ourselves away and become something better.
It's about befriending who we are already."
—Pema Chodron

"How've you been lately?" asked a friend in a gathering around a dining table. I'm usually not a rote, "I'm fine" kind of a guy. The pat question allowed me a few moments to reflect and respond briefly and honestly without pouring out the whole bottle. My response was something like this: "I've been on a learning curve over the past several months about trust—trusting my intuition. I need to learn to be more spacious and forgiving toward me."

Another person said, "How demanding and unforgiving we cultured and conditioned Americans tend to be toward ourselves." This round table wisdom triggered the nodding of heads all around, all in agreement. Then, I read the words from Pema Chodron above.

Let the word befriending wash over and through you today. It hints at the gentle capturing of love's presence. "What is a friend?" writes C. Raymond Beran. "I will tell you. It is a person with whom you dare to be yourself." So often, as Chodron reminds each of us, that person with whom you need to dare to be yourself is you—just as you are. Yes, JUST AS YOU ARE. At least my dog Lancelot gets it.

MAY 28

Letters from the Heart

"Words from the heart, put to pen, change the world."

My maternal grandfather and grandmother were estranged since my mother was an infant. He only connected with my mother through letters that he wrote to her. He would usually send them on special occasions. His words often took on an air of spiritual wisdom. I am fortunate to have copies of several of these letters. Here is an excerpt of a letter he wrote in May of 1942 as my mother was graduating from high school. The CAPS are his.

"Youth, vigor, enthusiasm, the world in front of you, and the world is yours. And, oh me, oh my, what a world it is, too! One big volcanic mess from one end to the other—the world being drained of its wealth in nearly all departments—physical, mineral. However, we can well do without a great deal we have had heretofore, and thought so very necessary to our well-being. Yet, there are two sources of power we should guard carefully, as they will loom large in after-war years, and in the reconstruction of this old world—that job will be largely up to you and your associates of this day. They are our SPIRITUAL and MORAL sources of power—they are most difficult, of absolute and definite determination, yet both are most powerful. They are invisible, but the very mudsill of our well being. So, in addition to the five-dollar bill I am enclosing as your graduation gift, I have this other gift for you: go to a quiet spot, and merely sit down with yourself and take an inventory of your spiritual well- being. While you are doing that, if it is done sincerely and conscientiously, you will know I am there with you, watching your stock-taking. Are you motivated by FEAR—fear of results, fear of being subject to ridicule, fear of possible failure? Fear should never be the handmaiden of youth. Are you spiritually alive and alert? Have you ever known the companionship of an invisible force, yet, always conscious of that force? If you have not, you have failed to educate your spirit along with your mind. Get out of the crowd and make a survey of yourself. Whither are you bound, and above all, WHY? Heaps of love, and kiss that sweet Mother of yours for me. Devotedly, Daddy"

MAY 29

Old Streets

"The past and future swirl in unison around me. I
am happy to be unmoving in their midst."

While walking familiar streets adjacent to lower, downtown Denver, I was surprised to see that the early twentieth-century buildings, which once housed my workplace, were gone. They were replaced by twenty-first-century buildings and businesses. Adjacent hundred-year-old buildings which remained were redesigned and given new life. The Sixteenth Street viaduct, once bustling with cars and busses, had vanished and was replaced with a wide, walking and biking thoroughfare, artfully designed with raised plant beds, sculptures, and benches. I loved the changes.

One particular landmark pub was a holdout. It was as if time stood still. There was no sign, no facelift, no redesign, no change in the menu.

Even the same wood benches, tables, and chairs, looking like antiques, were held together by much needed screws after decades of use. I ordered lunch and my sandwich was served, just like it had been long ago, wrapped in wax paper. Cash and checks still found their home in the same antique cash register. I was happy to be there.

There is the inner world of our present moment which is anchored in our past. In this space, we lament over what is no more, growl about the changes, as well as smile inside, and give thanks for what remains unchanged.

There is also the inner world of our present moment which welcomes change, cherishes the altogether new, and embraces visions of a future full of promise.

The heart in each of us is designed to be fully present to both of these worlds. Often we flow into our past and into our future within the same minute. Our hearts stand ready to reel us back into the present moment, giving rise to acceptance or appreciation for what has been, what is now, and what is yet to come.

Allow your heart to be the great integrator of all that flows through you. While breathing slowly into your heart, like the confluence of two rivers, see a flow coming into your heart from behind you (your past) and a flow from in front of you (your future). There, they come together, generating loving acceptance and appreciation for all that you are, past, present, and future. Feast on all that you are.

MAY 30
Write On

"Ask and it will be given you; seek, and you shall find;
knock, and the door shall be opened unto you."
—Jesus

Writing this book is a lot like real life. Day-by-day, I attempt to write new entries, connect with long-lost inspirations, discover ones I unwrap for the first time, and write stuff that doesn't even remotely catch a whisper of worthiness. It is slow and agonizing at times. Other times, it's fluid and fun. All together, it is outrageously time consuming. But, I write nonetheless.

I've been asked many times why I am doing this project. My response continues to be, "Because I know this is what I need to do at this time to come back into myself."

I am learning how to navigate and hack my way through all the inner noise of voices clanging together—rancorous judge, cynical belittler, grandiose pontificator, pirate of procrastination, and guru of perfection. Almost daily, I'm coming face-to-face with these meddlers and other sidekicks.

Many of you know what I'm yacking about. Similar voices show up in your life. Yet, there is a you and a me which have not conformed to all the confusing, ugly, and self-destructive ways of the clanging voices and their sidekicks. We have set our hearts on discovering something more deeply honest and courageous which helps to bring our more noble self back to life.

Some call this the search for God. Others might see it as a search for healing. Whatever it may be, remember, wherever two or more are gathered for a common heart-directed purpose, Divine Presence rises in our midst to meet the challenge of the moment. I feel the power of you and many millions of others alongside.

May the true and noble purpose for your life come to you and fill your heart. Ask, seek, knock, and write!

MAY 31

Hardwired for Love

"We cultivate love when we allow our most vulnerable
and powerful selves to be deeply seen and known."
—Brene Brown, Ph.D.

How many times in our lives, when presented with the opportunity to stand in front of others and reveal anything of a personal nature, have we felt vulnerable, frightened, or feared embarrassment? I have felt these feelings countless times. What is it about human nature that generates these kind of raw feelings? Some of us could be reciting the alphabet with eyes on us and still feel these same vulnerabilities. Why?

It's about the fear of rejection and humiliation. Being in front of others pushes that button. In our core, each of us longs to experience and recreate the presence of love for that is what we truly are. When we had our first few experiences in life of simply being ourselves and had something unloving be the response, we had a visceral reaction—confusion, pain. The more of these unloving moments we experienced while being ourselves, the greater the need arose to avoid them. Being in front of others recreates the visceral fear that a past, painful, unloving moment could happen again.

You are hardwired for love and acceptance. As you walk through life today, remember a time and place and the people present in which you felt love and acceptance. Take that feeling with you and more love and acceptance will find its way to you no matter where you are. New daily rituals and patterns that are congruent with the essential beautiful self and soul of you, allow you once again to experience you as you're hardwired to be.

June 1

Imprints and Inflammations

"The wound is the place where the Light enters you."
—Rumi

Emotional and psychological (E&P) wounds that recur can be tenacious, especially the ones which first occurred before the age of four. They seem to pop up almost automatically when the circumstances are right. They have no mercy and simply respond to stimuli that mimic the original wound. It feels at times like injustice. Something happens to us over which we seem to have no control.

Knowing this, what are the options? We could hide ourselves away or take drugs. We could rage at the world or decide to close our hearts once and for all. You see where I'm going with this. Of course, you may need to get professional or personal support.

E&P imprints are not all powerful. Let me bring you back to something I wrote in an earlier daily writing. "Remember that the heart is an expanded energy field connected to and extending out in a large circle around you. Breathe into and feel its amplitude and power circulating through you like blood through your veins. Take this keen awareness with you throughout your day. See what happens." An amplified deep resonance with this heart-space is a way to provide a soothing balm when E&P imprints become inflamed.

Massage these inflamed feelings with a simple heart-centered meditation. It could be as simple as this: place both hands over your heart, with the left hand on top of the right, thumbs touching. After a few moments of concentrated attention on your breath and heart-hand connection, say slowly this simple mantra: "Healing love come...come... come." Repeat this mantra several times with fifteen to twenty seconds in between. Spend at least three to four minutes in this resonance. Be a healing presence in your own life.

June 2

Being Truly Helpful

"There is only one of us here."
—Davis Hoffman-Roach

Would you rather give help than ask for help? At times, I have too strongly hinged my worth on helping people. In contrast, I have been far more reluctant to ask for help. I often have come face to face with not knowing what to ask for. Many of us can relate.

What I've also discovered is that over-focusing on helping others can serve as an effective buffer from feeling what is truly alive in me.

It doesn't have to be this way. Helping others can simply be an act of service—no agenda and no expectation of receiving a payoff.

Giving or receiving help is about making a real connection with the other and allowing that connection to provide the necessary energy and guidance to help in ways in which both are served and uplifted. This intimacy-effect ignites a spirit that is greater and wiser than when human beings are left to their own devices.

For example, I know from experience that when speaking to a group or large audience, the best way to reach everyone present is to establish genuine intimacy by speaking directly to just one person in the audience at various times throughout the presentation. There is a powerful ripple of connection and intimacy that moves through the space. Everyone is served.

Today, be aware of how you may be disconnecting from others. Help yourself. Practice some simple, deep breaths connecting you with your heart-space for a few moments. Feel what is truly alive in you right now. Bring this breath of connection into your relationships today. Watch how moments of cooperation and selfless service naturally emerge.

June 3

Spiritual Friends

"Gather your tribe together."

There are those in our lives who choose to stand alongside. They created room for each of us to stumble and fall. They stuck with us, in spite of our transgressions, and we stuck with them.

As we grow into adulthood, we also evolve into seeking out individuals who have certain qualities and frequencies. The day I graduated from high school, I was relieved and confused. I was relieved, because I was ready to move on beyond high school. I was confused, because I recognized I was feeling more and more like I simply didn't belong there with those classmates I had been hanging out with for years. Some time later, I began to understand that my soul was needing to be with those who my soul would naturally feel a connection— spiritual friends, rather than my old high school buddies.

These spiritual friendships are built on something more than a human connection and appreciation. They arise from a deeper well. We've said to each other, "It feels like we've known each other before." There is little pretense and resistance. We simply pick up where we left off, whenever and wherever that may have been. These are our spiritual friends, soul friends. We understand one another and much more easily bond and respect each other. We have parallel viewpoints about the universe and the spiritual presence which moves through us. It's as if we are members of the same tribe.

Feel gratitude in your heart-space for your spiritual friends past and present. Their presence has been, is, and shall always be priceless.

June 4

The Beauty Way

"Beauty is life when life unveils her holy face."
—Kahlil Gibran

When northwest bound U.S. Highway 287 gradually crests at the top of Togwotee Pass in Wyoming, quite suddenly the towering Grand Teton mountain range appears in full view thirty miles to the west. I've experienced that stunning view numerous times. Spellbound, I've always had to pull over, get out of my car, and absorb the imposing beauty of this glorious, geological masterpiece.

This is not a pitch for Wyoming tourism. It's a pitch for beauty. As writer Mary Oliver puts it, "You only have to let the soft animal of your body love what it loves." Beauty is the vibration of love softening us and coaxing us to set aside worldly concerns for a while. Like an answered prayer, it fulfills a longing inside of us for heavenly moments which heal and restore.

Beauty is personal and intimate. You know what it is when you see it or feel it or imagine it. It feels like a healing angel is hovering nearby. Walk the beauty way. Feel your heart, mind, and body aflame with her presence. Let yourself be loved by her today.

June 5

Breaking an Old Taboo

"When man lies in her womb, she is fulfilled, each act of love
a taking of man within her, an act of birth and rebirth."
—Anais Nin

Several years ago, I did something I had never done before. I gave a Sunday presentation in my spiritual community about the relationship between spirituality and sexuality.

Before I began, I gave a disclaimer that expressed my dismay that this was the first time I had given a Sunday talk on this topic in almost twenty-five years. It seemed preposterous, but it was true. I received a very loud round of applause. You would have thought I had just slain a fire-breathing dragon.

I spoke frankly about what traditionally had been an almost taboo topic. After that service, the room where we always held an after-service discussion group, was standing-room only.

The feeling in that group seemed unanimous. Sexuality needs to be brought out of the closet and become an integral part of our collective spiritual and personal dialogue. Secondly, the shame-and-guilt-based approach to sexuality needs to die and be buried quickly. Thirdly, the need for deep healing around our sexuality seems almost universal.

A healthy and respectful sexuality is essential for our well-being. It taps into the most natural and powerful generator of creativity in our universe. Enthusiasm, vitality, inspiration, ecstasy, rejuvenation, union, and passion are other expressions of this same energy.

Any personal rebirth and healing of your inner shame needs to include a wise, loving, and passionate relationship with your own sexuality. Listen to your own wisdom. I believe you'll likely come to the same conclusion.

JUNE 6

A Race of Time

"There are always a million reasons to keep
going, but never a good reason to stop."
—Wayne Muller

Notice what happens when a mother takes hold of her child and pours her love into her precious offspring. I was waiting in an airport and a mother and her son, who appeared to be about twelve, were intertwined in a loving embrace while sleeping. I couldn't take my eyes off of them. I was so nurtured by their expression of affection, stillness, connection, and presence.

Each day is a treasure. One-by-one, they come to us like a meadow full of natural abundance which we are walking into for the first time. The choice is ours to put both feet firmly in the present moment and set forth to gather bits and pieces of inspiration and redemption and eventually return them to the soil of our families and communities.

Consider your days as opportunities to put to rest the gospel of consumption. Commerce is vital. Consumption is not. In fact, consumption as a value and practice tears at the heart of being human. The one reality of everyday life that is being voraciously consumed by many of us is time. It's as if we're in a trance and running a race with no finish line.

We can still move efficiently through our days without running this race. It is not a speed issue as much as it is an attention issue. We need reminders to stop, not just stop being physically and mentally in motion, but stop unconsciously consuming every passing minute.

Ageless wisdom reminds us that there is a built-in divine design in our being which requires that we let our ears fall on the moment, slow down our breathing, and set down the tools of work and productivity at least one-seventh of our time. Move through this time by attending to what would be most nourishing, beautiful, and restful.

This quality of attention on what is truly rejuvenating is what you require from time to time. There is no urgency, task, or compulsive activity controlling you. You have found a very good reason to stop consuming time and start treasuring what time provides.

June 7

Falling Down

"A person of considerable strength,
when alone, may fall down."

I've witnessed very strong men collapse when cornered by their deep, unresolved feelings. Women, too. I include myself among them. It may have taken us decades to fall down. Others see through our defenses. The weight of truth and life finally slays us.

Inside, we are likely brokenhearted to a degree. It is a spiritual coup when the strong succumb to no longer holding it together. It is the beginning of putting ourselves back together in ways that divinely rewire us and crack open our hearts of compassion for ourselves and our human family.

We all have vulnerabilities. Some of us hide them better than others. Showing our vulnerabilities gets conditioned or trained out of many of us. The strong individualism of "stand on your own two feet" has been spoon-fed throughout our culture. The holy grail of excelling at all costs has exacted a severe toll.

Others of us have rejected this paradigm. Even that has produced side effects in the struggle to find our place. We long to ease these burdens for ourselves, friends, and loved ones. Eventually, even the strongest among us, sense the urgency to fall down and let go. And, fall we do.

The common thread that allows the strong to break open into vulnerability is the sense of being safe, having a safety net. To me, this is someone or somewhere or some group that provides a judgment-free zone into which we can fall and feel the heart of compassion.

Find your net of safety. Make it a priority. True strength arises when facing your vulnerabilities and the fears which generate them. This practice rewrites the story of who you believe yourself to be.

June 8

Marriage with the Infinite
by Dennis Rivers

"The Hubble (telescope) photographs of stars being born, and of zillions of galaxies filling up what were previously imagined to be empty quadrants of space, represent one of the most dramatic and inspiring streams of recent scientific information flowing into the mind of Earth spirituality.

There is another stream of information coming to us, not as dramatic as star pictures, but much more intimate, with lots of implications about the people we can become and the world we can create. This is the information about our brains, each person's garden of approximately one hundred billion neurons. One author called it 'the three pound universe.' Just as the Hubble telescope dramatically changed our view of 'empty space,' new brain studies are dramatically expanding our vision of the six inches between our ears. Current estimates are that the human body contains approximately one hundred trillion cells, including approximately one hundred billion neurons.

The community that we call our body also contains approximately a thousand trillion bacteria, most of whom do their best to keep our show on the road. One scientist made an estimate of how much information is stored in all these cells and came up with an estimate of around thirty-five trillion gigabytes, which is to say, really a lot.

So, while we might be inclined when looking at the vastness of the night sky, to imagine ourselves as mere specks in endless space, I want to invite you to explore the other side of the paradox. **We may be a speck, but we are also infinite.** Each person is a living universe, and as a culture we have hardly begun to mobilize our inner resources."[5]

June 9

Heartist

"Everyone is an artist in some way."
—Matthew Fox

Several years ago I reconnected with a friend who pours her heart into art. Standing in her studio, there were two new creations displayed on a wall that stopped me. They were captivating, as if they had emerged out of the primordial mystery. These almost accidental assemblages of color and form seemed to belong together. My question was, "How did you create these?"

Her answers reminded me that life is much like art. She described entering into the magic of the present moment and finding her way into the dimension of not evaluating, judging, assessing, or controlling. It was art as meditation and prayer and allowing that meditation process to reveal color, shape, texture, and form. She clearly had a feel for allowing Spirit and heart to join in creation. I would call her a "heartist."

Life as art happens as we allow ourselves to experience the present moment as a new canvas poised for the emergence of an original idea or inspiration. Each passing click of time is filled with the Divine Presence waiting to bring forth the beauty and creativity that we are.

Staying in the present moment, connect with your heart today. From this context and feeling, see all that is around you as art. Appreciate the creative explosion that is everywhere. Ah so.

June 10

Your Inner Guru

"There is no such thing as an enlightened individual, just individuals having many enlightened moments."
—Christian Pankhurst

Years ago, I attended a satsang led by a young man thought to be enlightened. As hundreds of eager listeners gathered around him, I had to ask myself, "Why have I come?" Here was a young man five years younger than me who was part of a lineage of gurus. As a world teacher of peace and goodwill, there seemed to be little that was extraordinary about him other than he was able to articulate simple concepts in front of large audiences.

Those we follow and shower with adoration are often mirror reflections of what we seek within ourselves. As Buddhist teacher Lama Yeshe expresses, "Our inner guru, our own clear wisdom, can accomplish everything. The practice of guru-yoga, therefore, is primarily a method for learning how to listen to this inner guru." Your inner guru is the mind in your heart. As Yeshe says, it is your own clear wisdom.

Heart-intelligence teacher Christian Pankhurst says that "you are me cleverly disguised as you." We are powerfully drawn to those who express and model who we long to be. We want to be like them. In reality, they are mirrors. The ultimate prize is turning the wisdom and love we experience through others into love and wisdom freely flowing through us.

Contemplate in your heart the love and wisdom you have cherished in someone else. Feel the power and gratitude of this experience. Now in your inner awareness see this cherished individual giving this love and wisdom to you. Receive this into your heart. Gently hold and claim this love and wisdom as your own.

JUNE 11

Memories

"What is past is prologue."
—William Shakespeare

Many of us have been long time advocates of doing what is necessary to learn how to live more in the present moment. I'm beginning to wonder if this is as important as it's been made out to be. Being attuned to living in the present moment has been uplifted as the holy grail of consciousness.

Whether our consciousness hangs out in the past, present, or future, what matters most is how we hold it in our hearts and the resulting actions we take. Because I'm sixty-two, memories now represent the large bulk of my turn of the wheel of life this time around.

Our past is still alive in us. Our relationship with it changes over the years as do our memories of it. Startling scientific research is concluding that specific memories can be targeted by non-addictive drugs and literally erased, or, at the very least, the emotional response to that memory can be greatly reduced or eliminated. We would welcome this breakthrough particularly for traumatic memories.

At the same time, we know that having memory is the laboratory for being wiser, more compassionate people. In other words, we benefit from learning from our mistakes and missteps. Many past experiences that formerly showed their painful fangs have transformed into tender teachers of healing truth for many of us. My mother gradually felt her way through a lingering inner disturbance which had been the result of recalling how disconnected and angry she had felt toward me when I was a teen. By going through, she softened and became a very tender loving mother to me the last thirty years of her life.

Even those memories that feel unresolved can energize the tensile strength of being a spiritual human. Over the years, even with these unanswered questions, what I would describe as an inner strengthening and stretching has led me to feel a humble acceptance of past events that remain unexplained and to gradually cut the cord of obsession that needs to have everything make sense.

The wisdom of the heart obliges us to have a sacred place at the table for our past with both its dark places and joyful oases. This realm of consciousness continues to offer us endless points of wise reflection, the most important of which may be that through these memories we discover the contrast between our human experience and the permanent light of Divine Presence that is our true self.

June 12

Gumption

"I can always look back and say, at least
I ain't led no hum-drum life."
—Forrest Gump (Winston Groom)

Yesterday, I reconnected with an old acquaintance for the first time in fourteen years. It felt timely. We realized the similarities of our lives. She had been completely absorbed in being a sole business owner for almost twenty years. She went on to say that she knew the time was coming soon to sell her business so that she could devote herself to her art. In her core, she is an artist. This had taken a backseat to keeping her business going. I nodded knowingly. The experience of being under the spell of a work commitment that is all-consuming was familiar.

Following the wisdom of the heart is an urgency to be ourselves and know ourselves no matter what we're up to. I feel this urgency amplified when I'm at a crossroads. One sign says, "stay the course," and the other says, "follow your heart."

What is required to blaze a new trail in our lives? Gumption. I had to look up the definition. Gumption is "shrewd or spirited initiative and resourcefulness." That's it. Gumption is essential for writing the script for a future that is uncertain. It calls us to bring forward out of dormancy our finest gifts of self-expression. Resourcefulness is heart-generated. All our mental, physical, psychological, and creative resources come together in our heart-space and synchronize in support of who we have come here to be now.

Become still and quiet. Bring simple attention to your breath. For a few moments, breathe slowly into that spot about two fingers below your navel. This helps you feel grounded and solid. Now bring to your awareness an issue that is needing to be resolved or a decision that is needing to be made. With your attention centered now in your heart, sense and feel that all your inner resources are joining together to assist you—one spiral of creative energy. This spiral is surrounding and enfolding you with the presence and power necessary to move you through what lies in front of you. Feel your resolve and strength. Give thanks.

JUNE 13
Lover and Beloved

"I have become the One I love, and the One I love has become me! We are two spirits infused in a (single) body."
—al-Hallaj

Ageless wisdom teaches that as we open to the depths of the heart, inevitably we will come to discover that love is our being, our source, our selves. Both lover and beloved reside within. By design, each of us is a deep well that receives love from an infinite Source and gives from that same Source. So, rather than being a dry and empty container aching to be filled with love, love is drawn from a fullness we truly feel inside.

I get it how this contradicts what almost all of us experienced. We learned that love is parceled out and comes to us because we earned it or got lucky. Aside from a few exceptions, religion, popular literature and music, family dynamics, and cultural norms have undergirded this lie. Our natural design has been hidden from us.

Today, begin again. Listen to the heart, listen to the heart deep within. Rewrite your story. Begin with these words: "In the silence of my heart is an ageless wisdom. I have ears to hear its message: love is my being and my source. Lover and beloved dwell in me."

JUNE 14

Please Release Me

"I can never close my lips where I have opened my heart."
—Charles Dickens

Saint Padre Pio transformed the Catholic sacrament of confession into an initiation for powerful healings. Countless thousands came to him. He would often sit for ten to twelve hours a day listening to the hearts of those he served. He was able to arouse a radical honesty that cleansed people of their darkest truths.

Confession to him was far more than a trite exercise of revealing very minor indulgences or offenses and concluding with some kind of rote formula for forgiveness. With each person, he viewed confession as a profound opportunity to be deeply healed and drawn closer to Divine Presence. Often, those leaving Pio's confessional would be ecstatic.

What I've come to know over many years of being a witness to the messiness of chronic shame, guilt, or worry in others, is that living out of alignment with our heartfelt values is destructive and painful. In fact, it can be crippling. What we hold against ourselves or another keeps us trapped inside our own self-inflicted wounds.

A healing power is generated when admitting to the Divine Presence or a trusted person the nature of our harmful actions whether it is one isolated event or a longtime pattern of behavior. Freedom comes from not hanging on. This release and encounter with raw honesty must truly be from the heart. Nothing else has lasting effect. You do it for you.

June 15

Wilderness Calls

"The love of wilderness is more than a hunger for what is always beyond reach; it is also an expression of loyalty to the earth...the only home we shall ever know, the only paradise we ever need."
—Edward Abbey

Wilderness lands are those spaces in our world that are largely untrampled and untamed. For millennia, humanity has imagined and sought to create and experience paradise. The ancient roots of the word paradise mean "to create a walled enclosure." In other words, let's create a space that is entirely self-contained and free of outer influences—a sacred space in which beauty and harmony are so wondrous, it is as if the gods lived there.

"Immediately the Spirit impelled him to go out into the wilderness." (Mark 1:12) Like our elder brother Jesus, we long to explore the wilderness. It draws us into spaces that are untrampled and untamed by the ways of the world both in nature and our inner lives. In these spaces, we breathe differently. We see and hear more easily the Divine Presence looking and sounding back at us. Ancient stirrings are aroused that remind us that we are beloved.

So, whether you go into your closet and close the door to find your sacred wilderness, or you drive your car to a parking area, get out and eventually walk past the sign that says "Entering a Wilderness Area," give thanks for the endless opportunities here on Earth to swing open the gates of paradise and enter in.

JUNE 16

Now I See

"Give up the right to strike back."

I went through months of having vengeful energy directed at me in the midst of a divorce. The reflex to strike back was strong. However, I was profoundly aware of her pain and I was deeply aware that giving life to cycles of revenge would only add to her pain and mine as well. It would serve nothing for me to act upon these urges except to once again magnify what I don't want—more suffering.

Many cultures are addicted to revenge and punishment. We see it in the policies of governments, in fundamentalist organizations, and right on down to online chats and personal relationships.

The following words that have largely been attributed to Gandhi, no matter how many times we hear them, speak truth: "An eye for an eye will make the whole world blind." Retribution begins on the inside. As Jesus often implied, whatever we think and feel in our hearts and minds is as good as done. Both Jesus and Gandhi are reminding us of how the laws of consciousness in our universe work without fail. Revenge begets revenge. Understanding begets understanding. Love begets love. Our inner choices have consequences.

I once read a story about a little girl who found out that her cat had been poisoned by her elderly neighbor who lived alone. The cat died. As her parents were conspiring about how to seek revenge on the neighbor, their daughter said, "Maybe she's lonely. What if we made some cookies and gave them to her or threw a party for her?"

This little girl inspires us to remove our adulterated blinders and see rightly. Resolution can only come by stopping the cycle of harm in our thoughts or actions by taking the courageous step of reaching out to connect. This is the way of healing, the way of the heart.

June 17

C'mon!

"Is your nose pressed against the glass?"

At eight years of age, I was straddled across the back of a working horse, gazing across the rugged redlands of Roger Mills County, Oklahoma. Just gazing. It was just me, the earth, and the sky. I was wrestled out of my gazing stupor by the distant waggle of Uncle Alec's voice: "C'mon boy! Stay with me. There's work to do!" Disrupted, I gathered myself and with a firm kick, my horse set off following Uncle A's buckskin, his favorite working horse.

Great Uncle A was a born and bred cowboy destined to be one for life. This tall, kindhearted man with a tall Stetson on top, was almost always seen with a clump of chewin' tobacco tucked in his cheek. He gave me the boyhood gift many times over of experiencing a made-for-TV world, his western land and soundscape of horses, cattle, and coyotes. Hanging out with the big animals, a thousand pounds or more in size, I felt so small and powerless in their massive presence.

Even long after my childhood passage with Uncle A, I would think of him and feel envy and awe. He lived a life he truly loved even with all the physical pounding. My imagination thrived in his world.

How's your imagination these days? Pay tribute to the longings of the child in you. Give back to yourself what you gave away in your adulterated world—a daily dose of imagination which creates a world you love. Let your body feel it. It'll do you good.

June 18

Real Community

"Darkness cannot drive out darkness; only light can do that.
Hatred cannot drive out hatred; only love can do that."
—Dr. Martin Luther King, Jr.

The willow tree in front of me is stripped bare. It looks cold, vulnerable, and alone in the stillness of this January morning. It reminds me to not judge by appearances. I know its annual transformation is coming in several months.

In a workshop I led, a young woman, while standing in the center of a circle, broke open, and expressed her hatred for her mother who had left her and her sisters when she was very young. She and her sisters became foster children. We let her vent and feel the rage she had obviously entombed inside for a very long time.

When she came to the end of her release, she was on her knees supported by several people close by. I asked her if she'd be willing to lie down on her back on the floor. She agreed. All of us knelt down beside her, and with her permission, each of us placed a hand on her. After a time of silence, we began to silently shower her with the energy of love and compassion while one of us whispered messages of love and support in her ear. As she and the rest of us had tears flowing, her final words were, "Truth is, I love my mother so much. I miss her terribly."

There is always a seed of genesis in each of us awaiting its time of germination. There are always photons of light gathering in the darkness of our life's experience preparing to brighten us when least expected. Being in community with others is the place where these phenomena occur most often. It is where we see all sides of one another. We face the opportunities to bring light into darkness and love into bitterness and hatred.

Some will leave, and others will stay and go through the human tunnel of truth together. Seek to find those who choose to remain when shadows and vulnerabilities appear and strip us down. This is where transforming love does its perfect work. This is real community.

JUNE 19

The Floodgates

"The waters are rising."

My life has been touched by the effects of devastating floods. From Colorado to New Orleans, the realities of extreme nature events have overflowed into my life. In one flood event, a friend died attempting to save others. Another nature event with raging storm waters resulted in me sitting with and counseling flood victims who had lost loved ones, jobs, and homes. When the floodgates open, so does the true spirit of community.

Gathering waters, especially storm waters, become a powerful force. What waters are gathering in your life that need attention? If real and present needs and feelings go unattended for too long they almost always rise to the point in which the floodgates are forced to open. You then either need to be rescued from the overwhelm or you pour out what is inside you in unpredictable and at times destructive ways. Like many of you, I have fallen prey to this on occasion.

Stress creates an accumulation of unresolved feelings and experiences. When there is an inflow of feelings, there needs to be a corresponding outflow or release, just as much as when we inhale we must exhale. This natural rhythm minimizes stress. Living well depends on it.

Be your own best lifeguard. Whether it is simple deep breathing practices or meditations or prayers or exercise or playing music, the options are endless to create a safe outflow of energy for what you may be damning up. Open the floodgates from time to time and let the waters flow out. Do it long before the waters are full to overflowing. Then you are better able to support those you love in doing the same.

June 20

Childish Things

"We are playing little kid games."
—Carolyn Myss

Putting away childish things makes sense. Yet, it is way easier said than done especially as we live with the onslaught of societal messages to the contrary as well as the deeply humbling reality of the effects of our choices. All of us have felt the weight of adult challenges pressing down on our shoulders, the weight of being an adult feeling cornered in an adult world that grips us tenaciously with its demands.

In these predicaments, the reality is that we don't put away childish things. We get overrun by the childish ways of an amped up ego which causes us to lose the ability to look more honestly inside. We do what we want.

You and I have justified living compromised lives, saying at one time or another such things as, "I do it because everybody else does it," or, "I'll get what is mine because I deserve it," or, "You hurt me so I am going to hurt you back but even more," or, "I'll lie about another to keep me from looking bad and to make them look bad." These childish ways are regressive and aggressive. We're frightened by the world and we act from this fear.

The heart-wise way of life is one of rigorous honesty and facing what we are doing to ourselves and others. But, we never walk this path alone.

We need a spiritual guide, someone who understands the realities of walking straight into our own egoic shadows because they themselves have faced what the great mystic Teresa of Avila called "inner reptiles."

Listening with deep compassion, the spiritual guide encourages depths of honesty which have likely never before been mined.

This is sacred work. It is the path to life, a life in which unconditional love is not a buzz word but a spiritual by-product of deep wisdom and compassion for one another.

June 21

Great Cathedrals

"God saw all that he had made, and it was very good."
—Genesis 1:31

One of the great cathedrals of the world stands on a hill in Chartres, France. Having visited this holy site, I can attest to the following words from Amberly Polidor: "People come for inspiration, beauty, God, or all three. The design of the cathedral involved sacred geometry, the use of numbers, angles, and shapes that mirror the principles the faithful believe God used in creating the universe." This great cathedral stands on a spot that for millennia has been considered sacred. Pilgrims have traveled to this site since before the time of Jesus.

A long-time friend recently reminded me of walks I used to take with her through Escalante Canyon in western Colorado especially in the spring when wildflowers were blooming among the ancient petroglyphs, giant red rocks, and vast blue sky. Everywhere you looked there was evidence of sacred geometry like the hands of a great potter had mastered the art of rock creation. Yes, this was and still is a cathedral, a holy place. I could feel Divine Presence there just as I'm sure the ancient petroglyph artists had experienced fifteen centuries ago.

The first time I walked the McKenzie River Trail near Eugene, Oregon was breathtaking. Giant fir and hemlock trees breathed their way into my being as the waters of the river echoed their healing presence all around me. This too is a cathedral. Admiring the great trees standing still and silent near the ever-present flow of hydropower is a divinely healing contrast.

Each one of us is a cathedral. The root of the word cathedral means "seat." In medieval churches, a cathedral was where there was a throne or seat of a bishop—someone who was deemed to have power and nearer to Divine Presence.

These many hundreds of years later, we realize that the seat of Divine Presence lies in everyone, the cathedral of soul and body. Once discovered, it is awe-inspiring. Yes, each of us is the embodiment of sacred geometry and the numbers, angles, and shapes that mirror the creation of the universe. Appreciate and be in awe of the wonder that you are. You have been billions of years in the making.

June 22

I Am New

The long yet steady stream of ebbs and flows,
Ups and downs, highs and lows,
Speak to me to return home, home to my soul.
Life, always cycling and circulating, resolving to settle me
And heal me and hold me.
I resist no more.
Having been alone in the madness of self-inflicted confusion,
I now breathe into the heart of fluid surrender and
Feel the silent rapture, a radiant infinite profusion.
Endless awareness overshadows all apprehension.
A Presence Divine rises up from the deep-middle.
I let it rise and wash me clean through.
I am grateful. I am empty. I am new.

At certain times in my past I've declared, "Nothing would surprise me any more." That voice is cynical and tired and weighted down by worldly uncertainties.

The adage, "Keep going, just keep going," is a powerful piece of wisdom. These are not marching orders about having a fighting spirit. This is more about staying the course. Hold firm in your heart to the piece of wisdom that all things come to you at the right time if you simply let them.

You'll be overtaken by a divine event. As my poetic expression above reveals, let it rise from the deep-middle of conscious awareness in you. Create the space today to breathe, relax, and turn within to your heart. Feel the power of allowing, allowing all things to come to you at the right time. Trust the genius of this eternal truth in you.

JUNE 23

A Swirling Eddy

"Vulnerability is about showing up and being seen. It's tough to do that when we're terrified about what people might see or think."
—Brene Brown, Ph.D.

I joined a large group on a guided whitewater raft trip in high water season on the Colorado River near the Colorado-Utah border. Most everyone boarded one of the four large rafts commanded by an experienced guide. I volunteered to paddle one of several small inflatable kayaks. I didn't admit I was a novice. After two hours of pure bliss and easy paddling, we landed on a sandbar for a break.

Those paddling the kayaks were then given instructions by one of the guides. They went something like this: "The water gets much faster below here. When you get in the river immediately start working to your left. Stay to the left because at the first bend there is a large whirling eddy to your right. You do not want to get sucked into it, because it will turn you around, and you will likely be sucked back into the fast water and flip over. If you get dumped in the river, it is critical to remember to put your feet out in front of you and lay back. Your life preserver will help you rise to the top of the big waves and eventually you can float down to an area where one of the larger rafts can maneuver to pick you up. Does everyone understand these instructions?" I remember saying, "Yes."

Off we went. Right away, I was surprised by the swiftness of river. I became so focused on trying to keep the raft from overturning that I blacked out the guide's instructions. I had veered too far right! Just like the guide foretold, I was being sucked into this giant swirling eddy!! In the eddy I had no control over what I was doing or where the raft was going. The eddy turned me around so that I was now facing upriver and in an instant I was sucked back into the current. The kayak flipped and I was thrown out.

The waves were house size, the water was wildly powerful and swift, and the force of it was pushing me under no matter how hard I fought to get my head above water. Quickly, I was taking in water and couldn't get any breath. I was in full panic-mode and feeling powerless against this mighty river. I thought I may very well drown. Then, like a flash, I heard the voice of that guide in my awareness, "put your feet out in front of you and lay back. Your life preserver will help you rise to the top." So I stopped desperately flailing against the force of the water and followed his instruction. Just like he said, I rose to the top of the giant waves.

Once my terror began to subside at the realization that I was likely going to be okay, I had the roller-coaster ride of my life! Downriver, where the waters weren't so swift and wild, I was pulled into one of the large rafts waiting for me there.

When we don't own up to our vulnerabilities and inexperience, we do so at our own peril. We get sucked into childish ego behaviors. Mine nearly took my life.

Owning and revealing your vulnerabilities can save you from painful outcomes. Wise are those who choose to be honest. By the way, my boyhood name was Eddie. At times, life gives us literal messages. Pay attention.

June 24

Freezing in my Tent

"It's a wonder, it's a wonder, it's a wonder every day."
—Jon West

The first night camping in a tent at 6,700' elevation, I froze. After a trip to buy a warm comforter to supplement the sleeping bag, I slept comfortably for the remaining nights.

This experience reminded me of my connection to my ancestors who lived close to the natural elements—rain, snow, extreme heat and cold, powerful thunderstorms, and winds, drought, you name it. They endured several years of living in an earthen dugout in Western Oklahoma. The raw nature of being in this world was a way of life and lent them the ongoing opportunity to respect and be in awe of the transcendent power and unpredictability of nature.

We all have, at times, been humbled by the puzzling ironies of this most holy place. It gives and takes away. It enfolds us in deep silence and roars with a mythological fury. It intimidates us with its awesome wonder and reveals to us a universe that tenderly opens our hearts. It overcomes all odds to sustain itself in the midst of unflinching exploitation, and, in other ways, reminds us of its razor-thin vulnerabilities.

These things could describe the divine-human being. You are a peculiar set of ironies, strengths, vulnerabilities, and wonders rolled into one far-out creation. Something spectacular has taken place in the universe to create each of you. Nature all around you is your ever-present mirror of this unmistakable truth. It all is truly a wonder even when I'm freezing in my tent.

JUNE 25

As We Are

"Joy....God has placed it all around us....It is in
everything and anything we might experience."
—Jon Krakauer

Remote Sagres Point at the southwestern tip of Portugal was for centuries considered the westernmost point of the inhabited world. It was often called "the end of the world." The vast Atlantic Ocean stretched out beyond the horizon into the oblivion of uncharted territory. Westward voyages were perilous and those courageous few who dared to go were true pioneers.

It is captivating to imagine why anyone would sail out beyond what they thought was the end of the world. Yet, each of us is part earthbound and part celestial. These proportions are unique in each one of us. Some of us almost always stay close to home like my brother-in-law's mother who had never ventured out of her small Italian neighborhood in Syracuse until she came to her son's wedding in Texas when she was near sixty. Others of us abhor the status quo and can't stay put any longer than the time it takes a damp towel to dry in the Arizona midday sun.

There are those of us who want a map and a well traveled navigator who knows the route very well before we go for a latte. There are those of us who seek to travel without a map, because we go where the spirit leads us.

Usually, we most admire and are in awe of great explorers and boundary-busting pioneers. With that said, I confess that I also admire those who have loved living in the same place for fifty-plus years and never seriously considered being anywhere else. They'd much rather venture to the front porch than to the wild places beyond the end of the world. That's astonishing not just to me but to many of us.

This all comes down to accepting ourselves as we are. Odds are, there will be others that won't. The measure of success is the degree to which we honestly value and appreciate the choices we have made. The world around us is a poor judge and rightfully so.

Closer to Enjoyment

"In order to be who you are, you must be willing
to let go of who you think you are."
—Michael Singer

During a recent transition period in my life, I reconnected and now am rooming with my longtime friend Samuel. He is distinct from almost all of my other friends and associates. Samuel genuinely enjoys life. He has a deep groove that sounds like, looks like, acts like, and smells like enjoyment. It's a bit sobering to realize how rare true enjoyment is in our society.

His brain-mind isn't preoccupied with the mouthpieces of society's minutia of insignificance. His attention is on staying informed and then deciding what he can bring to his community and world that uplifts and addresses what ails us. He does so with a clear and genuine affirmation of greater possibilities and progressive and inspired action steps, whistling and singing along the way. Yes, Samuel is frequently on his own everyday stage singing his favorite uplifting and heartwarming tunes. I've been humming and singing along with him, realizing that I could stand to rewrite the drama playing itself out on my inner stage.

His life isn't perfect. There are key longings that have gone unfulfilled. Yet, on he goes laughing and shedding light on what is beautiful and potent in our world. Now that I've been around him for a number of weeks, his energetic brushstrokes are splattering on me a bit and I'm enjoying it.

In my past, at times I've been reluctant to hang around people who truly enjoy life, partly because they reflected what had been missing from my own. I've been enjoying life more in recent months. In part, it is because I have been living with the question, "Who would I be if I truly enjoyed my life?" I give this to you to try on.

JUNE 27

Throw a Pot

"Mold me and make me."

I'm enamored with how potters throw pots on a potter's wheel. Once clay is centered on the wheel, it's still a lump of clay waiting for what's next. The potter's hands then act on the clay, pressing it down, digging into the heart of the clay, and opening a well. The clay is then stretched out, making room for growth.

All wheel-pottery can be understood by basic movements of clay: centering, opening, and shaping. Get these three movements figured out and you'll also know a secret to the spiritual life.

When working at the pottery wheel, if you can't center the clay, you may as well hang up your apron. When you watch a master potter, they make it look easy, but when you sit behind the wheel, it's not near as easy as it looks which I discovered while sitting at the wheel in an art class. You need to have a nose for the center—"cone it up, press it down."

There is a center to your life. To develop a nose for it, you may need to sit at your wheel for a bit. What I mean is, while you sit and notice the turnings of your mind, place your full attention on your heart. Therein, amid all these turnings, is your center. You'll come to know what all potters and lovers know—the sacred art of opening. From this heart-space, dig inside and ask to be opened like wet and stretchable clay in the hands of a master potter. Then, it is as if unseen hands begin to take what you see, how you feel, and who you are, and shape you into a new vessel.

JUNE 28

Out of Hiding

"I play in order to live."

One summer, I, along with many other college students from around the country, migrated to Glacier National Park in Northern Montana to work for the summer. I was one of the gardeners at the historic Glacier Park Lodge. Along the football-field-long walkway that led up to the lodge front entrance, the blooming delphiniums were prolific and seven to eight feel tall by mid-summer.

We gardeners soon realized that we could actually hide in these clusters of tall delphiniums. Tourists strolling only a few feet away couldn't see us. Often we'd be chuckling underneath our breath while tourists standing no more than six feet away would be conversing without realizing we were hidden close by. We created our own hidden world in the midst of all that beauty that allowed us to eavesdrop on private conversations of passersby. We'd then suddenly pop out of the delphiniums to everyone's surprise and we'd all laugh together. This kind of silliness energized all of what we did. More work got done and more fun was had by all.

Each of us has access to many expressions of wisdom and intelligence. One of these is play. I'm not suggesting you hide and eavesdrop on unsuspecting passersby. What I am suggesting is to get back into your body. Animate your life. Too much mental focus leads to too much madness and far less insight.

There was a tribe in West Africa that needed to address the question of improving waste disposal. Stay with me. They did what they have done for generations. They danced and sang and dreamed about this challenge and danced and sang some more. Visions and practical steps arose from using their bodies as playful transporters to higher wisdom and intelligence. Through this unconventional approach to tackling a real world concern, they were able to get the job done but in a much more creative, cooperative, and efficient way.

Apply this true story to your life. Call your childlike instincts out of hiding without retreating into childhood memories. It's not about reliving childhood. It's simply about opening to being alive in your body and allowing room for the art of surprise and spontaneity to have space to play in your world.

JUNE 29

The Work of Life

"At its best work (poetry) is an intimate conversation between what you think is you and what you think is other than you."
—David Whyte

I have worked at making a living for many years. Through those years, I felt a yawning gap between the work I was doing to make a living and what my soul was longing to express. Eventually, I was able to join the two. Many of us are compelled to do this. The edict to "get a job" is agonizingly empty.

With the mainstream job market constantly undergoing the shifts and tremors of this technological age, more and more of us are being pulled toward a livelihood we create out of our own inspired vision and ingenuity. Millions of us are together on this visionary expedition. Our individual work is to combine our wisdom, inspiration, creativity, and desire into a one-of-a-kind expression that serves our human family and expands the circles of lasting love, beauty, and well-being.

Actually, we all feel our hearts tugging on us to create our unique version of love in this world, be it through work, family, creativity, or service. This is our life's work—to flow the gift of our light into the heart of our world. It is for this that we all have taken birth. We temper our days with this calling.

In the spiritual tradition I have come through, there is a well-known teaching. Paraphrased, it says, "Divine Presence goes with you wherever you are, drawing you steadily toward the good." A willingness to infuse your life's work with the power of this spiritual energy carries you a very long way. Keep going.

June 30

Lasting Sustenance

"An integral being knows without going, sees without looking, and accomplishes without doing."
—Lao Tzu

For as long as I can remember, I've straddled two worlds inside of me. One world is the persistent feeling of wanting others to like me and wanting what I do to serve and support my community—others first. My other world is the deep need to do that which is right for me and my well being—me first. These polarities have often left me feeling caught in between, not knowing which direction to take. I have been caught up in my either-or world, as if there was a right and wrong choice.

Being in a service profession has often left many of us wondering how to truly serve others and how to truly take care of ourselves as well. How do we put the two together?

Here's my takeaway over the years. Beware of heavily relying on the need for outer confirmation and validation of who you are and what you do. This creates a hole in the bottom of your cup. This invariably leads to the compulsion to overwork because you are rarely ever able to fill your cup. There's a lot of wasted energy. Over-efforting is required.

Where there is great strain and effort, there is great stress. Where there is great stress, we are often found "trying to do the right thing" or trying to impress upon someone how good or noble we are.

The law of least effort reminds you that nature's intelligence operates with ease. There are no competing forces or wasted effort. When your actions are inspired by love—your natural inheritance— you are putting the law of least effort into action. Energy is amplified rather than depleted. You heal the inner split of seeing an either-or world. What you give to yourself, you give to the whole world, and vice versa. Let the world you serve come to meet you within the love, courage, and wisdom pouring through you from your own heart.

JULY 1

A Deep Well

"What's down there?"

John Sanford, in the preface of his book <u>The Kingdom Within</u>, recalls from his childhood in New England an old well which supplied water to his family homestead. He remembers this old well vividly, because at one time he could always draw up cool, clear water from its depths. In order to have water, family members had to be devoted to drawing up the water several times each day. This had been his family's experience for generations. Eventually, the family farmhouse was modernized and a new well was drilled in a different location with a modern electric pump installed. The old well was covered.

Some time later, John thought of the old well and with curiosity removed the cover and to his surprise discovered that the old well was bone dry. Wells are supplied with water flowing through tiny underground rivulets. The water keeps flowing into and supplying the well as long as water is consistently being drawn up. Once you cease drawing the water up and quit drinking from that source, the tiny rivulets begin to close up. Eventually, the underground water is unable to flow to that particular well. The water supply flows somewhere else or ceases flowing altogether.

Be devoted to drawing up from your depth that which is heartfelt and imaginative. Spiritual devotion to a daily heart-centered practice draws the flow of creative energy up and out into many aspects of your daily life, baptizing you with a refreshing outlook, particularly when you are laboring in something painful or obstinate.

It can begin with something as simple as focusing all your attention on your heart and breathing deeply, keeping your attention there for one to two minutes. This is like drawing up cool, sweet water from a deep well for the first time. You'll be so refreshed, you'll simply want more.

July 2

Through the Swamp

"Stay the course."

Life is a series of decisions, decisions, decisions. Like the scattering of millions of tiny seeds into fertile soil creates an abundant landscape of growth, we are hinged to the creative results flowing forth from the archive of our decisions. Wild stuff shows up.

About six months into my seminary studies, I was evaluated by a group of ten well-seasoned ministers. At the completion of a particularly difficult evaluation session, I was asked to leave the room and sit in a chair in the hallway. After an agonizing wait, I was asked to return to the room and again take my seat. One of them served as spokesperson for the group and said, "We believe you should stop now and do something else. We don't believe you will make a good minister." Now, more than twenty-seven years later, twenty-five of those in ministry, I look into the heart of that person that was me and attempt to comprehend what empowered me to bear that stamp of clear disapproval and stay on the path I had set before me. This is the wild stuff I was referring to.

So many of us have been there in these swamps where we feel like we're knee deep in alligators. We may get so focused on keeping the alligators at bay, we completely lose sight of why we ended up in the swamp to begin with. We're in the swamp simply because we are making a necessary crossing in order to get to the other side and keep going.

I had several close associates who reminded me that the alligators were doing what alligators do. If I hadn't received that piece of life-giving, heart-centered wisdom, then I likely would have been distracted and battling alligators for a long time to come. Fortunately, this wisdom saved me. I reconnected with why I had come to this point in my life. I kept going and continued to ask for support along the way. I made it to the other side of the swamp and way beyond.

I deeply relate to these decisive words spoken by religious reformer John Shelby Spong: "Our task is to call people to be deeply and fully human, so that we can live beyond our fears, so that we can be life-giving people, so that we can learn to give our love away." May your fears never stop you.

July 3

Master Teacher

"The goal of life is to make your heartbeat match the beat
of the universe, to match your nature with Nature."
—Joseph Campbell

These words are a beautiful summation of the heart-wise way of life. Everything in life leads us in this direction if we allow it. Dorothy in the Wizard of Oz is right. We are here to figure out how to go home.

Usually our hearts beat without us being consciously aware of their perpetual rhythm which are essential to human life and well being. Nor are we actively attuned to the heart's amplified field which is essential to facilitating the experience of our connection with each other, our natural world, and our universe and beyond. More simply put, we lost our way and simply forgot what we as children knew instinctively.

Our physical hearts have evolved into what they are today over eons of time. I see the heart as so much more than this amazing organ. It also is a highly evolved divine messenger and teacher located in our physical bodies. Hearts are continually teaching us that consistent flow, rhythm, and connection generate and regenerate life-affirming energy and stand as the keys to becoming a match with our grand nature. Life is about flow, rhythm, and connection.

I am encouraging you to attune to this master teacher cloaked in physical form. Your heart and its amplified field are teaching you non-stop how to live fully through all the changes of your life.

Flow, rhythm, connection—meditate on these things today. Your deep instinct and faith will likely begin to return.

July 4
This Old House

"Last night I lost the world, and gained the universe."
—C. JoyBell C.

Having passed through a long cycle of gradually accumulating things, I recently reversed that trend and released much of my stuff. What's left is in a small storage unit. Little remains in my house except silence and empty space. Inside this sanctum, it feels like a prayer is hovering close at hand, inviting grief and gratitude to ferment in my heart.

Silence and breathing space are the mystic's path to freedom—freedom from clinging to things of this world. We cling because we've been lured into believing that these things give us our identity. So, when we let things go, we lose our identity and worth. The mystic knows better. Their identity arises from the depth of love, spiritual presence, and connectedness they experience in their hearts and souls.

With most all of my remaining things stored away, I breathe into this hollowed out space inside myself and wonder what is to become of me. I humbly stand in this wilderness and ask that I be assisted in remaining open to embrace whatever lies ahead.

Join with me this day and return to the land of your soul. Become aware of your attachments of this world. Bring your awareness of them into your silent heart. For a few minutes, hold them all in this inner space and feel sincere gratitude and love. Remember, like your own child, all these people, beliefs, and things come to you and through you, but ultimately they don't belong to you. They belong to the Divine Presence from which they have been given life and form. In the depth of your heart-space, acknowledge this. May you feel all clinging cease even if only for a few breaths. Unconditional love hovers nearby.

July 5

Relief and Rapture

"When you surrender, the teacher appears."

After a very long and tense travel day in France several years ago, my wife and I and our traveling partners finally nestled into our chairs on an overlook at a café in the Provence village of Lacoste. As the sun began to set and cast its remaining light upon the hillside village of Bonnieux to the east, we were able to lean back into a sigh of relief and rapture at the view. We added a glass of local wine, and all the angst of a long day's travel went up in smoke. This is one of the desired outcomes of the dance of life—to have moments of angst and exhaustion dissolve into relief and rapture.

We were gifted with a number of these moments on our pilgrimage through France. A pilgrimage is a journey of sacred purpose in which doors open to new inner dimensions. Every experience along the way contributed to this intent. The journey itself became our teacher.

Wherever you are, let your journey through this day be a meaningful and powerful teacher. Feel an air of pilgrimage around and within you as you open to your sacred purpose. Surrender to it. May you experience unexpected waves of relief and rapture. Bon voyage.

July 6

The Healing Exchange

"The real voyage of discovery consists not in seeking
new lands but in seeing with new eyes."
—Marcel Proust

Some of us have been fortunate to have had a very healthy life. We likely attribute this to some combination of family genetics, lifestyle, diet, and good fortune. I am grateful for my well-being.

There is another very important factor in creating well-being. It is acting on the endless opportunities to exchange heart energy—loving another, helping someone heal, consciously expressing compassion for others, giving something back to the earth for its healing presence, and encouraging any kind of exchange of heartful energy. This energy medicine is generated from being in active relationship with the heart of life wherever it beats.

Healing never ends. We are always in an evolving state of relationship with the cycles of life and its ebbs and flows. These rhythmic dynamics are taking place on all levels within us and everywhere around us.

I notice this as I pass by a sculpted, green butterfly anchored at a popular street corner. This work of art stands there as a permanent memorial to Tammy, a loving friend and mother, who met her destiny unexpectedly at that corner. Every time I pass by, I feel this healing exchange of heart energy. The energy from her heart continues to contribute to my life and the lives of many others.

This ongoing healing exchange requires an open heart. There are reminders of this truth everywhere you are and everywhere you look. An open heart is needed to remove the armor from your way of being, so that you heal the fears which causes your heart to close. You then have the eyes to see and the heart to feel the infinite vantage points from which courage, love, and wisdom can awaken and inspire you.

JULY 7

Defenselessness

"In my defenselessness my safety lies."
—A Course in Miracles

I was getting a business up and running. There was a business owner who was a potential client. He was well-known in town and very successful. I wanted to call on him.

I mentioned this to several other vendors who formerly did business with him. They were unanimous in warning me to stay away from him. According to them and others in town, this person was mean-spirited and very difficult to work with. It was either his way or the highway. Their conclusions were that it simply wasn't worth my time. He was trouble.

Through my family influences, especially my grandfather and father, I learned to approach any person with genuine respect and a willingness to connect with the good that is within them. Therefore, against the advice of others, I went to visit this man who was described by some as the devil himself.

I entered his place of business and greeted him respectfully and with the feeling in my heart that there was an essential goodness in this man. He responded in a kind and friendly way. We talked for several minutes and I explained to him my work and how I could serve him. In the end, he became one of my best clients and advocates. His support and trust in me was critical in helping to build this fledgling business into a success over a number of years.

We can all relate to the power that we sometimes give to the opinions, biases, and judgments of others. When we do this, we often compromise our values and create blockades to opportunities and meaningful experiences and the abundance which flows forth from them. Judgments and biases toward others may simply reflect what we hold against ourselves or an important person from our past.

For your sake, take this story to heart. To whom in your life have you closed your heart and judged too harshly? There very well could be someone who deserves to be treated in the same way you'd like others to treat you. Reopen to the possibilities.

July 8

Friendship

"Walking with a friend in the dark is better
than walking alone in the light."
—Helen Keller

Friends are precious. They come and go. The birth of new friendships is as sweet as the loss of friendships is bitter. Most all of us have had many of both.

In the ebb and flow of human friendships, we at times seek permanence—a spiritual relationship that is unwavering and strong, one we can truly count on. It may be with Buddha, or Amma, the hugging saint, or Jesus, or a revered spiritual teacher, or simply a connection with Divine Presence. You experience this quality of friendship as an enfolding presence that is with you in every step and breath. As the last line of the Prayer for Protection expresses it: "Wherever I am, God is."

Human companions and friends often are reflecting points of Divine Presence. Notice how this is manifesting in your life. Divine Presence is making itself known to you through these friends. Friendship is a way divine light becomes visible in order that each of us may know we never walk alone. This knowing is priceless. Even the souls that pass through our lives and move on, leave a sprinkling of golden wisdom on our path.

Join with me in appreciating the gold that has been given to you through the intimate sharing of life's twists and turns with friends. Hold sacred space in your heart and mind for the many shapes, sizes, colors, and sounds of divine companionship befriending you daily whether as a memory, the beauty and power of the natural world, or a tangible presence. Take a deep breath and let it in. Feel appreciation.

JULY 9

Out of the Closet

"Your hand opens and closes. If it were always a fist or always stretched open, you would be paralyzed."
—Rumi

We all know what it feels like to have our heart-space closed down and contracted. Fear, betrayal, rejection, shame, and the like are the culprits. We feel trapped and unable to be ourselves anymore, as if suddenly, we are in a darkened closet unable to find a light switch or the closet door. It can become a paralyzing way of life.

In these moments we may instinctively contract into a fetal position. On one such occasion in my life, after sudden news of unexpected betrayal, I did just that. I was expressing my longing to return to the safety and comfort of the womb. It felt like the only thing I could do under the circumstances.

My contraction was an indication that I was about to have a new birth. I didn't realize it at the time. All I could feel was the pain of contraction. All mothers can relate. My contraction cycle eventually ended. It served a meaningful purpose.

I needed to learn how to expand and be someone larger than I had been before and not retreat into my old identity and body of habits. I was learning about living with a large heart.

The electromagnetic field of our physical hearts extends out beyond the boundaries of our physical self. This is measurable. To live large means to experience ourselves being present to this lighter, expansive version of our heart-space and to feel free, uninhibited, and appreciative of who we are.

We are both expansion and contraction, growth and gestation, beauty and being wilted, much like perennial flowers. Each has their time and place. Feel this as you breathe today, expanding, contracting, embracing how all things play together in harmony and fulfill a greater often unknown purpose.

July 10
Calling You Back

"What would you think if I told you that Gregorian chants create a harmonic vibration that has been proven in studies to eliminate fatigue, heal and cure disease and illness, extinguish depression, and enable the person who sings Gregorian chant to subsist on as little as two hours of sleep a day."
—Christina King

There were times while living in Grand Junction, Colorado that I would take a nighttime walk with a group under the full moon among the towering red rock formations of the Colorado National Monument near my home. The merging of silky moonlight, rocky monuments, and soundlessness was magical.

While walking along as a group, if wanting to say something, we almost automatically found ourselves whispering to one another, as if we had entered a holy shrine. Every so often, someone would simply stop and stand motionless and then everyone would stop. We were simultaneously experiencing powerful vibrations, waves of energy that were reorganizing our cellular and emotional sensibilities.

At times I sensed that I could almost hear the voices of ancient elders showering us with powerful messages of love and wisdom. Healings would take place on these walks. Lives were altered and visions of hope emerged.

Vibrations matter. You are a vibrational being. Come to terms with this. Your whole self is a holy shrine. You live with it every moment and you choose how to adorn it. A profound example of this is the research into Gregorian chant referred to above.

Grace is a vibration, a spiritual portal to infinite wisdom and healing presence and is accessible to anyone at anytime on our planet. It is the Great Spirit's way of calling us back to our true selves. Grace doesn't occur by chance or because our name was drawn from some giant hat. We participate in creating this experience by our choices, by the field of vibration that we generate.

Primers of grace like my walk in a moonlit canyon or the effects of Gregorian chant, serve to help us remember what is always with us. These primers are in our midst as specific prayers, practices, inspired moments, or the endless access points in the natural world.

Ask for grace to touch you. Then prepare to be surprised.

JULY 11

A One and Only

"This is my prayer....Cherish the day."
—Sade

In southern France, high up on a rocky mount, at a place called La Sainte Baume, is a large cave. This grotto, as a near 2000-year-old legend reveals, is the place where Jesus' companion Mary Magdalene went into seclusion for the final thirty years of her life.

My wife and I made the very long pilgrimage to this place. The final stretch was along a precarious one lane road which peaked into a remote valley. We followed the signs to a parking lot. Once out of the car, I looked up the face of the mountain in front of me and very near the top spied what looked like a Tibetan monastery clinging to the ridge line.

With great anticipation, we made the one hour trek up from the valley floor to the precipice that holds the entrance to this revered site.

The exposed side of the cave was enclosed, with a large doorway in the center that opens into the grotto. The interior partly serves as a place of worship for visitors and the Dominicans who live in the adjacent abbey on the cliff's edge. The only light from the outside penetrates through several stained glass windows. Various candlelit altars to Mary Magdalene are also found within the dark interior for pilgrims to make an offering of affection and prayer for her.

For more than a thousand years, souls from near and far have journeyed here to pay homage to her legacy and to feel the Divine Presence which hovers in this place. I deeply felt this collective presence of love which had settled in this hidden womb of nature like a great mother unceasingly pouring her heart out to her beloved offspring.

After leaving the grotto, I stood near the cliff's edge and gazed out over the broad valley brushed with late evening sunlight far below. I was immersed in the hushed beauty of the moment. I didn't want to leave and felt a bit of sadness at knowing that I may never return to Magdalene's cave.

Many first time encounters with a beautiful place or a lovely soul or a sacred spot may very well be the only time. If we know in advance that an experience is likely to be our one and only time, we approach it with a different set of feelings. We are likely to be much more in our hearts, for we realize this is it—no second chance or opportunity to have this experience. Tendencies toward apathy fade. Carpe diem. We seize the moment and wake up to the precious nature of what is about to happen.

There are times when you don't know whether what is happening is going to be the only time life will afford you this gift. Recall a time when you had a beautiful experience, a one and only, and how you cherished it. You likely still do. Light the flame of this powerful feeling and joyful appreciation and let it simmer within your heart today. May this day become filled with the scent of a one and only.

July 12

Changemaking

"Know the rules well, so you can break them effectively."
—XIV Dalai Lama

In order to have a reasonably functioning world, we need both rule keepers and rule breakers. Some of us are hybrids like me. I choose to follow certain rules, and at other times tend to lean toward bending or breaking the rules.

When setting cruise control on my car, I always set it above the speed limit even if it's just one mile-per-hour. I can't bring myself to go the speed limit when on the open road. Settling for convention or confinement to certain boundaries doesn't go over well with me at times. I know I'm not alone in this.

Living according to the parameters of others or society is at times disturbing to us rule breakers. Others of us stick to the rules, drive the speed limit, and conform to the boundaries set by society, workplace, church, or family. Rabble-rousers have been the bane of existence for rule makers and keepers.

Having been a rabble-rouser myself, I've gravitated toward those rabble-rousers who are also groundbreakers. There is more than defiance on their part. There is wisdom, the kind of wisdom that inspires all of us, rabble-rouser and rule keeper alike, to dig deeper and find the courage to live authentic lives and make our world a better place. They inspire us to put to rest the oppositional insanity to be right and decide to open out to a new way that transcends the mindsets of wrongdoing and rightdoing, rule breakers and rule keepers. These ripples of wisdom have flowed forth from the great change agents, be it Buddha, Jesus, Gandhi, and the like.

Follow their lead and live the life that you truly feel guided to live. Do what you do because you love this world and want to leave behind a better place for our children's children's children.

As a young boy, my great-grandfather Tom proudly walked me through his peach orchard and took the time to search for and pick the most delicious peach for me to enjoy. I knew that he truly cared about my life and the world he would soon be leaving behind. Inwardly, I can still see his gratified whimsical look and feel his well-worn withered hand on my shoulder.

July 13

Locate Your Heart

I recently rediscovered this excerpt from the book <u>Love Without End</u> by artist and author Glenda Green. It was quoted in part at the beginning of this book. These words stand alone as powerful testimony to a life transforming truth.

"Infinity is not a subject limited to vast spaces—or even to immeasurably small ones. Infinity is not about quantity at all. It's actually about quality. Let me tell you about the heart....The heart of which I speak is not the physical organ, although the physical organ is an appropriate symbol for the true heart, because the physical organ nourishes your body with lifeblood every moment. The heart of which I speak is the central focus point of your very soul. It is the lens through which your soul integrates all of your earthly emotions and all of your divine awareness into a focused point of infinite integrity. This point is on the threshold of your physical existence, at a point slightly below and behind your physical heart. Locate it.

This is the source of power your Creator has established within you, not your mind. Your mind is merely a servant, and it behaves well if it is given positive impulses; it behaves very poorly if it is given negative impulses. The heart generates all of the earthly emotions as well as the blissful emotions of the higher realms. But it is so much more than just emotion. It is infinite awareness, and the basis of all the higher consciousness you will ever assimilate. It is from this power, within the center of your being, that the entire script of your life is written. Live in your heart—not in your mind—to fulfill the script of your life or to rewrite it. Your mind is powerless to bring that about. But every desire of your heart will be fulfilled."[6]

And so it is.

July 14

Satisfy Your Hunger

"Appreciation is heart-math."

I've noticed through the years that most people will not admit that they hunger for appreciation. Mother Theresa has been oft quoted as saying that we hunger more for love and appreciation than we do bread. Underneath pride is a heart ready to open to receive appreciation. This hunger to be valued and appreciated will likely remain as long as you and I and our descendants continue on this path of spiritual completion.

I can be transfixed by simply watching a small child mesmerized in appreciation of something new. I am actually envious. That inner glow of appreciation is what I long to feel.

Become aware of appreciation's presence, much like having an invisible spiritual guide and companion. Sew seeds of appreciation wherever you are including quiet moments with yourself. Watch how subtle transformations occur and how appreciations flow back to you to complete an invisible circle. This could become habit-forming. Kindness will then follow you and flow forth from you wherever you are. Your only inclination will be to pay it forward. This becomes a value-added way to live.

July 15

Wyoming Wild

"True love is boundless like the ocean...and swelling
within one...envelops the whole world."
—Mahatma Gandhi

I long to stay aware of the endless expanse of what remains unknown
to me. This is why I love vistas and horizons which shake me into
remembering what I am beyond my skin and bones.

Living in a house on a hill just a few miles north of the central
Wyoming town of Casper, the eastern and western horizons dominated
the landscape. I had open unobstructed views stretching far in either
direction. Sunrises and sunsets frequently lit up the azure sky with
warm breathtaking color. This was one of those spots that felt as
if nature would soon reclaim for herself everything humans had
constructed.

Everything seemed wider and less tame atop this great plateau.
I often felt unnerved and stripped naked. When I first arrived there
one winter day, snow drifts were cascading over the rooftops of bilevel
homes. Fierce untamed winds were coupled with deep penetrating quiet
which urged my heart to open more.

Real love is similar to the energies of the Wyoming wildlands. It
has no container. This quality of love seeks not to squeeze us into the
prison cells of our made-up minds, but compels us to feel the wide-open
space of Divine Presence within us. If we allow real love to make its
home in us, our fearful controlling nature will be dismantled day by
day by day. Ask and you shall receive.

July 16

Turning, Turning, Turning

"To everything, turn, turn, turn. There is a season, turn, turn, turn. And a time to every purpose under heaven."
—Pete Seeger

For at least 3,500 years, walking the path through a labyrinth has been a way to unwind and connect with the larger story of life. There are no tricks or wrong turns. Start at the entrance and walk ahead. The path always leads to the center. I have greatly appreciated how walking through labyrinths has become a visceral tool for remaking myself.

There are a series of mostly one hundred eighty degree turns on the way to the center. Various labyrinth designs require anywhere from seven up to twenty-eight turns. Each turn is an opportunity to breathe deeply and let a barnacle-like thought-form that has been stuck to your consciousness drop away. Centered in your heart-space, you are consciously and physically making a one-hundred-eighty degree change. You feel the shift in your body. You do this through every turn.

By the time you reach the center you feel more like the unconditioned you. You stay in this awareness in the center of the labyrinth for as long as you want and feel and discover what has been lying underneath all those barnacle-like thought-forms and feelings—a clear vision of who you are and what you are here on Earth to do. You could describe it as your barnacle-free zone.

We are all making necessary turns and casting off lies and illusions as we get closer and closer to our center. We sense and feel in our whole body and soul Jesus' vision of the spiritual-human: A light; a city set on a hill that cannot remain hidden—a life-changing state of inner awareness that illuminates our purpose for being here.

The return journey out of the labyrinth represents the step-by-step commitment to consciously bring this new revelation of you into your daily life.

Life is like a walk through a labyrinth. With the turn of each day, may you move through your life more and more consciously centered in the strength and light of Divine Presence.

JULY 17

Breathology

"And God...breathed into his nostrils the breath
of life and man became a living soul."
—Genesis 2:7

At a conference I met a man named Stig Severinsen. I found out that Stig was the Guinness Book of World Record's holder for holding one's breath under water—more than twenty minutes! His life's work is called "Breathology."

Stig talked passionately about the science and art of breathing, both flowing your breath and holding your breath. In Stig's words, "Each of us has the capacity to utilize our breath and diaphragm in ways we never imagined, ways that profoundly alter the relationship between body, mind, and soul." He synthesizes the latest in scientific technology with techniques from ancient yogic teachings to create, through the breath, far greater states of well-being.

My chiropractor grandfather Doc almost always instructed me just before he adjusted my neck or spine, "Take a deep breath. Let it out slowly." Often, it is the exhale that is most important...a full exhale that takes twice as long as your inhale. It not only more effectively relaxes you and rids your body of toxins, it prepares you to be more receptive to what you need in oxygen and insight. May this awareness rekindle your interest in meditation.

Set your phone alarm for the top of each hour that you are awake today. After the alarm sounds, breathe deeply, inhaling through your nose. Then take twice as long to exhale very slowly through your mouth. Do this for the first minute of each hour. May you begin to breathe more consciously and fully and therefore expand your capacity to enjoy the life that has been breathed into you.

July 18

Indigenous

"The Earth is our Mother. We must take care of her."
—Kiva

We are all indigenous to Earth. All of us have recent as well as ancient and historical ties to this place. Two of my great-grandparents and their fathers and mothers were farmers and had a daily relationship with this living, breathing sphere. They lived much more closely connected to the cycles and seasons. Many of us have similar stories.

Recently, due to a winter weather event here in Western Oregon, our home lost power for five days. We broke out the candles and blankets and made the best of it. Without the stimulation of electric lights, computers, and other devices, the candlelit darkness at night shifted our attention toward conversation, reading, and staying warm by the wood stove.

As our technologically-driven world evolves and creates more and more ways to become stimulated, the truth that we are indigenous remains. Our molecules are akin to the creations of water, earth, air, and fire. There are growing numbers of us being drawn toward lifestyles, work, and spiritual practices that reconnect us with our love and respect for Earth Mother.

Let me state the obvious, yet all too often taken-for-granted truth. This abundant planetary organism provides the air we breathe, the water and food that sustains us, the substances needed to create all things, the fires to keep us warm, and the usable light that gives life. Each of us is this organism in miniature.

As an indigenous inhabitant, wherever you are, walk a circle of prayer today as so many have done before you. May your heart express and feel words and songs of appreciation for Earth Mother. She does take such good care of you.

July 19
The Flow of Eternity

"Eternity is within us."
—John Shelby Spong

It is a marvel how well fish can negotiate being in fast-moving water. While we humans wrestle with staying upright while standing in or moving through swift waters, fish have evolved to be the perfect inhabitants of these currents, holding almost still as the waters move through and around them.

I have spent many days of my life walking through or near moving waters. It speaks to me and I listen. It catches my eye and I watch. Because of recent rains, I have had the good fortune of hearing and seeing water flowing outside my upstairs window as it cascades toward the ravine below.

The sound and sight of water flowing by is soothing in the same way a melody rearranges our nervous system or a hug of encouragement releases anxiety. These moments of letting life touch us more deeply become a revelation of our connection to eternity and the oneness of life.

This is not high-minded wordplay. Every day presents a kaleidoscope of wildly various sensory touchstones. The Divine Presence in all life is unmasked as we experience more completely every passing moment by consciously connecting with the movement of life around us. It reveals oneness. Our most natural state is to allow this oneness to flow through us.

Bring into your awareness a memory or place that is a touchstone for connecting with the feeling of the powerful flow of good in your life. Breathe into your heart and let this flow take you into the center of your being. Eternity is there.

July 20

Learning Intimacy

"I ache for...intimacy that touches the sacred in all that is life."
—Oriah Mountain Dreamer

For me, the longing for intimacy hovers nearby most of the time. It shows up in many forms. In one form, it is two people getting to know each other while gradually coming out from behind their veils of protection. It is a privilege for another to experience what is behind that sacred boundary.

Behind it are our most valuable gifts: our true feelings, our longings, our losses, our values, our loves, our fears, our bodies, our precious belongings, our shadows, our shattered dreams and visions, and our current dreams and visions. All these entry points into intimacy are priceless. Do not open them easily. Do it with someone you trust who will the treat the gift of you with respect and care.

Take the example of sharing your dreams and visions. They are like your children, original creations, one of a kind. Care for them so that they grow and root more deeply within you. Share these inner gems with those who you believe will treat them honorably and understand their value.

There will be times when cracks will happen. You open and risk with someone ill-equipped to hold what you've offered with wisdom and love. You learn from it and hopefully don't close down. There is practically nothing worth closing over.

Wisdom blossoms through the cracks and mistakes of life. Shake the dust off your feet and give thanks for those who know you, love you, respect your dreams and visions, and tenderly care for you.

July 21

The Whole Truth

"Half of our spiritual nature and legacy as human beings has been eradicated by the omissions of history."
—Sandro Botticelli

Several of the renowned artists of the Renaissance such as Botticelli were known to have captured history in their paintings, history that was omitted by those considered history's recorders. There were spiritual secrets, teachings that church authorities despised, which lay hidden in many of these paintings. Today, we are still left with having to look around the smoke and mirrors of recorded history to discover the broader story, the whole truth.

I mention this because each of us has a record of our own history (or her story) and that record is so often influenced and shaped by our own biases and inner messages that it leaves us as refugees from the whole truth.

I'll give you an example. About twenty years ago, I met a woman who came to me for spiritual counseling. She was devastated. Her husband had suddenly left her, she was pregnant with their first child, and financially broke. She recalled various episodes of abuse and neglect from her childhood and how they had traumatically affected her. She talked about these things for long while and I listened with compassion.

Then, I redirected the conversation and asked her what she remembered about her childhood that was life-affirming. This took some doing. She had to look beyond her painful feelings. Eventually, she recalled a friendship in which she experienced happiness, strength, and possibility.

We explored further. The more I asked her to recall what was affirming in her past, the more she remembered. Eventually, you might say, she opened herself to the whole picture of her life.

It was about a year later that I saw her again. She was a beautiful young mother, creating a life that held the space for the whole truth of who she was—compassion for her troubled past along with plenty of welcoming room for inclusion of the life-affirming aspects of her experience.

The mind can be like a trap that captures and keeps a partial version of your historical record. Your consciousness and perceptions can become locked inside this half-truth. The whole truth includes what is often previously omitted or obscured which usually is your spiritual story and the wisdom and light it reveals. Let the **whole truth** of who you are and what you have experienced be remembered and told.

JULY 22

A Wonderful Drill

"For breath is life, and if you breathe well
you will live long on earth."
—Sanskrit Proverb

When I was nineteen living in Texas, I took a summer job working in a local factory that machined parts for oil drilling equipment. I worked in a metal building with no air conditioning. Most days, the temperature hovered between 95 °F and 105 °F. My job was to stand in front of a large drill press machine and repeatedly cut and drill steel parts to fit very precise specifications. Between the heat, sweat, oil lubrication used to prevent overheating of the drill bits, standing all day, and the monotony of repetitive motion, during the first three to four weeks I thought I would be drilling my way into insanity.

Finally, one of my coworkers, who had been a long-time drill press operator, approached me and offered this advice: "Each time you start to repeat the same drilling operation, take a long deep breath. You'll be happier in your work." This was a man who had been doing this same kind of repetitive work for more than twenty-five years. I thought to myself, "Twenty-five years of this???!!! He must know something."

So, I tried it...a long, slow deep breath at the beginning of each motion of pulling down on the drill press. We had quotas, up to as many as two hundred per hour for the simpler parts. Therefore, that meant two hundred deep breaths per hour. My experience quickly shifted. I noticed I did far less clock watching. The oppressive heat as well as my stress seemed to ease, and I made far fewer mistakes. The combination of conscious breath and rhythmic movement altered my space-time experience. I was happier in my work. Wisdom comes from the most unlikely sources at times. Stay ready.

In tai chi, the ancient art of movement and breathing, it is said, "Everything in heaven and earth breathes. Breath is the thread that ties creation together." When your breath and movement become consciously threaded together, you will be happier. It's a wonderful drill.

July 23

Meet Up With Your Heart

"I am still learning how to love myself."

Most of us are aware of the statistics on heart attacks and heart disease. One in four Americans are affected by heart-related or hypertension problems. Many who find themselves with physical heart troubles end up facing a surgical knife.

A colleague of mine found himself having a fifth open-heart bypass surgery(yes, fifth!). While on the operating table, he experienced an opening of his deep heart. This experience changed him. His thirty years of corporate ladder-climbing ended very soon after. There was an unexpected emergence of feelings of unconditional love. This turning point ushered in a new life purpose and work for him that eventually inspired the lives of thousands.

In order to open ourselves to the wisdom and power of the heart, hopefully most of us will not need to face a surgical knife. There are far less invasive approaches to becoming heart-wise, which, over time, radically alter us physically, emotionally, energetically, and spiritually. As Rumi reminds us: "There are two kinds of intelligence. One is like that acquired by a child at school. The other...is the gift of God. It gushes continually from the house of the heart. Seek the fountain from within yourself."

Alter the statistics of your life. Begin today to give your heart a chance, not only the ways you take care of your physical body, but the ways you relate to your spiritual heart, your deep, divinely given wisdom. Have a meeting with your spiritual heart and decide you are going to become a devotee of this most sacred gift. It's time.

July 24

Doing Whatever It Takes

"The smart dogs ran off."
—Kabir

The words, "I'll do whatever it takes," are seared in my awareness. In those times when I have been knocked down by painful life events, these five words have saved me.

There was a time in my life that I was feeling very disconnected from my sense of purpose and spiritual direction. It was distressing. I felt I needed help to understand what was happening with me. I was willing to do whatever was needed to breakthrough this cloud.

Through a series of events, I decided to attend a ten day spiritual intensive. After the first day, it was clear that this experience was designed to break me down emotionally and physically. Break down

I did. Once this happened, particular messages were delivered by the leaders of this group, messages that didn't sit well with me.

Fortunately, my reason for being there had been strong and clear. I was able to keep what I felt would truly serve my transformation and let the rest flow on by. I was clear that I was there to flush out whatever was inside of me that was clouding my connection with my heart, soul, purpose, and life direction. I got what I needed from the experience.

There is a very fine line between the willingness to be cleaned out of old remnants of pain and suffering, and giving ourselves away to something or someone that has "the answers." One is for love and healing so that we can more clearly fulfill who we have come here to be. The other may provide relief of suffering. It also may diminish us.

I pass this on to you. There is a time and place for opening to receive the love, support, and inspiration needed to feel and be your own true spirit once again. Do whatever it takes to stand in your strength and stay in your heart. However, in response to anything or anyone that attempts to diminish or demean you, even if they claim it is for your good, as Jesus said, "shake the dust off your feet" and move on.

July 25

Being a Satyagrahi

"The inner journey is one in which all violence subsides
in the human heart—only love then remains. Over time
and practice and perseverance, fear is put to rest."
—Mahatma Gandhi

How do we address the causes of violence, harsh judgment, and fear-mongering in our communities and in ourselves? Often, we respond from what I call the trinity of fear: fight, flight, or freeze. When did these responses ever help anyone except in cases of pure self-defense? Never.

Addressing this reality calls us to practice what Gandhi called satyagraha—"holding fast to truth/love." It is a life-changing practice in which you become so infused with the power of love and truth, that fear, hatred, and violence dissolve even in the heart of your adversary. Hearts of stone become hearts of compassion. It never becomes about embarrassing the wrongdoer or adversary. The appeal is not to one's fear or weakness. "It is, must be, always to his heart," Gandhi declared.

When life changes come unexpectedly, or events take place that are emotionally disturbing, the tendency is to collapse under the weight of fear and anger. From this, we react and hurl our fears and frustrations at others.

There is another way, the way of the satyagrahi. Gandhi gives us a good starting point—make our lives about learning how to put fear and violence to rest in our hearts and minds.

What one inspired action could you take today to begin to put a long-held fear or adversarial reaction to rest? Consider this in your heart.

July 26

The Blessing Way

"He had a face like a blessing."
—Miguel de Cervantes

On my altar is a picture of an image of Jesus with hands held upward about shoulder height, palms facing out. This mudra or hand gesture is an ancient Middle Eastern form of blessing and meditation.

You do it. Close your eyes for a few moments, breathe deeply into your heart, and when you feel all systems slowing down into a more restful place, gently lift both your hands to about shoulder height, keeping them open and relaxed with palms facing out. Hold this gesture for a minute or two. Keep your attention on breathing slowly and deeply into your heart. Notice what you sense and feel.

Now direct your conscious awareness toward someone in your life. With loving, kind, and generous intent directed toward them, continue to breathe fully with your hands still in the position of blessing. Continue this for a minute or more and then complete your blessing meditation by bringing your open hands together in front of your heart, holding that sacred gesture for several seconds.

This blessing meditation is simple, doable, and doesn't require years of training to experience an overflow of warmth and goodwill. This synergy of heart, hands, and breath is designed to help relieve suffering, the suffering of those for whom we extend a blessing. Also, it clearly creates a circle. Love and blessing flows out to others and then returns to us.

We all benefit from more and more of us giving our hearts and attention to compassionately extending our divine inheritance to the larger circle of life. A few minutes a day is sufficient. This is the healing path of Divine Presence calling us to lift our hands and open our hearts and allow the power of love to recreate itself over and over and over again. Today is a good day to follow the blessing way.

JULY 27

Hearts Full of Love

"Just let your love flow like a mountain stream....
And let your love bind you to all living things.
—The Bellamy Brothers

Connecting heart to heart is what most of us naturally do with our children when they are small. It feels like our hearts are full of love and subtle invisible energy comes flooding out. The hearts of our children receive it and radiate it back.

When this exchange of subtle energy between a child and a parent stops, it is confusing and often painful. This stoppage is caused when one or the other closes their heart. I experienced this from my mother when I was a small child. I actually have recollections of what it felt like. It hurt. I became angry for reasons I didn't understand. I knew my mother had love inside of her, but it was as if it became stuck there. Her heart closed toward me and I didn't know why. The flow of subtle heart energy between us was rare. I translated this into the message: "Mom doesn't love me."

Decades later I realized that was not true, but for all those years I felt and believed it was. What I came to know was that my presence in her life as a boy-child triggered her painful feelings of living her entire childhood without a father present. To cope and go forward, she closed in order to keep those feelings at bay and be able to do the things that stay-at-home moms were expected to do.

This is a lifelong challenge for all of us. How do we feel the difficult feelings and not close our hearts? Wisdom and practice. The wisdom that develops through years of experiencing the excruciating effects of a closed heart, not only yours but the hearts of others, leads to deciding that it is far better to feel what needs to be felt than to hold back. And, practice. Practice flowing energy out to the world and receiving it in return while consciously keeping your heart-space open. The benefits are endless.

My mother's heart gradually and beautifully opened to me later in life. My heart then opened to her as well. I remain grateful.

JULY 28

Flowing

"May what I do flow from me like a river, no forcing and no holding back, the way it is with children."
—Rainer Maria Rilke

While on vacation, I made a Sunday visit to a spiritual community I had previously served as minister. Wanting to be unnoticed, I headed for the back row so I could slip out near the end of the service. It was summertime and I was dressed accordingly: T-shirt, shorts, sandals, and ball cap. Next thing I knew I was being pulled aside at the scheduled start time by a volunteer and informed that the minister had taken ill. I was then asked if I would be willing to provide the message during the service. It took me a few seconds to get my knickers untwisted so to speak and to be able to nod my head yes.

Sure enough, with no preparation and in beach attire, I stood up and presented a talk on the subject of finding the courage to be yourself. Most everyone there seemed to take it in stride. I enjoyed it in spite of some cranky voices in my head. So much for wanting to be unnoticed.

Sometimes we cannot run or hide. Life has something else in mind. Many of us tire a bit of hearing the four words, "go with the flow." Yet, we must admit they contain a powerful truth. It almost always is harmful to push back against what is needing to express and move through us.

Visualize yourself as a flowing stream. Feel the ease of movement which never ceases. Even though you may not know what lies ahead, you do what comes naturally for all streams—you keep flowing.

July 29

Nothing to Lose

There was a period of several years when my mother was either very near her time to die or moving away from it. Back and forth she went. At that time, I was very aware of my connection with her spirit and energy. As I allowed myself to accept that she was going to take leave soon, I could feel that I was shedding a skin or two of old resentments. Away they went. The shedding of the physical body, whether it is your own or someone you love, is the ultimate clarifier.

Today, I pass on to you these powerful words from the late Steve Jobs. Let them rest in your heart and mind.

"Remembering that I'll be dead soon is the most important tool I've ever encountered to help me make the big choices in life. Because almost everything—all external expectations, all pride, all fear of embarrassment or failure—these things just fall away in the face of death, leaving only what is truly important. Remembering that you are going to die is the best way I know to avoid the trap of thinking you have something to lose. You are already naked. There is no reason not to follow your heart.

Your time is limited, so don't waste it living someone else's life. Don't be trapped by dogma—which is living with the results of other people's thinking. Don't let the noise of others' opinions drown out your own inner voice. And most important, have the courage to follow your heart and intuition. They somehow already know what you truly want to become. Everything else is secondary.

Believing that the dots will connect down the road will give you the confidence to follow your heart, even when it leads you off the well-worn path, and that will make all the difference."

Thank you Steve. Today, let your heart-space expand to include those who have taken leave of this life experience and let them serve as the inspiration to wait no longer. Cherish your life and follow your heart.

July 30

Faith

"There is no lack of faith, only variations in how we use it."

We all have faith. It's a matter of where we place it. We can place our faith in the past and its stories or virtues. We can place our faith in what's inside of us, be it creative or destructive. We can place our faith in the stories that emerge from the world around us that are largely influenced by the story-makers and media as well as family. We can place our faith in a deity, a power greater than ourselves. We can place our faith in proven facts like a scientist. We can place our faith in what feels safe.

For me, my faith is a montage of several of these sources. My core values are steeped in a willingness to take leaps of faith. I've taken many. It is who and what I am. These choices to leap run the gamut from what feels like a no-brainer to what feels borderline reckless. Leapers like me know there is risk involved. We measure the risk and decide that the nature of the leap being taken justifies what risks are apparent.

The main thing is, what is the story about you that you are telling yourself and others? It is this story that shapes your faith. The roots of faith are love or something unlike love. Your story, therefore your faith, could be harbored in fear and its cousins. Or, your story and faith could arise from "I love and appreciate what the Divine Presence is creating through me. I feel its roots going deeper and its branches reaching farther each day."

What is the story you have created about yourself that you are performing each day? Is it a story of your soul's noble purpose or a tale which leaves you reduced to some caricature of yourself?

We need our stories to instill a faith rooted in love and its power to transform. This is our universal story. Make it your own.

July 31

Love Me

"When the dawn seemed forever lost, you showed
me your love in the light of the stars."
—Loreena McKennitt

The vision we all catch a glimpse of and naturally embrace with our hearts and long for in our gut is that there is a beautiful life unfolding before us. Each of us is here to do our part in co-creating this vision.

When we are witness to simple acts of loving kindness, no matter the source, we notice an expansive and hopeful feeling in our being. We may be moved to tears. This has gone on for as long as we have been divine-human beings because these acts of the heart trigger a deep memory of our human as well as our divine connection.

One small act does not go unnoticed, one kind word is not meaningless, one loving thought and intention is not insignificant, and one shift in consciousness toward a heart of love is not unimportant.

Within your heart, listen closely. There is a discernible cry, a call reverberating throughout our communities, our world, and the universe. It comes from the Spirit of all that is alive in you, me, and all living things: "LOVE ME." With absolute certainty, the foundations of our universe are ceaselessly regenerating this encoded message. It can be heard and felt in the voice of a child, the voice of a loved one, the voice of an animal, the sounds of nature, the chords of great music, the images of great art, the light of a star, underneath fear, and within your own heart.

Consciously connect with this feeling and voice inside your heart. Let it resonate there for a while. Feel yourself opening to be the love and receive the love which belongs to the universe and you.

August 1

Unhooked

"Be still and know..."
—Psalm 46:10

Even though I have been known to wet a line on occasion in my life, I have never been altogether comfortable with fishing. Hooking fish and removing them from their natural habitat has always caused me to squirm.

Like a fish that is hooked and pulled out of its natural state, we too become hooked by thoughts and feelings and are pulled out of our element, out of our flow, out of our right minds. We lose ourselves in the myriad of hooks vying for our attention.

Aware of this human predicament, I sit near the Willamette River and listen to the flow of water. I sense that you and I are more like fish than we realize. When we become aware of being in a river of hooks, let the wisdom of the heart arise. Like a fish bending with the flow and finding a still place in the rushing waters, this inner wisdom draws us to toward a more watchful place within. From this watchful awareness, choices are made which keep us connected to what serves our soul's development and gradually free us from the hooks of distraction.

We each have a flow in which we know who we are and why we are here. Hold a meditative prayer in your heart-space today that you are open and ready to be in your flow in which you are wise, watchful, and free from all hooks of distraction. Be still and know that this is so.

AUGUST 2

Secrets We Keep

"Only when we are brave enough to explore the darkness
will we discover the infinite power of our light."
—Brene Brown, Ph.D.

"We are only as sick as the secrets we keep," is a well-known and discomforting saying. Even mentioning the word secret gets a few stress hormones circulating through us. Aside from the small and insignificant ones, like not telling my aging mother that I didn't like her cooking when I was a boy, or, the ones which are truly for our safety or the safety of others, the secrets we keep act like neural-emotional viruses eating holes in our well-being and integrity. The more secrets we keep, the more armored, shame-ridden, and afraid we become.

The following is only to be done in an environment in which significant trust and safety have been established and trained support is close at hand. As part of a seminar I attended, we broke into small groups of four to five. We were instructed, one-at-a-time, to say aloud, "What you don't know about me is..." and then complete that sentence by revealing a secret for which we felt guilt or remorse. Each of us was asked to do this three times. I didn't go first. While I was listening to the others express their revelations, I could feel a growing fear in me.

When my time came, I felt that if I said what I was about to say, I would immediately be rejected. That didn't happen and I felt my inflated fears losing air.

Fear of rejection can be overpowering and hold you hostage if you let it. To be able to safely speak to another person about the dark secrets of your life and the underlying guilt or remorse, initiates the dismantling of the spider web of fears that give guilt or shame a home. This leaves room for your light to brighten and your love and acceptance of yourself to expand.

AUGUST 3

Through the Clouds

"Nonviolence, which is a quality of the heart,
cannot come by an appeal to the brain."
—Mahatma Gandhi

I've posed this question countless times to groups or audiences: "What is it you long for the most?" Usually a sizable majority quickly answers, "Peace." The Buddha said, "It is better to conquer yourself than to win a thousand battles. Then the victory is yours. It cannot be taken from you, not by angels or by demons, heaven or hell." These words of wisdom speak to something often hidden within—a meta-energetic, indestructible, inner peace.

If you are disturbed or afraid now, you're feeling something like this: "I can't nor do I want to be peaceful. I'm hurt. I'm angry. I'm irritated. I'm ready to do battle." Your instinctive personality is looking out into the world through eyes of fear and alarms are going off. You then believe that being hurt justifies hurting back, experiencing injustice justifies vengeance, and receiving harsh judgment validates taking the perpetrator apart. You've lost your soul. When you unpack the ripple effect of this psychological trap, you see that everyone suffers even more.

Get ahold of your heart. Make an appeal to that which is deep inside of you. Your heart knows what you are longing to experience. Like a demonstrator holding up a placard for peace, stand strong for what you TRULY want—victory over violence and hatred through transforming yourself.

The peace which passes all worldly understanding is always awaiting you behind your clouds of fear. Go through these clouds. Ask for someone to stand by in love, support, and non-judgment. What you receive will reconnect you with your soul. What you then give to the world is sourced from soul power. The path becomes illuminated to lasting peace and you'll inspire others to put down their swords as well.

AUGUST 4

Powerful Energy Medicine

"May I be a wishing jewel, a magic vase, powerful
mantras, and effective medicine. May I become a wish-
fulfilling tree and a vessel of plenty for the world.
—Shantideva

A first grade teacher asked her students to spend some time drawing and sketching a picture with pencils and crayons...whatever picture they were guided to create. The teacher noticed one student who was passionately drawing her picture. She approached the young girl and asked her what she was drawing. The young girl responded, "I am drawing a picture of God." "But," said the teacher, "no one knows what God looks like." "They will soon!" affirmed the determined little girl.

May we all come to know this level of inner certainty, determination, and self-assurance especially in today's world in which there is a disproportionate amount of worldly power in the hands of fewer and fewer people. This first-grader reminds us that we can be a "wish-fulfilling tree and a vessel of plenty for the world." Her expression of authentic power that is not conditioned by ideologies or self- imposed limits has an air of unstoppability.

So often we forget that the power of our self-expression lies in the energy field we create and call into play within and around us. The heart is the power supply. Words, actions, and creative expression are only as effective as the energy from which they arise. This is a core aspect of spirituality.

Our physical health, emotional balance, cognitive acuity, and spiritual power are fully actualized when they are an outgrowth of potent and effective energy medicine. The earliest followers of Jesus described this energy medicine as the Holy Spirit. The yogic tradition describes it as prana and in the Chinese tradition it's called qi (chee).

I'm glad there continues to be a steady stream of unadulterated little ones to remind us of what is within us.

August 5

This I Pray

"My spiritual goal is to one day walk into God and disappear."
—Thomas Merton

Through the first twenty-five years of my life, prayer didn't make sense to me. When the minister of my boyhood church would stand center stage behind this massive wooden pulpit, bow his head, and "talk to God," nothing was happening within me. There were times when curiosity would take hold and I'd look around during a prayer to see what other people were doing. A good many were devotedly bowing their heads and seemed to be feeling something or napping. Some had their eyes open and more than likely were either contemplating what they'd be eating for lunch or wishing they could sneak out the side door. So was I. My father, who always sat to my right, kept me from taking off.

In my mid-twenties, I met Grace Faus. I viewed her as a tall shining tower in the midst of newly planted seedlings. I learned from this sage of eighty-plus years that prayer was the experience of changing oneself from the inside rather than attempting to bargain with the so-called master of the universe. "Go within," was her mantra. I began to turn my attention in that direction.

A few evenings ago as I sat with friends around a dinner table, I was asked by the host to offer a prayer. Even now after having offered thousands of prayers in hundreds of settings, I could still feel that curious little boy of long ago. As always, I paused to take several deep breaths and feel what was in my heart. After several moments of silence, what was in my heart flowed out. It was simple and real. I felt a slight gearshift inside. Only a minute or so had passed by. I have learned much. May this help you in your inner life as well.

AUGUST 6

No One Left Behind

"The bird a nest, the spider a web, man, friendship."
—William Blake

As told by Professor Michael Nagler, there's the powerful story of Marcela Rodriquez and Karen Ridd who were peace volunteers in war-torn El Salvador. For no apparent reason they were arrested by the Salvadoran National Guard. Marcela was from Columbia and Karen from Canada. Word got out to both the Columbian and Canadian governments about their arrest. They were blindfolded and taken to a prison in which inmates were routinely subjected to torture. Mistakenly identified as terrorists, they were fiercely questioned and intimidated.

Then, good fortune for Karen, her government had placed sufficient pressure on the Salvadoran regime and they agreed to release her. As she was about to be released, her blindfold was removed, and she saw Marcela still blindfolded, face to a wall. Feeling grateful to be alive, she was escorted out of the prison to be handed off to a waiting Canadian official. When she approached the official, she suddenly turned around and walked back into the prison having no idea what might happen to her. She couldn't leave her friend behind especially knowing the inhumane way she was being treated.

The Salvadoran soldiers were enraged. It is reported that one of the soldiers immediately handcuffed her, called her an expletive, and then added "Now you're going to receive the treatment a terrorist deserves." However, Karen's actions had an effect on the soldiers. They angrily questioned her. She did her best to explain why she had come back: "You know what it's like to be separated from a companero (team member)." Obviously, they felt the impact of what she had said. Soon after, both Karen and Marcela were released and they walked out together hand in hand. This story was not reported by mainstream media.[7]

In her book <u>Human Nature—Revised</u>, biologist Mary Clark states that every human being seeks three things above and beyond food, clothing, and shelter. They are bonding, autonomy, and meaning. She wisely put bonding number one. All of us have this deep human need. Call it a spiritual law. The flame of community, intimacy, and bonding never dies out. All hearts understand this to the core. If you know of someone in isolation, and it may be you, give them some love today.

AUGUST 7

Stay Open

"We are gods in training."

I've done a great deal of letting go in my life as have many of us. From loosening ties with my family of origin, to two long-standing meaningful relationships, to a near thirty year identity as a minister, I've withstood these tests of letting go, but not without scars and thundering movements of grief. In and through these woundings and releases, there is a crossing of a wasteland inside. My deep feelings have touched the bitterness of loss and the bare powerless reality of staring into the unfamiliar. You know what I mean.

These crossroads are where the greatest challenges lay. Our choice is to close and contract into the fear and pain of loss, or, even with the wound and suffering, to remain open.

Spiritual teacher Michael Singer writes, "If you love life, nothing is worth closing over." "Okay. Remain open. Remain open to what?" we ask ourselves. Remain open to the transformative nature of life itself. This is going on all around us in the natural world and in the endless examples of unimaginable turnarounds and discoveries within the hearts of those remaining open to being remade.

We are "homo-spiritus"—unbounded spiritual creators beautifully bred with a human being. Whether it is science or ageless spiritual wisdom, we are being led into realizing that physically, energetically, emotionally, and mentally, we are the light of the world. If we accept this, we stand in the doorway of a new life no matter what we've lost.

Notice today where you may be contracted, afraid, or frozen. Bring that feeling into your heart-space. Breathe into this moment with the intent to open. Then acknowledge silently that there is a light in every scared and closed place of your life which is inviting you to open once again. Relax, breathe, and give thanks.

August 8

Three-Hundred-Sixty Degrees

"I've been to the mountaintop."
—Dr. Martin Luther King, Jr.

One of the things I find exhilarating about reaching a mountaintop is being able to see great distances in all directions, a three-hundred-sixty-degree view. Aside from feeling the accomplishment of completing the climb and ascending to a high altitude, it feels like I'm standing in the center of my life, and in all directions, I can stretch out and feel the full circle of me. Wherever I look, my vision is not limited by obstructions and I'm still on the ground.

We know what it's like to feel obstructions and not be able to experience the full spectrum of being human. There are many examples. One of the most common ways this happens is related to joy. We feel joy happening for a moment. Then, a switch gets tripped. We turn off the joy, because there is a reactive voice inside our heads telling us that the joy is too good to be true and not to get our feet too far off the ground—don't get too high or too open to this energy of greater aliveness, because "the real world" will descend upon us. The fear of crashing from a big high to a big low creates a barrier to joy.

We all can relate to the voices within us that exist for the sole purpose of reigning us in. We become stuck in an adolescent paradigm in which we're still giving fearful and controlling parental energies too much power. We rarely have access to a three-hundred-sixty-degree experience of who we are, because we aren't living from the center of our lives. Our mountaintop isn't accessible.

Today, take the time to stand in your center. Stand up if you can. With eyes closed, while feeling your feet firmly planted, in your inner awareness go to your favorite mountaintop or high spot wherever it may be, real or imagined. (pause) From this vantage point, while turning to look in all directions, simply say and feel, "I see in all directions. There are no obstructions. I am open to all of me." Breathing slowly, stay with this vision, this feeling, these words. Tomorrow, I'll have a continuation of this experience.

AUGUST 9

The Four Directions

"Our religion is not one of paint and
feathers; it is a thing of the heart."
—Handsome Lake

There's a powerful expression coined by Paul Tillich—ground of being. It is that feeling and knowing in the depth of our hearts and in our bodies of being connected to the Divine Presence within all life.

Today, as a follow up to yesterday's experience, take a few moments to do this simple, but powerful ancient ritual. Please allow spaces and pauses to breathe and feel the connection with the earth and all that is around you. Locate the four directions.

It's beneficial to stand up. If you can't, right where you are is okay. While feeling your feet firmly on the ground or floor, take several slow deep breaths into your heart. Relax and feel yourself standing strong and connected to your essence.

Now, facing east, acknowledge in your heart and mind those aspects and experiences that are new and just now coming into expression. Feel the full flow and gift of their presence in you.

Next, turn and face south. Connected to the earth and to your deep heart, acknowledge and feel your passions and what you stand for in life. Take a few moments and let this awareness flow freely through you.

Following the circle around clockwise, face the west. In the same grounded, heart-connected awareness, acknowledge your obstacles and fears. Without remaining stuck there, shift your attention and acknowledge the transforming power of infinite love and creativity that is present in and around you and in all situations. Feel the power of this transforming energy that assists you in every aspect of your life.

Turn and face north. Acknowledge the wisdom and generosity that has come to you from all sources in your life. Feel this expansive presence in you...overflowing abundance. Now feel this abundance flowing from your heart out into your world especially to those you love and serve.

Complete the circle by turning again to face east. However, this time center your full attention on the Divine Presence within you. Feel the earth beneath you and its strength and support. Deeply appreciate being connected in your heart to all that you are. Namaste.

August 10
Meditation

Meditation.
It is soft, yet wild
Like a tough and tender child.
Free me, find me, fulfill me,
Inside, outside, upside down,
Falling and feeling and finding
The hidden, the hollow, the universe of
endless heart-pounding power...
Meditation.

Silently, I wait, voices loud and long,
Sounding out from the wall of bewilderment.
There is also a spot in this world so quiet, so subtle, so me,
That calls me to the flowing breath.
A sign so bright and clear says, "Stop and be and root your life
Like a tree longing to know the sky so blue."
Meditation.

The invitation is ceaseless.
The great ones are quietly praying that
my resistance to love's presence
Drop away into the disappearing universe of forgotten lies.
A giggle then arises to say,
"Open to the spirit of the wise inner voice,
The juice of the sweetest fruit.
Drink, eat, remember, release, live."
Meditation.

Our planet is turning, turning, turning, and
You and I are turning, turning, turning.
Sit in your soul
Where the waters of light run free and effortlessly

Into the fields of heaven so near, right here.
Peace, be still...
Peace, I feel is slowing me down
To simply be, see, and gleam.
The buzz of busyness now lands softly on a tender rose.
There is no place I'd rather be.
Meditation.

August 11

Dramatizing

"When people ask what I write about, that's what I
tell them: 'The drama of human relationships.' I'm
not even close to running out of material."
—Joyce Maynard

Drama is an element of everyday life that can't be denied. Some of us seem to delight in it and allow it to take over and serve no purpose other than to become like a drunken monkey throwing up royal messes into the midst of our lives.

Through bitter experience, many of us have learned that if we too often enter into our own personal dramas or someone else's, we become too exhausted, too distracted, too upset to be able to do those things we love and need to do.

As well-known author Julia Cameron suggests, a powerful tool you can use in your dramatizing-removal practice is to make a list of one hundred things you personally love. Before you start, pause for a few moments and center and breathe into your heart. Now number from one to a hundred on a page and make your list. It may take you an hour or two. Keep a copy of this in your wallet, purse, desk drawer, or on your personal altar.

When dramatizing is lurking, pull out this list and read it as I have done on a number of occasions. It compares to changing a TV or video channel from something dreadful to something healing and uplifting.

My list includes such things as: soft warm blankets on cold nights, visions of France, and a newly painted room. This will help to redirect your energetic flow toward a sense of appreciation and well-being and counterbalance the harmful effects of auto-stressing and overindulging in dramatizing.

AUGUST 12

The Heart of Being Fully Human

"Where your treasure is, there will your heart be also."
—Jesus

You are reading this today, because you feel tremors of longing deep inside which point you toward the heart. With or without a religious orientation, like so many others, you are drawn to this ageless spiritual teaching of Jesus scrolled above. You feel its truth. You can't practice or experience it authentically without being connected to your heart of hearts. To ignite the treasures of heaven within you and in most cases to even have the breath of it touch you, you have to be in close relationship with your heart.

We are multi-dimensional beings with unlimited capacities to create in the short time we've been given. Our mental and physical faculties are essential for this migratory flight. Heart energy is the presence and power in our lives that forms our understanding of who we truly are in our essence and why we are here. It sets the course for our lives and provides the anchor of self-awareness that makes it possible to have a fulfilling experience of being our unique selves and truly making our homes and villages better places to live.

Many of us have come to the center of our existence many times through moments of truth, moments of great challenge, moments of great joy, or moments of great suffering. A large majority of the time, somehow, we found our way through and kept going.

These events of our lives can serve to lead us from our spiritual waiting room through the doorway that says "The Unknown." Beyond this door we are called to face the world and our lives as they are with all their unpredictabilities and bring our open and wise hearts to each day. In so doing, we find our way through our labyrinth of experience to meet up with that which is real, lasting, and life-altering. Our heart-space will touch, empower, and lighten all things. It's not perfection, but it places us firmly in the midst of being fully human even with all its rough edges.

Today, with your inner vision, see your heart-space as being larger than you, extending several feet out beyond your physical body in all directions. Carry yourself through the day in this large way. Remember, you are powerful beyond measure. Use this power in service of a greater good today. Feel the grandness of being alive and connected to your heart and the hearts of others.

August 13

Intangibles

"The heart has its reasons, which reason does not know."
—Blaise Pascal

Without exception, my mentors and guides have had subtle energetic qualities. These subtleties created an essence about them that was so much more than what brains create. This is what attracted me to them and what I have taken with me. Many of you reading this have experienced these same subtleties in yourself and others, the kinds of intangible energies which have inspired you and altered your perception of reality.

For centuries, the brain has been the center of attention when it comes to explaining what makes us tick and our source of intelligence. We have plenty of things in our world which are extensions of our brains: computers, ipads, cell phones, bridges, motors, etc. The influence of these more impersonal devices and systems is everywhere present.

Many of the popular spiritual and self-improvement practices are centered around the activity of the mind. They are simply more spiritualized forms of largely cerebral-centric influences. This human reality is slowly changing. Our understanding of who we are and what constitutes our essence is evolving.

Less well-known, but gradually emerging, is a more informed understanding of the heart. As a pump it is a marvel. Science is confirming that the heart is so much more than an electromechanical pump. It is becoming evident that the heart is a powerful center of wisdom and intelligence that supports higher brain and immune system function. The heart also serves as an inner compass and choreographer inspiring meaningful ways to be, create, and connect that are far less stressful and more fun. It is the heart which stands as the central creator of these intangible subtleties mentioned above.

Envision your heart as your center of intelligence and wisdom. After a few moments of feeling centered in your heart, sense that your brain is revolving around it and releasing the conductor's baton. While your brain beautifully and automatically performs all of its natural functions, it is your heart which is now conducting your life in your evolving world. Relax and allow and give thanks.

August 14

A Never-Ending Dawn

I share this vision with you from best-selling author Deepak Chopra:

"I once read that Jesus, Buddha, and all the saints and sages exist for but one reason: 'to precipitate reality upon the earth.' In that moment I saw humanity as a giant pyramid, with each person perched in his or her own unique spot. God descends to earth like a fresh spring rain, and at every level this grace is received differently. For some it feels like love, for others like salvation. It feels like safety and warmth at one level, like coming home at another. I'm not sure where I belong in the pyramid, because I have chosen to be a climber. I push myself to keep moving up, inspired by occasional glimpses of the level of consciousness I must attain.

One day I will reach the very pinnacle. At that rarefied height I doubt that I will see an image of Buddha or Christ, or whoever has been blessed to come before me. They will have vanished into the ether. Above me will be only the vast expanse of All, the infinite blissful plentitude of God. But my impulse won't be to look upward, but not because I am afraid to see the divine face to face. I want to look down instead, because you will be coming toward me, barely a few steps back. We will see each other at last in the light of God, and in that moment of recognition what I can only describe as love will arise like a never-ending dawn."

AUGUST 15

Failing Upward

"Failure is an opportunity."
—Lao Tzu

A well-known parable from the far east tells of three men standing around a vat of vinegar. Each man dips his finger into the vinegar and tastes it. One man reacts with a sour look. The second responds with a bitter face. The third smiles. The smiling one is usually understood to represent Lao-Tzu, the writer of the Tao te Ching, the foundation for Taoism.

Failures in life are like dipping a finger in a vat of vinegar and tasting it. We choose how to respond. In the Taoist tradition, rather than failure creating a descent into sourness or bitterness, failure is seen as an ascent that places us one step closer to happiness.

To me, failure occurs when I make a choice that I know violates my inner guidance or values when there is no real and present danger. I allow fear or conformity to take a bite out of my integrity. Ugh! It could be a large or small bite. I don't expect that you or I walk away from these bites with a smile on our faces. A failure of courage can leave us stirring sourness and bitterness around and around in our heads and through our bodies creating a toxic soup that we feed ourselves. There is a better way.

After several moments of breathing into your heart, ask the question, "What do I take with me from my personal failures that would contribute to my future well-being and happiness as well as those I love and serve?" Stay with the question. Notice what comes to you. Then, from your heart declare, "What's left doesn't belong to me."

This is failing upward. From the Taoist wisdom tradition, this is the only way to go.

AUGUST 16

Playing the Game of Life

"Play your best, look out for your teammates, and have fun."
—Earl Conrad

During my growing up years in Texas where football was the state religion, my father was a junior high football coach. He had a strong competitive push, but it was always couched in a spirit of fair play. As a young boy I often was able to attend practices. I noticed how he blended tough talk with encouragement and an emphasis on togetherness. His coaching philosophy was not "win at all costs." It was: "Play your best, look out for your teammates, and have fun."

Today, we still find ourselves largely in a cultural pool that is obsessed with winning. We adore and idolize winners and are deeply disappointed when our team is on "the wrong end of the score."

What I notice is how this cultural DNA affects us especially in relationship with ourselves. In spite of wisdom handed forward to us from elders, as adults we often tend to be unmerciful on ourselves. Our inner judge and jury are quick to convene and issue guilty verdicts and edicts for not measuring up to some unforgiving standard of acceptability and success in life. This is a chronic condition in our culture.

Your life is not a competition. May any tendency to measure yourself as either a winner or loser ease up. Take to heart this wisdom: "Play your best, look out for your teammates, and have fun." Let this philosophy of life rub off on you today. The heart of a child still beats within you.

August 17

Heart-Sense

"How many times have you been advised,
'Don't give your power away'"?

Today a loved one called me asking for support due to a very upsetting event that had just taken place. I knew stress hormones were invading her body and feelings of anger and frustration were heightened. Both reactions were effecting her physical heart and her state of mind. It was clear that her capacity to stay in a zone of wisdom, balance, and power was severely weakened. She was hyper-tense and having a small moment of insanity. The reactions of her mind had literally hijacked her ability to respond in empowering ways that would truly be helpful to her.

In order not to react and become hyper-tense, these situations require heart-sense. This necessitates being able to remain consciously connected with your heart and its powerful moderating energy. Heart-sense insures a flow of communication to your brain which minimizes its out-of-proportion, fear-based reaction to what is happening. Your neurological, biochemical, and energetic systems all benefit.

Recall a recent event in your life in which you reacted and became noticeably upset. For this or any future upset, apply the "Freeze-Frame" technique developed by Doc Childre and The HeartMath Institute. Access the steps at this link http://www.pbs.org/bodyandsoul/203/heartmath.htm. Scroll down the page and you'll find these simple steps which will strengthen your heart-sense muscle. When practiced consistently, your whole self benefits. You're worth it.

August 18

Holding the Balance

"In our heart, we seem to know that sadness is as
essential to life as joy and have learned that we benefit
from a good cry as much as a good laugh."
—Paul Pearsall, Ph.D.

There's a gentle spring which cascades down a slope next to the McKenzie River trail in Western Oregon. It softens the hard clay over which it flows creating a silky smooth mixture that when applied to the skin has a soothing, moisturizing, healing effect.

When on the trail, it is always the one place that stops me. Ritually, I take a deep breath and run my hand over the silky clay and spread it on my brow. I reach down again, this time to cup the pure water in my hand for a satisfying drink. It's a baptism and communion all in one.

This natural interplay of pure flowing water and hard clay brings home the truth about balance and its powerful healing energy. Life is flow and ease as well as firm and unmoving. Both of these polarities have their place.

Living with heart is a path of widening our capacity to be present and open to the juiciness of life which we experience across life's full spectrum. Feeling deep sadness and emotional suffering can carve us into beings of compassion and healing wisdom. Expressing joy and having a sunny uplifting disposition can create space for self-confidence and creativity. These two different human dimensions help to create a whole person who welcomes and values tears of sadness as well as tears of joy. The embrace of both is at the heart of being a divine-human.

The Gold of Kindness and Generosity

This reading could be a doorway into reimagining the whole of your life and aligning your aspirations and actions with your most treasured personal and spiritual values. Consider this:

- Spend some time and energy giving something back to life, to the human community. Are you for getting or for giving?
- Recirculate perfectly good unneeded stuff.
- Aspire to connect heart-to-heart with others which is the level of relationship in which we truly hear each other.
- No longer use the past as an excuse to be unkind.
- Do your money and time investments match your personal and spiritual values? Do a "spiritual values audit" of your monetary and time spending and consider a radical redistribution of your financial and energetic outflow.
- What do you truly appreciate and do well? Build your life on these things.
- Daily, be still, get quiet, and consciously reconnect with your heart, your breath, and your dreams.

May these considerations speak to you. May the golden rule prevail in all your relationships even if it means clearly insisting on respect by saying "no" to another's unkindness. Grow kindness and generosity in your heart and community. Pass this on.

August 20

Underneath It All, There You Are

"Your ears thirst for the sound of your heart's knowledge."
—Kahlil Gibran

Our experiences from early childhood aren't something we snuff out. They are, for the most part, hardwired into our system. However, we can create a way to turn these experiences into the ground from which we take wise and inspired action that aligns us with our true and noble self.

We come into this world tender as a blossom. We open to the life before us and experience the vulnerability of being at the mercy of those around us. Even when what comes our way is painful and distorted, underneath all the conditioning remains an essence untouched by the world's lies. Gradually, through the wisdom and power of our deep hearts and with the help of others, we discover this light hidden under the lid of life experiences.

No amount of force or reason will shed your conditioned self. It's a matter of fostering an ongoing connection to your deep heart. This moderates and calms the early childhood effects to your brain and nervous system, gradually opening your inner awareness to discover the very same you that came into this world as a light for all to see and cherish.

Dedicate some time today to asking the full light of your soul to return. Do this as you place your attention in your heart. Ask this light to pour into you, all of you, all the nooks and crannies of your being, even the dark and gloomy places. Feel this healing and restoration coming over you now.

From the Rampart

"There are...those who build walls. Those who protect
walls. Those who breach walls. And those who tear down
walls. Much of life is discovering who you are."
—P. S. Baber

Perched atop a hill in southwestern France is the tiny village of Rennes
Le Chateau. Over the past century it has become a destination for
pilgrims seeking insight into its mystique and legend of hidden
treasure. I found myself there walking slowly and tenderly upon this
hallowed ground on a misty July afternoon at the foot of the Pyrenees
mountains.

At one point, I stood upon the rampart (a wall built for defensive
purposes because of fear of attack) that had been built there long
ago and gazed out upon the various villages scattered about like
brushstrokes on the distant hillsides. There were momentary breaks
in the thick low-lying clouds. The sunlight streaking through added
colorful highlights. I found myself listening to the whispers in the
wind and letting my sight dissolve into this visual kaleidoscope. I felt
a healing power in this place.

This healing presence and power is within and around us always.
We more consistently feel it when we slow down. I mean really slow
down. The impulsive urge is off the accelerator. Our senses cleanse
and any tendency to strain is diffused. We embrace each moment as it
passes through.

Taking the inspired action to slow way down allows the miraculous
healing power of a Holy Presence to free you to see, hear, think, and
feel in life affirming ways and to gracefully disassemble walls of fear.
This power of Divine Presence is your ever-present hidden treasure.

August 22

All of Me

> "Come take my body, come take my soul, come
> take me over. I want to be whole."
> —Julie Flanders, Emil Adler

We crack into pieces. Each one of these pieces has an identity and usually shows up for very specific reasons at very specific times. For me, I have embodied Ed as minister, teacher, fearful child, frustrated controller, lover of women, playful imp, musician, gardener, a lonely man, etc. I once attempted to take inventory of my many selves and stopped at fifty. They come and go. I am forever being recreated.

Each of us is a highly sophisticated creative and complex puzzle of talents, energies, and identities. This isn't indicative of mental illness. It's what happens when we interweave our eternal threads as spiritual beings with our natural gifts and interests along with the choices and experiences we have passed through. Some of these pieces become altered by fear and suffering. They generate feelings of brokenness and shame. The rest we cherish.

Those pieces we despise, like scared children, also need to be loved and understood. This I discovered as I sat weeping by myself over the loss of my marriage. A friend came to me and led me through an inner experience of realizing how over many years I had systematically discarded pieces of me and exiled them to a lonely, isolated place inside. I wept even more realizing what I had done to myself for so long. As I began to find a place in my heart for these discarded parts of myself, I knew that they were worth redeeming. There was gold hidden in those dark places that only love could reveal.

Begin to look for the beauty and unity in your own multiplicity. Give yourself room in your spiritual heart to see with new eyes and feel with a heart-tuned vibration. Look neither for the cracks nor broken pieces, but embrace the amazing sum of who you are...all of you.

Grief Meets Love

"The Compassionate Friends is about transforming the
pain of grief into the elixir of hope. It takes people out of
the isolation society imposes on the bereaved and lets them
express their grief naturally. With the shedding of tears,
healing comes. And the newly bereaved get to see people who
have survived and are learning to live and love again."
—Simon Stephens, founder of "The Compassionate Friends"

One weekend several years ago, while tossing frisbees to one another,
three local teenage boys were overwhelmed by a large "sneaker" wave
and lost in the rocky crags of the Oregon coast. These sudden endings
leave one speechless. I've walked along there numerous times. It is one
of my very favorite spots where ocean collides with land. Such beauty
and passionate waters bringing such tragedy stirs every imaginable
human emotion.

In smaller communities, it is like family. When something tragic
happens to someone, especially a young person in the prime of their
life, we either know the one affected or at least we likely know someone
who is not far removed from the ones directly affected.

Life expressed through the human experience is fragile even for
those who feel invulnerable. Having sat with and looked into the eyes
of parents who have lost children prematurely, no matter the cause,
there is a depth of emptiness within them that is unlike anything else.
It is up to the community around them to be responsive and gather in
love and support to help in whatever ways are needed. Thank goodness,
real people, who have gone through the loss of a child, are available
to support other grieving parents through the Compassionate Friends
group.

Take this to heart today. In truth, real love never dies. Wherever
you are, give a moment right now to those in your life who have lost
a loved one whatever the reason. This could be you. Silently pray and

pour your heart of love into the Divine Presence which connects us and stirs us to love one another.

Waste no time. Do this now.

AUGUST 24

Become the Sky

In Milt Cunningham's novel, <u>Where Trails Cross</u>, he tells the dramatic nineteenth-century story of the movement westward of those seeking a new life and the inevitable tensions that unfold when that movement crosses over into the lands of native peoples. Near the final page, Milt allows the reader to look out upon the Rocky Mountain plateau through the heart, mind, and vision of Little Coyote, a young native warrior:

"He stood for many long moments absorbing the greatness of the country, the unknowable empty sky. He was part of it all, one with the bear, one with the eagle. An eagle circled high over him, hovered, and swooped down and across his vision. Its eye burned his. But this time, instead of floating out below him over the far prairie, it screeched once, and flapped its wings, rising higher and higher. It became a small dark bird, a speck, then nothing. A great spirit-blanket of peace settled over him. His soul was at ease, his torment gone. He raised his arms once more to the sky and stood, hardly breathing. His spirit soared out and up with the eagle."

On several occasions, Milt and I talked about his days of growing up in the Big Horn country of Northern Wyoming and being a ranch hand. I spent several years living in Casper, Wyoming traveling the vast spaces of the Wyoming plateau, so we shared stories of our fondness for those vistas and how, in the Wyoming winds, comparatively few are left standing. Even now, population centers are often "five days ride" from each other. It is a place where you easily forget where you are.

Today, may your spirit soar out and up with the eagle. It's necessary on occasion to forget where you are. Sometimes, we become too gravity prone. Raise your arms and from your heart say a simple prayer to lift your spirit. Become the sky.

Have Mercy On Me

"My yoke is easy and my burden is light."
—Jesus

Live with eyes wide open. Feel your passion. Follow your bliss. These declarations are not the easiest things to do. We aren't some kind of turnkey operation. Everything about us isn't quite in its perfect place. Each of us has at least one kind of obsession or addiction or glaring fault. We cringe as the imperfections of our humanity get rubbed all over those we get near.

When we begin to start tackling these imperfections, as renowned writer Anne Lamott imagines, it is "like trying to put an octopus to bed." We think we have our lives under control and sure enough a long, clinging arm escapes from under the covers waving wildly. We can't maintain control over all of it. Something seems to almost always poke out or become as obvious as the mid-afternoon sun in Death Valley on a clear day.

Imperfections, vulnerabilities, and shadowy aspects will always be with us. Many of us feel we have made a run on the bank of healing what's supposedly wrong with us. That door may feel closed. There seem to be few options. Actually, that door always remains open.

It is kindness and mercy that I often find are missing. If the chance presented itself, we'd run as fast as possible and throw ourselves into the arms of Amma, the hugging saint, or Mother Theresa, or Jesus, or Kwan Yin, the Buddhist goddess of compassion, and plead to have all our dark and unhealed places taken from us. We long to feel this rarified kind of unconditional love and mercy. Go ahead. Imagine it. Feel their arms and their love embracing you.

Many of us simply need to wail, to fall down, and fully let go with someone there to reassure us that everything will be alright. In light of our shared vulnerabilities, I pray that endless mercy and compassion find their way into your heart and when needed that there are arms to hold you. Namaste.

AUGUST 26

The Bottomless Purse

"What's in your purse?"

My partner cleaned out her purse one evening and dumped the contents onto her bed. Via Skype, she then described to me some of what was strewn across her bed: sand, a Life-Saver package with only the unwanted lime green ones remaining, a package of soy sauce from a recent lunch and forgotten about, a name tag, a deck of cards that I had given her, a tube of triple antibiotic cream for medical emergencies, a note pad, an inhaler last used two years before, two tea bags, a honey stick, tampons, a hairbrush, a package of Mentos, a travel toothbrush, and several outdated appointment cards, to name a few.

Women's purses have mostly flustered me. If I'm asked to find something in there, I reluctantly dig and dig and dig and, almost always, that certain something eludes me. "I can't find it," is the familiar refrain. "Where could it have gone?" I murmur to myself. She then comes to my rescue, opens the purse, and within three to four seconds, "voila," she finds the missing object.

After decades of having similar experiences, I finally figured out the secret to locating one specific item roaming loose in a woman's purse short of dumping all the contents out. You need a set of eyes trained to discern what to look for, and a pair of hands trained to recognize what you feel. I have an untrained pair of eyes and hands. Now, unless it is a larger object like a pocketbook or a small cat, I simply say, "no" to purse explorations.

Many things in life are like the bottomless purse: desktops, bathroom drawers, garages, or our storehouse of feelings and aspects of self-expression. What gets put in often gets lost or misplaced. Some of what gets tossed there isn't worth retrieving.

A few things though are valuable and worth finding again. On occasion, consider taking a simple inventory. What have you lost or unconsciously tossed aside that are valuable aspects of your true and noble self? One personal example for me that had been misplaced and later rediscovered is a healthy and vibrant sexuality.

It is never too late to be surprised by what remains dormant in you. May you have the hands to feel, the eyes to see, the mind to remember, and the heart to discern what lies within you just waiting to be brought to the light of day once again.

August 27

Uncharted Territory

"The art of living is the ultimate creative act."
—Lama Surya Das

I've posed this question to groups several times over the years. If you had the power to go anywhere during any era past, present, or future and spend thirty days there and you would have all that you need in food, clothing, etc., where would you choose to go?

I've discovered that a large majority of those responding said that they wanted to return to a time before the industrial revolution when, on a daily basis, humanity was connected to and intimate with nature. A small number wanted to go into the future. I responded to this question by seeing myself spending thirty days with Lewis and Clark on their expedition especially as they entered the northern Rockies at the headwaters of the Missouri River.

My desire to experience an expedition into uncharted territory revealed to me that which I already knew about myself and the journey of my life: Living a full life requires a willingness to embrace the unknown, as well as internal preparation, and a trust in myself and the spirit within which guides me. Each day unfolds before us as not just existence but as a revelation of our place in this great adventure of life!

If you were to imagine where you would go for those thirty days, your response would likely reveal some insight about the current longings of your soul and some pieces of guidance about your life's direction and intention. You can only create in the present moment, yet you are more than this present moment. Each soul is the summation of the past, present, and possible futures. Reach inside yourself. There is uncharted territory waiting to be discovered.

August 28

Spirit-Breath

"How many years can some people exist
before they're allowed to be free?"
—Bob Dylan

My family and I lived in Casper, Wyoming for several years. Sometimes referred to as the windiest place in North America, I would often drive up the switchback road on Casper Mountain to a well-known lookout point in which I could not only see almost endlessly into the distance, but I also could experience the full force of the westerly winds often gusting to sixty mph or higher.

This was also a favorite launching spot for area hang gliders. Securely fastened to their wing-shaped craft, they would take off running and launch themselves over the edge of the mountain, disappearing and falling out of sight below! Then suddenly, as if they were in an invisible elevator shaft, they would rise up and quickly be soaring into the distant heights above. Lifted by an upward circulation of air they would drift and soar for a very long time high in the sky. The wind had become their support and uplift. It was an unforgettable inspiration. I marveled at their courage and trust.

Dylan's lyrics point toward being held captive. Turn that into self awareness. Are you allowing yourself to be free? The answer is in your breath. Start becoming aware of your breathing patterns. Feel your breath moving through you like an uplifting wind, inspiring and leading you in life. Conscious breathing rhythms increase your capacity to feel the juice of freedom even when you are vulnerable. You let go and trust more easily no matter what is happening around you. Softened, loosened, and relaxed, you are then able to see more clearly, think more clearly, open more easily, and flow through life in balance.

Follow your breathing rhythms today for at least three one-minute periods. In these conscious, mini breath sessions, adjust your breathing so that there is more of a full and deep flow. Breathe into the space between your navel and heart. Relax, let go, and open and attend to your breath, knowing that it is a divine transformer. It then becomes your spirit-breath like a great uplifting wind inside of you.

August 29

Pray Rain

"Imagination bears no limits."

In the book, <u>Secrets of the Lost Mode of Prayer</u>, by Gregg Braden, is a story Gregg tells of his friend David with whom he had the following experience. In Northern New Mexico where David and Gregg lived, they were experiencing a drought and badly needed rain. So they set out on a long hike to a sacred site in the mountains to pray.

When they arrived, David quickly prepared himself and sat quietly. After a relatively short period of time, he gathered up his things and told Gregg he was finished and ready to return to the village. Quite surprised, Gregg said, "'I thought we were here to pray for rain.' 'No,' he replied. 'I said that I would *pray* rain. If I had prayed *for* rain, it could never happen.'" Looking back at David, Gregg asked, "If you didn't pray *for* rain, then what did you do?"

"It's simple," he replied. "'I began to have the *feeling* of what rain feels like. I felt the feeling of rain on my body, and what it feels like to stand with my naked feet in the mud of our village plaza, because there has been so much rain. I smelled the smells of rain on the earthen walls in our village, and felt what it feels like to walk through fields of corn chest high, because there has been so much rain.'"

Gregg continues, "Following the prayers of rain, he (David) described how feelings of thanks and appreciation were the completion of the prayers, like the 'amen' of Christianity. Rather than giving thanks for what he created, however, David told me that he felt grateful for the opportunity to participate in creation. 'Through our thanks, we honor all possibilities...'"[8]

Prayer is more about knowing not asking—something we do to ourselves. Prayer is not an intervention as much as it is communion, a deep feeling, an inner creation ignited through the feelings and visions of the heart. Acquaint your heart with this flight of creative imaginings. Put this into practice today.

AUGUST 30

The Community

"There's a place for us, somewhere a place for us."
—Stephen Sondheim

For millennia, souls have come together in circles to learn, care for one another, celebrate, and stretch the old boundaries of experience and possibility. Buddhists have experienced the gift of the Sangha (community). Villages have been the strongholds of love, support, and genuine warmth across the globe. Hindus have joined together in satsangs, sacred gatherings of students and teachers. Facebook has spread the gospel of community far and wide. The Muslim faithful have devotedly come together daily to pray and commune for centuries. Jewish devotees have been celebrating Shabbat for millennia.

Native peoples, as they have for a very long time, continue to gather for pow wows, ceremonies, and loving support. In monastic enclaves that revere solitude, members still cherish the glue of community through shared work, study, and meals. Christians have formed churches and communities of faith around the globe. Co-workers spanning the world of commerce turn to one another to create a sense of belonging.

We are individuals with widely diverse personal and spiritual interests and curiosities. All our lives are richer, because we are willing to empower the gathering of wisdom from all corners of life, not because we seek to establish sameness.

We are about joining in community. Through all the highs, lows, and changes, we prefer being together with others, not alone. In our visions, all have a place and are embraced with love and understanding.

Feel appreciation for all the times in your life you have been cared for, uplifted, and illuminated. Let this flow over you. If you are now seeking once again to feel that sense of belonging, begin with this simple prayer: "There is a place for me, a place of love and support. I feel it coming to me now as I open to receive it. And so it is."

AUGUST 31

Waking Up

"The origin of suffering is attachment."
—Buddha

Things happen to us out of the blue. I was once accused of violating a highly sensitive sacred trust by a person I had vowed to serve. Immediately after he leveled the accusation, he left the building making it clear he would never speak to me again. For several minutes I just stood motionless and stunned, because what he accused me of doing was horrendous and completely false.

Over many years, by necessity, I've learned to be more present to what I'm feeling when such unexpected potentially hurtful things occur. Chasing after the tail of why something happened or who's to blame or exacting justice has always prolonged the hurt and kept me stuck in a painful loop of reflexive nonsense.

What matters is staying in contact with the feelings moving through us and being responsive to supporting ourselves in coming back to our center. There is a saying, "Use everything that occurs as the means to waking up." In other words, dissolve the dualistic battle. Stop struggling against what happens.

The well known spiritual teacher Krishnamurti was once asked, "What is the secret to your happiness?" He answered, "I don't mind what happens." Being in resistance to what takes place often prolongs the pain, suffering, and confusion. Resistance leads to reaction. Reactions breed more hurt, therefore more suffering.

Let go of your end of the rope. Be present to what you are truly feeling. When you are able to feel more rather than resist more, what you experience hurts less especially in the long run. You become increasingly alive rather than having your life energy siphoned away via forceful resistance or by your ego's attachment to having its way no matter what. You then are a wise and artful presence in the midst of whatever comes along. This is the way of the heart.

September 1

Matrimony

"We are all meant to be mothers of God."
—Meister Eckhart

Come with me into a brief exploration of matrimony beyond the marriage statistics we're all familiar with. Matrimony is derived from two words that literally mean "the condition or action of mother." From this, I could state the obvious: Marriages create the container for procreation, the birth of children to occur—a powerful and essential action of the mother.

What else? The Great Mother of spiritual and religious tradition embodies and creates the essence of relatedness in this realm, like soil to a plant, fish in water, an infant and its mother, a dog and its human companion, two lovers in irresistible embrace, strawberries and chocolate. We can't get away from this powerful connection, even if we conspire to disconnect.

Why do untrained individuals at great risk run into burning buildings or dive into dangerous icy waters to save someone they never met? The spirit of relatedness flows through our hearts like blood through our veins. Matrimony is happening in so many places.

While attending a Lynne McTaggart seminar on her well known book The Bond, at Lynn's instruction, all in attendance were given five to seven minutes and asked to split off into small groups. She gave us clear instructions what to do for that time.

It went like this. One person in each group volunteered to share with the rest of their group a present difficulty and their feelings about it. In my group, a woman volunteered and shared her real life concern for thirty seconds. She then stood quietly in the center of the group. The other group members took about three minutes and joined hands and together focused inwardly on healing, positive intentions and visions for the woman in the center.

Once the collective intention time was completed, the woman with the difficulty shared how she now felt about her concern. She said that she experienced a very significant shift in just those few minutes. Her feelings of stress had dispersed, and she had renewed optimism about her situation. None of us had ever met until those moments of consciously connecting.

You could say that we humans have tied the knot. In ancient traditions, cords made of three strands would often have a knot tied in the middle. The three strands represented self, all others, and the spirit of relatedness made possible by the Mother of all that is alive. The knot reminds us that we have a powerful bond and are eternally related and tied together. Healing our sense of separation in every aspect of life is the loud and clear cry of the Divine Mother.

Thank you for being her hands and feet and courage in action. She is everywhere, in all of us.

September 2

From a Particle to a Wave

"Let the old dissolve."

A gifted healer I knew had an unusual approach to healing. When entering into her healing state of consciousness, she frequently used the phrase, "from a particle to a wave." She would repeat this phrase a number of times and create a powerful healing presence. The experience was mesmerizing and effective.

That experience has come back into my awareness from time to time. Each time it does, I sense that I am being reminded of the necessity to dissolve perceptions in me that are set in stone and resistant to change. For example, certain illnesses and injuries are the outpicturing of resentment. Resentment is a revealing word. It is an inner disturbance that is repeatedly being "re-sent" from the past via a thought, belief, feeling, or memory. It then becomes calcified in consciousness at the cellular level, is resistant to change, and contributes to illness or injury.

Now, take a few moments to become centered in your heart. Then, set the clear intention to dissolve resentments while hearing or repeating the phrase "from a particle to a wave." This energizes a transmission to the consciousness within your cells. This transmission activates what I call God particles which are always present within your cells. By activating these particles, a "wave" of movement and energy occurs at the cellular level that dissolves the effects of resentments. It is the nature of living organisms to be creating new life, new cells, new visions, new viewpoints. The nature of a wave is to go forward and not stay put in old resentments or life-denying patterns.

Remember, the heart is the transmitter. When thoughts and feelings move through the heart-space, they become much more effective in generating a lasting, healing effect. This is truly one of the treasures of the heart.

The Messiness of Love

"We do not decide which way the wind will blow.
Some things in life only heaven knows."
—J.D. Martin

When speaking to my son who was going through a difficult divorce, he mused that he could have never ever imagined being in the situation he was experiencing. He and his wife had made a vow years ago when they got married that they would not duplicate my broken marriage. They would do it differently.

Human love and intimate relationships are unpredictable. They change form and appearance, often unable to sustain the bond between two people who at one time believed they were very much in love with each other. At other times, that love bond is sustainable. You can say about certain couples that the bond is such that nothing in this world or beyond could ever separate them even death. They are destined to be together. You could say about other relationships that nothing in this world or beyond could possibly keep them together. They are destined to go apart. The bond is brittle.

We are not all-seeing or all-knowing. We are in the great adventure of truly learning what love is and what love is not. In our shared human experience, love, or the closest we can come to it, will always have some degree of imperfection and risk blowing through it.

Yet, it is our destiny to bond with others for we come into this world from the womb of inseparability. Separated at birth, we are destined to make the return to what instinctively is our source—oneness.

So, accept it. Go with it. Birth is messy and often agonizing. So is acting on the longing to return to love, to the bond of oneness. The wisdom of the heart knows this and allows for the imperfections.

In your heart, acknowledge the love bonds that you have shared with loved ones in this life, both those which have come and gone, and those which have remained. Feel the love, the love which brought you together. Let that love move through you from the top of your head to the soles of your feet. Appreciate the bonds of love which have enlivened your life.

SEPTEMBER 4

All Ways Home

"There's always, there's all ways home."
—Steven Walters

Countless times I've been in settings in which someone expressed the feeling of being home. Once, after a particularly painful and emotional admission in a support group, I returned the next week and noticed I felt at home with these people I had only met a few weeks before.

One of the sweetest joys of life is the experience of home, not only as a place of familiarity, comfort, and love, but also as a heartfelt unconditional appreciation for being a participant in life right where we are. Nothing needs to be added or taken away—life, just as it is. As renowned poet Maya Angelou expresses it, "I long, as does every human being, to be at home wherever I find myself." Each of us, just as we are, being accepted and welcomed by others, results in being opened to love's tangible presence.

I would love to hand over that experience to everyone...for love to be so real and beautiful that you would know that you have come home.

Yet, this wish is not within my control or anyone else's. I envision it anyway and will continue to do so. Join with me in being an advocate for the homeless, not only those among us living without a roof over their heads, but those of us yearning to find our home of love and acceptance inside.

Take this mantra with you in your deep heart throughout your day. It's adapted from a well-known song. "Home, come on home. All who are weary, come home."

SEPTEMBER 5

Embryos of Renewal

> "Return to yourself...and when you get there, you will
> discover yourself, like a lotus flower in full bloom,
> even in a muddy pond, beautiful and strong."
> —Dr. Masaru Emoto

Women and men still gather in circles to sound out a rhythm. On one such occasion, I signed up to participate in a transformational weekend with about thirty other men. We came having no idea what the agenda for the weekend would be. All details were surrounded in secrecy. Soon after our arrival we were herded together into a small room. About thirty minutes later, we began to hear drumming in the distance. There was a bit of nervous murmuring among ourselves about what might be in store. Several of the two dozen staff members then entered the room and blindfolded us. Connected together by a rope, we were led outside and down a path as we closed in on the growing sounds of drumming.

Eventually, we were ushered into what seemed like a large darkened building. Any minimal perception of light through the blindfold disappeared. My vision was plunged into complete blackness. Numerous drums were being loudly played with great energy in powerful rhythms. I lost perception of my separate body and became immersed in the pulsating body of sounds everywhere present. It was as if I had plunged involuntarily into the womb of a mammoth beating heart. This electrifying moment unzipped me and left me deeply shaken. It was what I needed to begin to feel the essence of me, the truth of me, the heart of me.

Return to hearing or feeling the beating of your heart. Pick up a drum or rhythm instrument and play along with the rhythm of your heart. If a sound seems to want to express itself alongside this rhythm then sound it out. These rhythms and sounds are the embryos of renewal and allow your mental and emotional muddiness to settle. Something beautiful will rise up in you.

SEPTEMBER 6

Cosmic Creation

"The great miracle of life is that there is
something rather than nothing."
—John O'Donohue

The beauty of conversation is that I often hear or say something I never heard before. One of the beauties of writing is finding myself writing something I didn't realize I could put into words. This is very similar to what poet David Whyte says about writing poetry: "You overhear yourself saying things you didn't know you knew."

The intrinsic beauty of the natural world is that it continually reveals to us sights we've never seen before, smells we've never smelled before, sounds we've never heard before, colors we've never imagined before.

The beauty of authentic intimate relationships is that they bring to light what previously was hidden within us about love.

Any creative endeavor takes you to places you've never been before. To allow your life to be framed by your limitations is tantamount to abandonment. You are unlimited. This truth doesn't deny your human limitations. It only puts them in their rightful place and invites you to reimagine yourself in light of your cosmic heritage. Set your heart on this powerful medicine today.

Take a Drink

"If all God's creatures...came to God for love, all at the same moment and they all took all the love they could ever want or need in that one moment, it would be as if a tiny bird took a sip of the ocean."
—Baba Virsa Singh

Perched about five hundred feet above the Oregon coastline is the Cape Perpetua lookout point. Standing there for the first time, I was instantly startled when looking west over the vast Pacific Ocean stretching out like an endless blue blanket. The feeling went right into my heart. How humbling it is to be witness to this liquid marvel, thousands of millions of years in the making, which continues to be an integral aspect of planet Earth's creative engine.

The heart of what it is to be human remains an emerging work of art. We are in an enormously active discovery period. Each of us is a vast universe in miniature with a breadth and depth that has no end. The individual and collective multiverse of creativity and wisdom which flow from our hearts are breathtaking.

Through all this is an amplified presence, an invisible field of energy, which unveils itself in our midst as an endless array of heartfelt manifestations. When we experience this presence, we give it a capitalized name: Infinite Love, Spirit, God, True Source, Divine Presence, the Unified Field. This Presence has also been thousands of millions of years in the making. Like the oceans, the universe, and ourselves, this Presence is still actively percolating.

We are like that tiny bird taking a sip of the ocean. Inexhaustible Divine Presence is available to us. When we open to it, we become Infinite Love made visible. It is a communion. Drink in this truth in honor and remembrance of this Infinite Love, our everlasting True Source.

SEPTEMBER 8

Heart-Wisdom

"Blessed are the pure in heart for they shall see God."
—Jesus

A few years ago, one of my longtime friends who has a sharp intellect and is a respected sage in his community, was given unexpected feedback from his therapist. His therapist advised, "You need to open your heart." He considered that for a bit and then responded, "Okay. How do I do that?" His therapist's response didn't seem to help with the question. He again asked, "How do I open my heart?" After several more back-and-forths, the session came to a close. My friend left without having any clarity. Years later he is still left wondering how to open his heart.

Consider approaching the question a bit differently. Ask it this way. "How do I open to the wisdom and power of my heart?" Science is now revealing that the heart also generates energy and information that comprises the essence or soul of who we are. Research confirms that the heart's electromagnetic field is measurable. This field has been found to be as much as five thousand times more powerful than the electromagnetic field created by the brain.

Creating a greater capacity to skillfully and naturally tap the resource of your heart-field is what it means to open to the wisdom and power of the heart. Imagine and see your heart as an energized space within and around you. It is like being a fish in water. Consciously see and feel yourself in your heart- field.

It is through your conscious relationship with this radiating heart-field that you generate clearer guidance, uncover surprising levels of creativity, open to genuine love, become a source of inspiration, become more receptive to healing, and feel the joy of greater aliveness. As the famous transcendentalist Henry David Thoreau wrote, you are living "with the license of a higher order of beings."

Today, centered in your heart not your head, ask and hold the question, "How do I open to the wisdom and power of my heart?" Repeat this throughout your day and make note of what comes to you.

SEPTEMBER 9

Earthmates

"We are part of a giant intergalactic bond."
—Lynne McTaggart

We are inherently one. We find ourselves often in the feeling state of needing to belong and be in community with others. Where does this come from? What's the source?

There's a game-playing strategy called the Nash equilibrium. A group of players is in Nash equilibrium, if each one is making the best decision that he or she can, taking into account the decisions of the others. Expressed another way would be: "my best response is what is also best for everyone else."

We are born to care, connect, and live this truth of oneness, nurturing, and support. We are in this life together. Every attempt to deny or forsake this spiritual, cultural, and scientific truth leaves us isolated and disconnected from sacred purpose.

This divine design lives through all of us as this seamless cloth. We know it's present each time the impulse arises to pay forward the golden rule even in very small ways. This could be placing our hands on the shoulders of someone in pain, saying a ten second prayer of support for our earthmates in the midst of disaster, or listening to another with presence and compassion for a brief moment. There are those among us who have been willing to lay down their lives for another even someone they don't know.

There is no end to the expressions of our bond. It is in this wholeness that we live, move, and have our being. Take someone's hand today or simply ask for their attention and say from your heart, "I am glad you are with me."

SEPTEMBER 10

Manifesto to Myself
by Suz Aird
(Adapted from Brene Brown's
"Wholehearted Parenting Manifesto")

"Above all else, I want to know that I am loved and lovable. I will learn this from my words and my actions. Lessons in love are in how I treat others and how I treat myself.

I want to engage in the world from a place of worthiness. I will learn that I am worthy of love, belonging, and joy every time I practice self-compassion and embrace my own imperfections.

I will practice courage in my relationships by showing up letting myself be seen and honoring my vulnerability and yours. I will share my stories of struggle and strength with others who can hear them with compassion. There will always be room for both. I will teach compassion by practicing compassion with myself.

I want to know joy, so I will practice gratitude. I want others to feel joy, so I will support mutual learning on becoming vulnerable. I will cry, face fear, and experience grief with supportive others. I don't want to take away pain, and I am committed to sitting with it as we teach ourselves how to feel it.

I will laugh, and sing, and dance, and create by myself and with others. I will always give myself permission to be authentic. No matter what, I always belong wherever I am.

As I begin my wholehearted journey, the greatest gift I can give myself is to live with love in my heart and dare greatly. I will not teach, love, or show up perfectly, but I will let others see me, and I will hold sacred the gift of seeing myself, truly deeply seeing myself."

Long Live the Music

"All this singing is just one song."
—Rumi

It is the anniversary of 9/11. Stand with me in the gathering winds of a shared vision that sees the emergence of a world free of hatred and terror and the consciousness that spawns such things. Pause and feel these prayerful winds with me for a moment. In these winds, I begin to hear the music that once again cures the temporary blindness that shadows of fear create.

Several years ago on the eve of 9/11, PBS' "Great Performances" featured the stunning presence and voice of eleven-year-old Jackie Evancho. I sensed a collective sigh that helps so many of us lean into life's sometimes maddening contrasts. This very young being was seventeen months old on September 11, 2001. The sound of her voice, like the healing hands of a guardian angel, mends the muted spirits of wounded hearts and echoes the words of author and priest Matthew Fox: "No beauty dies, no grace is lost, no warmth is forgotten."

Wherever you are, as you read this, be still and know, be still and know that Matthew Fox is right. Beauty, grace, and the natural warmth of the human expression shall always prevail. Today, or in the next few days, listen to your favorite music that opens you to beauty, grace, and warmth. Join in the circle of millions lending their spirits to tenderly hold in healing prayer all of those individuals and families directly affected by 9/11. Long live the music and its power to shower us with beauty, grace, and warmth in this world!

September 12

Intervention

"In my deepest darkest moments....Sometimes
my prayer was 'Help me.'"
—Iyanla Vanzant

We can't always pull ourselves up by our own bootstraps. We may be stuck in helplessness and unwilling to ask for the help we need. Interventions could be life-saving.

Those of us not on the precipice of some imminent downfall, could also benefit from an intervention, the kind of intervention which turns the tide of temporary insanity into enjoying life. This temporary insanity goes by a thousand names: stress, burnout, binging, anxiety, numbness, etc.

So much of this has to do with being fragmented. In speaking to a loved one today, she was frightened by her experience of suddenly going blank at work. Her brain seemed to shut down for several minutes. She thought she may have been having a stroke. Like so many of us, she inwardly juggles too many thoughts, too many responsibilities, too many unknowns, too many concerns, too many fears, too many choices, and too many feelings of being out of control.

She needs to intervene for herself. What would this look like? She needs a stroke, but something more like a stroke of genius. She needs to once again find her heart, her center, a single voice within her.

Intervene in your life. While connecting with the Divine Presence in your midst, call all inner voices, thoughts, feelings, and needs into your heart-space. Ask them to conspire to serve the whole of you, the heart of you—to serve the single cause of healing the fragmentation within you and restoring you to balance and being able to enjoy and value the gift of life.

Facing Fear

"What lies behind us and what lies before us are
tiny matters compared to what is within us."
—Ralph Waldo Emerson

Buddhist nun and respected spiritual teacher Pema Chodron tells this
story: "Once there was a young warrior. Her teacher told her that she
had to do battle with fear. She didn't want to do that. It seemed too
aggressive; it was scary; it seemed unfriendly. But the teacher said
she had to do it and gave her the instructions for the battle. The day
arrived. The student warrior stood on one side, and fear stood on the
other. The warrior was feeling very small, and fear was looking big and
wrathful. They both had their weapons. The young warrior roused
herself and went toward fear, prostrated three times, and asked, 'May I
have permission to go into battle with you?' Fear said, 'Thank you for
showing me so much respect that you ask permission.'

Then the young warrior said, 'How can I defeat you?' Fear replied,
'My weapons are that I talk fast, and I get very close to your face. Then
you get completely unnerved, and you do whatever I say. If you don't
do what I tell you, I have no power. You can listen to me, and you can
have respect for me. You can even be convinced by me. But if you don't
do what I say, I have no power.' In that way, the student warrior learned
how to defeat fear."

This effectively illustrates the degree to which we may choose to
give power to fear. However, it is illusory power. It has no power of its
own. For what is within us and moving through us is always greater
than any fear.

Take hold of this teaching: "If I don't do what fear says, fear has no
power." You discover this when, like all great inner warriors, you feel
the fear and keep going. You decide to not allow it to stop you. The
fear then withers and dies for it has no life to sustain it. There is a Great
Spirit in you which is far more powerful than any fear.

September 14

A Great Reservoir

"Without a generous heart there can be no true spiritual life."
—Buddha

The great, high-desert places of the western U.S. call to many of us. They have powerfully called to me. It has to do with expansive, wide-open space. Beauty may or may not be evident, but the space that stretches far out to the distant horizon is much like entering into a grand dimension of myself. In this space, I feel that I can stretch out and ride the free spirit of the wild horse inside of me. There are no limits, just the peace and passion which oozes out of the heart of being free.

Our inner spirit is an energy source that naturally taps into dimensions of the unlimited. This spirit is also effortlessly generous and giving of itself.

Like a well-known parable teaches, generosity is sensing and feeling in your heart of hearts that you are much more like a great reservoir than a glass of water. Put a teaspoon of salt in a glass of water, and the water tastes bitter. Put that same amount of salt in a great reservoir, and the water still tastes sweet.

Bitterness, dropped into the midst of a muzzled spirit, will turn everything bitter. When that same bitterness is enfolded in a self-awareness that is expansive, it becomes integrated and quickly insignificant.

Breathe into the expansive field of energy around your physical heart. Therein lies the reservoir of generosity and depth in you that then can flow into all that you feel, think, say, and do. Your naturally large and spacious spirit just needs resuscitating.

SEPTEMBER 15

Real Love

"The one I love lives inside of you."
—Heather and Benji Wertheimer

Winding our way along the north shore of Lake Superior on a warm, blue-sky, summer day, my wife and I arrived near our destination and parked our car. With musical instruments in hand, we walked amid evergreens down a long winding trail to where it opened onto the beach of this great lake. There, in this gorgeous setting, beautiful music was played and two loved ones exchanged vows and gave their hearts to one another.

We are all aware of the statistics for committed relationships. Beautiful loving ceremonies don't guarantee longevity. Many relationships falter and die as did the one mentioned above less than a year later. Others falter but survive and renew. Some become a repository for the alchemy of real love. This harvest of love grows even when broken cups of human vulnerability lay in pieces on the floor of togetherness.

I heard heart-intelligence coach Christian Pankhurst describe human love as "the experience of feeling felt." Feeling felt and known strikes a resonant chord in me. Human love simmers and becomes something even richer when we are willing and able to truly feel into both the sacred heart and the vulnerable cracks in ourselves and each other.

In the words of Kahlil Gibran, "All these things shall love do unto you that you may know the secrets of your heart, and in that knowledge become a fragment of Life's heart." This is the path of real love.

SEPTEMBER 16

See Rightly

"I was blind, but now I am beginning to see."

Rigidity has been a bugaboo at times for many of us. There's a place for conviction and standing our ground. Yet, there are plenty of times when standing our ground has turned into sinking knee-deep into some strange kind of glue that is stuck to us. It's the glue of senseless stubbornness. Often it's because we are not in the mood to admit that we are wrong, or we don't want to get out of our sour mood. We feel justified in staying right where we are. We've shut down our heart-space. We've been evicted.

How we act in these situations is much more about what we are feeling or not feeling. This feeling or unfeeling usually has little or nothing to do with what is happening in the moment. Are you with me?

The glue that we are stuck to is an old feeling like exasperation or an unfeeling like numbness. In the Hindu tradition these old imprints are called sanskaras. Our senseless stubbornness or numbness is a reaction to this old imprint that arises, the distorted lens through which we perceive what's happening. We're usually blind to this.

To truly loosen what is glued shut within us, we must identify what's actually going on. Reopen the heart. Stop and feel. It's best done with someone who has no agenda or need to get something from us. They serve as a filter. If this option isn't available, then write it out... all of what this old energy is about. This is not a moment for mental effort. How many times, in an attempt to pass through the effect of being stuck, has mental effort made the situation worse?

Underneath rigidity and resistance to the deeper truth is a beautiful purpose—to reconnect with your joy and creativity. From the wisdom of a children's tale, The Little Prince, the fox so wisely reveals to the little prince, "The secret is 'it is only with the heart that one can see rightly; what is essential is invisible to the eye.'"

September 17

From a Star

"You are the light of the world."
—Jesus

While star gazing on a clear night, we can be ushered into the infinite. We are spellbound as we come face-to-face with the deep. We are awed by how comparatively small and vulnerable we feel, like one microscopic electron bouncing around in this endless multiverse. And, we are awed by how grand it is to know and feel we are players in an arena without end. Almost anything can happen and it does. Almost anything is possible and this is true.

Within the heart is often where what can happen and what is possible meet. From miracles to disasters, we show up and keep going. We are enormously resilient.

Here's what we do know. From a quark to ourselves to a galaxy, light is actively a part of this evolutionary impulse to be and create. Each of us is like a star in endless space. We can shine and inspire or we can dimly exist. Our vulnerabilities and personal disasters can forge us into fearfulness or open us and allow the frequency of our original blessing born of infinite light to be our handmaiden.

The word disaster literally means "from a star." Even disasters can serve to inwardly rearrange us and generations to come into beings who are awe-inspiring and filled with light. We are accountable to pass this teaching on to our children's children's children.

Begin with you. Sit quietly for several minutes breathing slowly focused on your heart. Then after a full inhale, either chant out loud or silently in your inner awareness the sound "ahhhhh." This sound chanted openly and repeatedly turns up the wattage of light in your cells. Keep your attention on your heart. Bring this simple practice into your most vulnerable moments as well. Fears will break apart amid this sound.

SEPTEMBER 18

Storms of Decision

"Each entered the forest at a point...where it
was darkest and there was no path."
—Joseph Campbell

Very near my wedding day, the guidance from my heart was very clear that I needed to call off the ceremony. I succumbed to my fear of others' reactions and judgments. I agreed to go ahead with getting married. It was a significant compromise for me. Through the years, this relationship had many meaningful and affectionate moments as well as several near-endings. I value my former partner and my twenty-two years with her, but my heart was rarely in the relationship and I suffered because of it. So did she. For the most part, it was the calculations of my mind that kept me in it all those years. It was a persistent voice that argued a convincing case.

It is usually not easy to follow the heart especially when you know that others you truly care about will be affected. These moments feel like being buffeted by the winds and rains of a powerful storm while on a journey to a desired destination. You can stop and take shelter. The safety and comfort of shelter may dissuade you from going any further, or you may brave the elements and keep going even when fear is present.

The everyday reality of listening to and following your heart is a great and noble test. The calculations of the mind may offer valuable pieces of guidance. The question of what to do remains.

Do you listen to your head or your heart? At times, the choice is clear-cut. At other times, it's not. You may pray, wait without choosing what to do, seek the wisdom of trusted friends, or relinquish the decision to the Divine Presence within you. Eventually, as I have concluded in my life, in matters of the heart, taking imperfect action is better than no action at all.

SEPTEMBER 19

Eternity

She who squanders her love for security's sake will lose it.
She who bequeaths her love for eternity's sake will find it.
Give it away, yes, give it away.
It's not love unless you give it away.

In the disappearing darkness of endless echoes
Lies love's great cause, a shimmering light.
And I am me no more—just a ripple of I Am
Flowing from the beginning dream.

What is the timeless past of all that is
But a fragrance of love's enduring message
To come out of the ego's lair and live
And fully be the revelation of one heart.

I crawl beyond the edges of willingness
And let my soul swim in the Source of living water.
There, my world of foolish loneliness dissolves,
Vanishing in the arms of eternity.

SEPTEMBER 20

Pass it On

"To all my friends in far-flung places...when again
I'll see your faces, no one knows, no one can
say, and none can name that happy day."
—Chuck Pyle

Let's consider all those who have passed through our lives and given us something of real value, some as brief passersby and others as long time loved ones or friends. Gather them together in your heart and mind today.

I was very well aware of the many friends and loved ones in my life as I took personal time to walk through a nearby cemetery to meet up with the lives and spirit of some of those who have come and gone in my community in the past century. After about an hour of walking through these lives and the lives of those I love and miss, I came across a memorial plaque for a woman that had died at my current age. Next to her spot was a beautiful lily, the only live plant in this entire section of the cemetery. She had passed on many years ago, but someone was still bringing flowers to this sacred spot in love and remembrance of her.

I've been in many cemeteries and done many graveside services, but I have never experienced what happened next. I received this inner nudge to take the live lily and pass it on to someone I loved. One of the unwritten rules of conduct in cemeteries is to not tamper with plants left at gravesides. As I was about to walk away, I once again got this strong nudge that I was supposed to take this lily and pass it on to someone I loved. So, I stood in front of this woman's memorial plaque, said a prayer of appreciation for her life and the giver of the flower, and picked up the flower and carried it with me.

About ten minutes later I arrived back at the home of a cherished loved one. I gave her the flower and thanked her for her love. It was Easter evening.

May we each recognize on this day that amid all the shadows and light of this human experience, we have been gifted with human companions who have accepted us, loved us, and provided for us in so many amazing ways. They are our resurrection, our life. In honor of them, pass on a gift of love to someone today.

SEPTEMBER 21

Rejuvenation!

"There is a better way to live. You can be totally rejuvenated."
—David Wolfe

Some of us have been fortunate to encounter shining lights. One of those for me was Mary Wessel. I met her once right after either her 103rd or 104th birthday. Mary was a pioneer in what she accomplished in the world and how she lived her life. She single-handedly started five churches in Montana in the 1920's. She traveled vast distances and was present with each fledgling group weekly, making her way around the state by train. This regimen went on for years.

Mary embodied rejuvenation. Life sizzled in her. For ages, rejuvenation has been the subject of intense study and exploration. A prime example has been the search for the "philosopher's stone" which seekers have believed to be the elixir of life, a substance that would bring immortality. The search for the golden key to total rejuvenation continues.

Consider this question. Could it be that death is a human belief and life an eternal truth?

Rejuvenation emerges over time as we cleanse ourselves of toxicity—the habits, beliefs, misunderstandings, and foods that are "deathening." I'm reminded of all the years I have spent waiting for certain people to love and appreciate me. This shadow of incompletion has hovered and denied what was always with me—love without conditions within my own soul. This sad, love-defying twist of misunderstanding is an example of toxicity which many of us know all too well.

The true story about each of us begins again today. Turn to your physical heart. It is the physical manifestation of the invisible Source of your being. In an average eighty year lifespan, it beats about one billion times. It's sending a lifelong message that reverberates through you without ceasing: beyond the veil of physical form you are essentially indestructible energy, the image and likeness of Divine Presence. In this Presence, slow down. Open up. Tune in.

September 22

Conception Day

"The moment one definitely commits oneself,
then Providence moves too."
—W. H. Murray

You or I didn't have any say-so about the day we were conceived, unless our soul was somehow intervening from the other side. I appreciate that I was ushered into this mortal existence. Most of us feel the same way. Some of us would rather have had different parents. Some of us deeply appreciate our parents.

Once we arrived at adulthood, we gathered up what we'd been given as a child and young adult and began to separate the wheat from the chaff. We began to see and identify what truly belonged to us and was worth keeping and what needed to be tossed into the fiery furnace marked "dung heap."

This sorting out process may continue for a long period. Some of us eventually come to a place in which we strongly feel that our physical birth and everyday human experiences are woefully insufficient to satisfy our hunger for meaning. We're stopped by this feeling inside. We stare into our lives and wonder what we're doing here. This questioning may come at any time and more than once.

To address this question, consider the miraculous nature of conception itself. This extravaganza of creation which was our own initiation into this life experience, continues to reverberate through us like endless waves lapping onto a waiting shore. Our calling is to commit to listen with the heart for this pulse of conception-creation and unite with it.

A way to do this is to allow deep time for making love with the question, "What am I here for?" Even several minutes each day of holding this question tenderly in your heart-space knocks the dust off your connection to your pulse of conception-creation. You receive guidance that molds you more beautifully with your unique life purpose. As Murray described, "then Providence moves too."

SEPTEMBER 23

Becoming Heart-headed

"Our heads can be so stubborn at times."
—Doc Childre

Our heads may wrestle with the intuition and guidance we've received from our hearts. Our minds persist in mind games because they judge the wisdom of the heart to be an imminent threat to its known patterns and calculations.

By deciding to follow my heart and its wisdom and write this book, I've met up with some powerhouse judgments and calculations from my head that said very clearly, "Don't do this." I'm now more than two-thirds along and beginning to better understand why it has been necessary to move in this direction. It is instilling in me a new emerging identity that is clearly necessary for me to be the person I have come here to be now. I needed to make a clean break from my former profession and identity. There will continue to be new insights that will confirm why I needed to follow my heart.

Leading from the heart always has elements of mystery like a journey to a place we've never been before. Behind most all great discoveries are moments of inspiration, unexpected occurrences, gut feelings, or unusual dreams of revelation. To deny these sources of heart-wisdom is to deny who we truly are.

The ageless wisdom of many sacred traditions teaches that as a divine human being, you light the lamp of happiness when your heart and head join in harmony. As you enter into today, through conscious breathing, keep your attention on your heart and send a message to your mind. Feel a current of energy flowing back and forth. May the prayerful message be, "Let's join in harmony and creativity. We are in this together."

September 24

Powerful Partners

Gratitude is transformational. It invites us to drop whatever is distracting us, connect to the heart of our lives, and weave together golden threads of affirmation. These threads, which are born out of all the ways we sincerely feel gratitude, join together to form a rope that pulls us up and out of stuck places and habitual negativity. Expressing gratitude randomly, wherever we find ourselves, helps to clarify what's truly important.

Heartfelt gratitude generates a healing power. It has helped me look back over my entire life and feel acceptance. I hold this for all of you reading this today. We all have suffered, some more than others. It pains us to realize how much suffering we have endured, because we are connected in love. Through our suffering, we have plunged into dark places and risen somehow. We have discovered deep truths about ourselves as a result.

While suffering remains, as St. Paul writes, "love endures all things." I can say with certainty that having endured suffering and faced my inner darkness, I have created much more room for love to roam. This is true for so many of us. Through the entire landscape of darkness and light, love is still present. There is no lack, only an abundance of it. This is what life can reveal and what serves to unravel everything into an awareness of how courageous and resilient and caring we are. We learn what we are made of and how much love floods into our lives every day, if we open to it.

Gratitude is a constant teacher pointing out how far we've come toward full acceptance of the omnipresence of unconditional love. In this acceptance, previously unknown resources appear within and around us to assist us in facing whatever feels unfinished and unloved.

Right now you stand at the apex of your life. Remember, gratitude is not so much about making your past okay. It is much more about assisting you in accepting and bringing to clear understanding who you truly are and using this heavenly kiss as the lens through which you interface with the whole of your life.

Who you are right now and have always been is a one of a kind creation, living and expressing in a unified, energized field of unconditional love and potentiality. The more you clearly feel this, the more love flows into every dark corner of your life, past and present, and reorganizes your relationship with everything that has happened. Love and gratitude are dynamic, life-changing partners. Your deep heart knows this is so.

Loving, Cracking, Breaking, Loving

"All you need is love...all together now."
—John Lennon

Freezing rain has been falling for a while and turning into ice wherever it lands. The weight of gathering ice is too much for some limbs and trees. They are cracking, snapping, and falling. The sound is somewhat disturbing.

Relationships become like this. Partners become overly icy. One or both snap under this weight and fall into separation. We can remain in these relationships for years while still feeling separate. I know. Part of what goes on in these situations is that one or the other feels stuck in a cocoon which often is caused by the ongoing experience of not being able to evolve through the changes that are certain to occur within each person.

If only a relationship would let out a cracking sound when it's about to break. It would get our attention. There are forewarnings: silence, distancing, loss of inspiration, absence of playfulness, depression, sexual coolness, being overly controlling, to name a few. If we'd give any one of these our full attention, we could be moved to knock off some of the ice.

Emotional balance, the ability to evolve through changes, and real love for the other, combine to form the fertile soil for relationships to strengthen and deepen as they meet the tests that are certain to take place. If one of these is missing, then the relationship gets brittle, heavy, and will likely break. I'm writing from experience. Real love must be present above all else or nothing much works in the end.

What matters and what I have been very fortunate to experience is to truly love another and be loved in return. May you be as fortunate as I have been. Let this day be a time to cherish those moments of good fortune that have come your way in this life.

SEPTEMBER 26

Driving Into the Sky

"You are the sky. Everything else—it's just the weather.
—Pema Chodron

There are certain earth locales where land meets sky and we touch the Infinite. Be it day or night, it's as if we lose all sense of being earthbound. While driving across Eastern Oregon, the highway started a long straight climb with endless sky as a backdrop. After a mile or so, it seemed like land and gravity were giving way to this magical blue magnificence. I was driving into the sky.

Throughout my life I have appreciated the gift of sky especially certain locales in the Western U. S. where I could see from horizon to horizon. These vistas are a set up for looking more closely into our life patterns and taking an honest inventory of how we see ourselves. These experiences have an element of risk, the risk of exposing ourselves to the ways we make ourselves small. It's only human to do so. We do this in relation to others, those who we see as greater, smarter, wiser, or more attractive. This way of minimizing leads to losing sight of our priceless value.

The great vistas of planet Earth urge us to take heart and feel the wonder of it all. Rather than feel small, they invite us to open to how grand we are. They are a mere reflection of a divine creation that is designed to duplicate itself as grand vistas and skies and us.

Let the awe of being in this creation help you come alive like never before. Say a prayer, breathe a breath, love another for the sake of the Infinite in you. Open to the spirit of the sky.

SEPTEMBER 27

The Heart of the Mystic

"Release heaven into life by living fully on earth."

Many of us have mystical leanings. Whether you are a closet mystic or unabashed in your mystical fanfare, we likely share in similar proclivities. We revere regular quiet alone-time. We have powerful intuitions that we are urged to follow. We have an ongoing sensual love affair of wonder with nature and its healing power, beauty, and aliveness. We are often drawn to look beyond appearances and download the subtleties of the invisible which orchestrate the oneness of life. We feel passion for connection and intimacy. We allow music to accompany us into realms more terrestrial. The mystic expressing through the philosopher Plato concluded, "Music gives a soul to the universe."

As mystics, we choose to live outside the turnstiles of worldly certainty and dare to take the view of Einstein: "The finest emotion of which we are capable is the mystic emotion. Herein lies the germ of all art and all true science." The mystic emotion is a passion to look right into the face of mystery and say, "Here I come!" This is in spite of the fact that we can't see what is in the dark unknown, but we know that the source of infinite creative wisdom awaits.

This day give homage to the heart of the mystic in you. Be still and quiet for a moment. Breathe into your deep heart and say to your inner mystic, "I love you and thank you for your presence which shows me the oneness of life. I feel your strength, wisdom, and passion which connects me with my essence. And so it is."

SEPTEMBER 28

What the Eye Cannot See

"The kingdom is spread upon the earth and men don't see it."
—Jesus

Scientists and physicists have determined that there are two different theories to explain reality. One is Einstein's general theory of relativity which explains the macrocosmic universe of large things such as planets, solar systems, and gravity. It has predictable laws and uses equations to explain how things work. A second theory, more recently discovered, called quantum mechanics, explains the inner workings of the smallest microcosmic particles. According to this theory, at this strata of existence, what is observed appears to be chaotic. Two radically different explanations of life exist side by side.

These incompatible points of view motivated researchers to begin the search for a "theory of everything." What eventually emerged was the so-called "string theory" which puts forth the idea that all life and form is made up of extremely tiny strings of energy that vibrate. Different forms of life simply vibrate with different frequencies. In order for this theory to make sense, some quantum theorists now believe that there are extra spatial dimensions that we simply cannot see that are crisscrossed with one another and form the energetic matrix for all things in the universe, no matter how large or small. This matrix keeps the whole cosmic symphony of life in tune and working in harmony.

Allow your heart-centered awareness to open and feel into that which you cannot see—this unifying and magnetic power and presence saturated with energy and intelligence. You are an instrument in this cosmic symphony which is constantly being conducted through and all around you—a most amazing whole of energy sizzling with life. Let this elegant awareness and order pour through you like a prayer. Science and spirituality are interweaving into one cord of awe-inspiring amazement.

September 29

A Butt Kickin'

"If you want to succeed in life you need to be brave and show up."
—Brene Brown, Ph.D.

Several years after I went through a heartbreaking divorce, I felt I was beginning to open my heart to a woman who I had been dating for a while. One day I screwed up the courage to say to her that my heart was opening to her and it was scaring me. I let her see my feelings of vulnerability.

The day went on and we enjoyed being with each other. Two days later I called her and she told me pointblank that she never wanted to see or talk to me again. When asking her why, she said she didn't want to talk to me and hung up. That was it. That was the last time I ever spoke with her.

When we put ourselves in the arena of life, at times we are going to get our butts kicked. If we let ourselves be seen and known, stones may be thrown at us. We may be rejected and judged. We may scare others. To me, this is far better than closing down and losing the courage to be ourselves. I've had my share of butt kickings as well as retreating inside myself.

Daring to be courageous means you are going to be called to open your heart and allow the world to find out about your passions, values, and vulnerabilities. These moments may strike fear in you and often involve embracing the unknown. If you choose to withdraw into your comfort zone, you'll be protected from truly being seen and known. That may be needed on occasion. It doesn't change the truth that you get from this life what you are willing to express and experience.

Through it all, the key is to grow in love for yourself, so that, no matter what you choose, you will be right with your heart and soul.

SEPTEMBER 30

Belonging

"We belong in this world."

By nature, all of us have the inherent desire to belong and be included. Belonging is central to feeling fully alive, creative, and self assured as well as knowing we are part of something larger than ourselves. When this basic need goes unmet, we feel like an outsider whether it is being outside our families or fellow workers or community. A restless insecurity and alienation sets in.

There may be more of us who color ourselves outside the mainstream than there are insiders. I include myself in this esteemed group. Many of us feel we have never quite fit in. We carry with us a bit of an outsider's edge. The desire to belong may even be more potent for those of us out on this edge.

There is an innate wisdom and implant in most humans that reminds us that we all belong. I witnessed the segregated society of the mid twentieth century in my hometown. I was creeped out by the established norms which taught that people who looked different than me were not to be included in the mainstream. As one of the ones included, I felt like I didn't belong in a society that treated people like this. In my heart I knew this was inhuman. I was disturbed by it.

Because you have been born on this earth, you belong. There is a place for you here. Reaffirm this in your heart today. In the grand scheme of this endless universe, wherever you go you are right where you belong. Welcome!

OCTOBER 1

A Card Stuck in a Wall

"These things I have done, you shall do, and even
greater things than these shall you do."
—Jesus

I was with my family at a hotel restaurant in Wyoming. It was a very quiet evening with few others in the dining room. After we had ordered, a magician and trick artist who appeared to be about seventy years old was roaming the dining room. He came up to our table and presented himself in a very friendly manner. He asked if he could perform card tricks for us. "Sure," I said, all the while thinking to myself that it felt odd for a magician to be there. He did a couple of tricks which seemed within the realm of your average card trickery.

Then, he asked my seven-year-old daughter to pick a card out of the deck, look at it and remember it, show it to me also, and place it back in the deck. She did these things. He then told my daughter to hand me the deck. He then asked me to shuffle and cut it several times which I did. I placed the deck back in his hand.

Quite unexpectedly, like a whirling dervish, he did a full three-hundred-sixty-degree turn and, without forewarning, threw the entire deck of cards at the wall next to our table. Cards went everywhere. We were rather startled to say the least.

Then, we quickly noticed that one card, and one card only, stuck straight out from a tiny slit in the old barn-wood wall paneling and just hung there like an apparition. We couldn't take our eyes off of it. He then asked my daughter to remove the devilishly dangling card from the paneling and look at it. She and I looked. She gasped and I tried to be a cool dad, but inside said to myself, "What the h... just happened?" It was the card she had picked. The magician calmly picked up the cards scattered about, smiled, and walked away.

I've talked to other magicians since then and described this trick. Every time, they've looked at me with complete disbelief.

Get this. The restaurant in which we witnessed this amazing feat was a customer of mine. Several days later when I went to make my weekly sales call on this restaurant, I told the head chef about what had happened. He looked at me and started to puff up with anger when hearing about some old guy hurling cards against his dining room wall. He checked with both his dining room manager who had been present that night and the server who waited on us. He told me that they both confirmed that no such person had been hired to do magic tricks and that no such magician was seen or heard by anyone else at work that night.

After hearing this, I can tell you that from that day forward I became much more curious about Jesus' vision that we have "greater things" in store. Whatever it was that happened that night, it confirmed that there is so much about who and what we are that we have yet to discover and were we to make this discovery, we would be astonished.

Rather than settle on your apparent limits, open and widen your focus today. Envision being a vast open space as large as the space between where you are and the moon. Feel the vast expansion of such spaciousness. You are so much more than you believe you are.

OCTOBER 2

Impressions

"Sunrise and sunset...We love the beauty of both."

My great grandma Juliu (the spelling is correct)was born in 1881 in the Oklahoma Territory. At thirteen, she married my great-grandfather Tom, a twenty-year-old farm boy. I came to know her through the many summers my family spent on their small hilltop farm near the tiny remote hamlet of Reydon, Oklahoma. She was a time-tested, self-made survivalist whose gentle demeanor was crisscrossed with a no-nonsense, get-it-done attitude. I had a fond fascination of her even though she sometimes made me nervous.

When I showed up, great-grandma would put me through a bizarre annual boy ritual. She would tie on her waste apron with extra long straps so that she could wrap them around her and with authority tie the apron off in front of her long dark dress. It was like she was preparing for battle. She would take hold of my hand with her gnarly soft left hand. In her right hand she firmly clutched a cleaver. Off we'd march to the chicken coop. I was unable to say no.

Wide-eyed, I'd watch her well-aged wide body nimbly chase down, then corner and deftly squeeze by the neck a frantic squawking hen. I'd then grimace and close my eyes tightly as she swiftly beheaded this helpless creature on a well-used tree stump. I'm purposely leaving out several details I'd rather forget.

She would then insist I help her de-feather and clean what remained in order to prepare the chicken to be fried in god-knows-what. It was memories like this that lead me as an adult to be a vegetarian for many years.

Short clips of life can make large imprints on our hearts and minds. We gather up thousands of these and store them away only to retrieve any one of them at any time anywhere. We are impressionable. That's only part of our story.

On the other hand, your daily life can be organized around your childlike ability to hatch innocence and untarnished spontaneity any moment. Invite yourself into the present moments of this day. Feel your heartbeat. Clasp your hands together. Close your eyes and be still. Take your place in this moment. See and feel yourself at the starting line. Your slate is clean. There is so much that is new calling to you. Get going.

OCTOBER 3

The Truth in One Word

"Love never ends."
—St. Paul

More and more over the years, I've come to the same conclusion. Aside from all the theories about the technicalities of the ongoing journey of the soul, it's about love—the vibratory frequency of this life-invigorating energy. The more unconditional love we embody, the closer we come to mastering the relationship between spirit and matter. We know this to be true.

Life provides countless moments to turn fear into love. When we shed fear's clinging presence, our energy field flows according to our love. What we call death is simply another moment that opens us into the heaven of unconditional love, whether it's death of unnecessary fears or our physical bodies. Out of every moment, every choice, every relationship, every joy, and every upset comes the siren song of love. Life on Earth is refined to the question, "How fully have I embodied unconditional love?"

This life experience is about being love now for that is who you are. Bring heaven into play now not later. The truth in one word has been, is, and shall always be: love.

OCTOBER 4

Relearning Geometry

"Geometry existed before the creation."
—Plato

The sounds, emotions, and words we sensed and felt while in the watery fluids of our mothers' womb resonated through us creating specific patterns in our cellular and emotional makeup.

Dr. Masaru Emoto's research with water crystals proved that sounds and words dramatically alter the molecules therefore the geometry of a water crystal. Uplifting and soothing sounds and rhythms or loving and wise words create crystals of breathtaking beauty and symmetry. Harsh sounds, erratic rhythms, and fearful words turn water crystals into malformed, non-symmetrical shapes. From this research we can easily postulate the long term effects that sounds, emotions, and words have on the development of our consciousness and potential.

We came into this world like highly evolved sponges. We absorbed our environment to our benefit or detriment depending on what came our way. Because we were porous and open, we either took on the distortions and illusions being fed to us from our adult ancestors, teachers, and companions or we drank in their expressions of noble effort, real love, and goodwill. We mostly became habitat for the wisdom or ills of previous generations.

As adults we have broader options. In spite of this truth, some of us still feel tethered to the abrasive burn of childhood sounds and words by a seemingly overpowering gravitational pull. Others of us are able to mentally and emotionally dissect our childhood. We keep what enriched us and grow in love and wisdom. We grind up the rest into a fertile fluid which fuels the urgency to take flight and become the spiritual architects of a new inner geometry, a rebirth. Some of us are a mix of all three.

Find a geometric design or symbol that speaks to your heart. There are so many wildly intricate and beautiful ones. One I encountered just yesterday is the sri yantra, a geometric symbol which encompasses almost all symbols. By visually meditating for only three minutes a day on a geometric shape that appeals to your heart, you will start to redesign your sacred geometry. Nothing in your inner life is set in stone.

OCTOBER 5

It's a Stretch

"I'm afraid of heights!! 'Well then...jump!'"

Lancelot, my nine-year-old companion, is a greyhound crossed with a blonde labrador retriever. He can really stretch out, not only when he runs, but also when he rises from a nap and fully stretches out back legs to front like a stretch limo. This brings energy back into his leg muscles as well as stretches his spine. He instinctively knows what to do to prepare for lift off.

I love certain yoga poses. What is often called Marichi's pose is one of my favorites. I love the way this twisting pose stretches my spine and adjusts my sacrum. Marichi literally means "a ray of light." When stretching the spine, it does feel like I am letting more rays of light radiate through me. I always have more energy after doing this pose.

Stretching is a physical need and a consciousness need. What's a stretch for you? Sometimes, before you and I stretch out beyond our known limits and conformities, the best primer is to stretch our physical bodies especially the spine. Often, before doing a speaking presentation, I physically stretch my spine. This always provides more energy, greater openness to inspiration, and better mental flexibility. More light shines through.

The spine is a vertical masterpiece. Keep it stretched and you are likely to tap unknown spiritual capacities flowing through you from the infinite. Stretch out!

OCTOBER 6

A Movement with No Name

"What will guide us is a living intelligence that creates miracles every second, carried forth by a movement with no name."
—Paul Hawken

While stopped in my car at a traffic light, I watched three people carry a woman into a nearby business to tend to her after she fell on the ice and couldn't get up. The number of individuals in our world who serve to create a better life for all Earth's inhabitants is truly remarkable. I'm witness to this outpouring frequently. The heart of caring and oneness is alive and very well.

Every week numerous acts of altruism occur in our communities. Multiply these acts of generosity by millions and this is what often goes almost unnoticed in our world every single day.

So, take notice even when it comes to you. You are to be thanked. You are part of this mega-movement of loving your neighbor as yourself that is ever-growing in numbers and impact.

There is so much love in this world and it is finding ever-increasing channels of expression. Population growth has its great challenges. How do we care for all the children, mothers, fathers, working folks, and elders of our world and support one another in living lives that are fulfilling? The resolutions to this question come through this irrepressible spirit of love, ingenuity, and generosity inherent in the human heart. This spirit is expanding every moment and will not be denied.

Thank you for letting others into your heart as you care for them. One day you'll be asking someone to do this for you.

OCTOBER 7

Finding a Mate

Every breath and pulse of life hums a
symphonic alchemical masterpiece
of eloquence and magic that is the constant call of remembrance.
You each have emerged from a Source of
beauty and terrestrial harmony,
a universal prayer resounding in the echo chamber of each moment.

This Source is indestructible.
She is a tapestry of tradition and awkward surprise,
heard and felt through sounds uttered in caves,
aroused around fire pits and appearing as a newborn in sweet purity.

While walking in winter woodlands, look for signs—
a large stone, unmoving, whispering, "touch me."
Moss, multiplying as you move, softens your vision,
coloring the damp earth and barren branches
with an overspray of serenity.

There is an effusion of hobbit-like wind-chiming
guiding your inner positioning system.
Turn here, stop now, listen, listen, listen.
You notice the pull in your groin urging a step onward.

Every sound is a note of a sacred chord leaving
the flow wanting for nothing.
In the unbroken rhythm of a hundred thousand years
you are etched in the living library of purpose.
Now ask the Holy One to come and be your mate.

OCTOBER 8

Beyond Hyperbole

"Again I tell you, it is easier for a camel to go through the eye of a
needle than for a rich person to enter the kingdom of God." (KG)
—Jesus

This saying is likely hyperbole, an exaggeration used to get our attention
and convey an important teaching. It does get our attention.

It's similar to the hyperbole in this parable: "God's kingdom
(KG) is like a treasure hidden in a field for years and then accidentally
found by a passerby. The finder is ecstatic—what a find!—and
proceeds to sell everything he owns to raise money and buy that
field." (Mt. 13:44)

In either case, the message is about something extraordinary, so
extraordinary as to seem almost impossible to attain. If this kingdom
is realized, the average person is more likely to discover its secret access
code than someone with riches and worldly power.

In other words, we can't buy our way or power our way into KG. It's
something far more sublime than what money or status could buy. Also,
there's a feminine air about it, because the original word for kingdom
in Jesus' Aramaic language, malkuta, was gendered feminine.

All things of Earth, in time, come and go. The sublime, all powerful energy and light which gives life to all things throughout this grand cosmos, has found expression as us and as countless other manifestations. It does not come and go, but remains and creates.

In our tiny corner of the cosmos, this energy and light has become the great venue of exploration for science, spirituality, art, the written word, and architecture. It far transcends earthly value. You can feel it, sense it, nurture it, and endlessly create from it. As a sentient being, you can join in celebrating it through love, ecstasy, and generosity.

This was the direction Jesus was pointing. He could only point. The rest is up to you. What an extraordinary treasure is within and all around you. In two thousand years, we have greatly evolved in our understanding of how to access this treasure and care for it. No hyperbole is needed to be in awe of this truth.

OCTOBER 9

A Lingering Question

"You'll just be completely blocked and hopeless and wondering
why you shouldn't just go into the kitchen and have a
nice glass of warm gin straight out of the cat dish."
—Anne Lamott

Opening the channels of creativity is so often a mystery. There are prescriptions for when you get blocked. Here's a few examples: Just do something...begin, even if what you are writing or drawing or singing seems completely senseless; stay with it and something valuable will eventually emerge; start laughing and keep it going for at least five minutes; put on loud rhythmic music and dance and move wildly until you're ready to drop; take a long vigorous walk; pray like there's no tomorrow; you could follow Anne Lamott's suggestion above. Sometimes these things work to arouse creativity, sometimes they don't.

Staring at an orange resting on my desk, questions arise. What inexplicable, innumerable steps had to take place in order for this intricately designed edible object to exist and for it to be here in front of me waiting to be consumed? The same question applies for each one of us except for being edible and waiting to be consumed.

Consciousness is what gives flow to this river of creation. Being here having consciousness aroused in me in these ways reminds me that I have won a universal creation lottery. Same is true for you who are reading this. Billions of years and trillions of molecules have conspired to put us here in this form, in this spot with this animating eternal spirit expressing itself as us.

I still feel the excitement of eyeing my new red bike on Christmas morning 1958, the burst of joy when I was present in the birthing room for my children's births, the gripping sadness recalling the final time I said goodbye to my mother, and the hilarity I experienced when reading Anne Lamott for the first time. In creation, sequential time steps aside and allows the present moment to fill us with whatever emerges from all that we are.

In the stillness of this moment, let your heart-space come to the forefront of your awareness. Marvel at the creation of you, the wonder of you, the lingering question about what you truly are. Creativity begins here.

October 10

Confessions of a Heretic

"The gospel in one word is love."

A heretic is usually defined as "someone who believes contrary to the fundamental tenets of a religion or spiritual way of life they claim to belong to." I am grateful to be a part of this growing wave of contrarians. Many of us see Jesus as a contrarian. We view him as the torch bearer for a unique spiritual way of life that combines an eastern philosophy of "seeking the kingdom within" with the sweeping and redemptive teaching of unconditional love and forgiveness even of our adversaries.

Jesus never gave this deeply spiritual and profoundly human way of life a name. Those involved in this movement shortly after his earthly departure were often called followers of "The Way." This "Way" was just that—a way to be fully human, to open the corridors of our hearts to the inner temple of Divine Presence, and to break the hold of religious dominance and fear.

These contrarian heretics, what I've called "raretics," have been murdered, imprisoned, tortured, ridiculed, demonized, rejected, and told they are doomed to eternal suffering. We have mostly emerged from these dark ages, but much of the rhetoric of self-professed "true believers" who are critical of these contrarians remains.

As I see it, the presence and power of love is for everyone no matter your religious or non-religious values. Rather than condemn when other's beliefs or visions differ, do unto others as you would have them do unto you.

I suspect that a good number of you have been hereticking along with me for a while. Keep going. Follow your heart. And, when you see me, wink if you're a heretic. I'll wink back.

OCTOBER 11
Pedal Strokes

"Walk in another's shoes."

I greatly admired my son Zach's efforts as a competitive cyclist. He worked his way up to great heights in the sport of cycling only to meet up with its growing drug culture. The reality of this and the growing effects of living a one-dimensional life, eventually led him to walk away from something he had poured his whole life force into for ten years and ten's if not hundreds of thousands of miles.

At one time, I was so inspired by Zach that I decided I would train to ride the Iron Horse bike race in Colorado. Train I did, riding the steep hills of the Colorado National Monument near my home for about nine months. I entered the Iron Horse and completed the fifty mile ride from Durango to Silverton which included ascending and descending two mountain passes exceeding 10,000 feet in elevation.

Here's what I learned aside from needing the right equipment and a pair of strong and healthy legs and lungs. The training was worth it. What it taught me was how to stay in the moment. One pedal stroke at a time is all I need to focus on and the Great Spirit breathing through me will get me to wherever I'm going. Projecting ahead will only create small energy drains.

What stood out most of all during my training and the race itself were all the moments I would think of Zach and the countless millions of pedal strokes he had made through the years, many of which were done while he was training alone on his bike on some road somewhere in all kinds of weather.

It became evident to me later that I trained and entered the Iron Horse as a way to more deeply connect with and understand what Zach had been experiencing for years. I had always been a spectator. I needed to know my son more fully and what was in him that would inspire him to keep going when no one else was there to push him. What became clear was that he had great heart and courage. I can say, on this his birthday, that he still does.

One of the most important journeys of our lives is to touch and experience what is in the heart of another and to know them as they truly are. Otherwise, we are missing one of life's precious gifts.

OCTOBER 12

Reconciliation

"I want to be remembered back into alignment
with my self and my purpose. I want to live
with the opportunity for reconciliation."
—Christina Baldwin

Many of us have experienced rejection by someone we deeply cared for and loved. I ended a marriage of twenty-two years. The reasons languished in me for a very long time, until one afternoon when I knew, for the sake of my well-being, I needed to end it. Her experience of rejection was deeply painful.

The beginning of the end of my first marriage of fifteen years quite unexpectedly came crashing in upon me with a long distance phone call out of the blue in which my wife very plainly said, "I no longer love you or want to be married to you. It's over." That was it. I, too, experienced the deeply painful reality of rejection.

Along the spiral of life, rejection is a powerful heart-wrenching creator of needed change. It offers us the space to stand back and look at ourselves with honest eyes. Rejection could point us toward our own insecurities that have formed into addictive, contracted behavior. The shadow sides of our conditioning are there to look at, if we are ready and willing to lean toward them.

When feeling rejection, our worth as an individual and soul feels at stake. It's as if we are in a hall of mirrors with no way out. Wherever we look, there we are. It's a deep dive initiation whether we like it or not, whether we are ready or not.

Get your breath and go forward. Various options can be taken to address what you feel. Most importantly, I learned I needed someone who knew me very well to be a live, honest mirror and tell me just what they saw in me—the good, the bad, and the ugly.

In short, rejection opens the corridors of our lives to what is likely long overdue: being reconciled with what always lies underneath the scars of life—a child at heart who only wants to be loved. Take good care of that child.

OCTOBER 13

Loving Touch

"We humans are made for touching. We are covered with skin, not a hard shell. In fact, the average human has eighteen square feet of skin embedded with five million nerve endings, each ready to be triggered by touch. Do you suppose this is some accident of nature? Hardly! Our skin is there for relationship. It allows us to experience and receive the world. Think about it: If touch didn't feel good, there would be no pair bonding, no sex, no mothering, no fathering, no species, no survival! We are hard-wired for touch."[9]
—Christopher Uhl

Whether or not we received consistent affection as a child is one of the most powerful indicators of the choices we make as adults as well as our overall well-being and success in the world. This is clear. A variety of scientific studies confirm this.

We don't need these studies to confirm the power of affection. By affection I mean heartfelt, loving touch. Loving touch becomes an extension of your real love for another.

I have spent much of my life sorting out the ripple effect of receiving very little loving touch from my mother. My relationship experiences and choices have clearly pointed out to me the results of bringing my childhood yearning for loving touch into my adult life. In my mid-thirties, I changed careers and chose to become a minister in a spiritual organization whose culture encouraged appropriate hugs and touch. There were many touchy-feely folks there. Years later, I became aware of how this choice was influenced by my strong need for touch that had largely been missing from my childhood relationship with my mother and my adult relationship with my wife.

One other thing I have learned about loving touch and affection is that people can change. Later in life, my mother was able express affection and loving touch toward me. This was because her heart had opened. This continued on for her final twenty-five years.

May your deep yearnings for loving touch and affection be truly fulfilled. You are deserving.

Taking Up Residence

"It doesn't interest me if the story you are telling is true. I want to know if you can disappoint another to be true to yourself; if you can bear the accusation of betrayal and not betray your own soul."
—Oriah Mountain Dreamer

In the more than twenty-five years of serving spiritual communities, in all but one, I have come into disjointed environments that called for healing, mending, and compassionate care. These tinderboxes of emotional and spiritual uncertainty repeatedly drew out of me my mothering instincts.

Here's the catch, as I'm sure many of you mothers can attest as well as some of you men: a disconnect arises with your individuality, your soul. So much essential energy and attention is given to the community-family-collective consciousness, it leaves a gap between the two halves of your life.

Have you felt like you've been living much of your life as a tenant in your own soul? Like a tenant does at times with a rental property, you may neglect your spiritual residence, your individual soul. Your heart breaks tiny pieces at a time.

A wise friend has reminded me several times that you can't give what you don't have. What you would like to give is yourself, a self that is spiritually, physically, and emotionally balanced and inspired. As I frequently counsel others, you must be committed to taking care of yourself, the beautiful manifestation of Spirit's sacred imaginings. Then, the self you give in every relationship and form of expression is your best, truest, and clearest light.

Take up residence in the life that you have been given. Love yourself.

OCTOBER 15

What's Your Take On All This?

"We are called to be architects of our lives not its victims."
—Buckminster Fuller

The heart knows that any moment can serve as a turn of fate, a sudden lift into clear vision, a lifelong influence, the leading edge of our destiny urging us along. Infinity is in the palm of our hands and in the chalice of our hearts.

My partner and I were talking one day about the series of events that had to have taken place in order for us to meet. The almost endless number of decisions made, tangents taken, inspirations received, and events occurring from pre-birth to the present in order to create the opportunity to meet, were almost as complex as what was required to map the human genome.

Do things happen as a result of random occurrence? Or, is there some kind of labyrinth we are moving through which has a clear purpose or meaningful completion embedded within it? This is where you and I come in.

If you hold that the events and relationships of your life are the result of random occurrences, then you are likely to view your life as a series of accidents or coincidences or lucky or unlucky moments. You believe that life happens to you. Or, you consciously choose to engage with the mapmaking of your life and observe and participate in it by bringing your sincere willing heart and conviction that you are a key player in co-creating direction and end results. This generates a powerful energy that attracts meaningful and purposeful experiences that have your fingerprints all over them.

You are then a player with the Great Spirit. Life doesn't happen to you, it happens through you. You'll better understand when to be the artist and when to be the clay.

OCTOBER 16

Put Your Whole Self In

This message is written for children. You decide if it still fits the life of an adult.

When you decide you want to create something new, you may begin slowly, wondering whether you've made the right choice and have the skills and confidence to finish it. Maybe you want to run a marathon or paint a picture or help a friend or learn math or write a poem. Usually, it's a matter of staying with it. You keep going day by day, week by week, for as long as it takes. Like the hokey pokey, you stay with it until you finally are able to put your whole self into it.

What does it mean to have your whole self in? It means having your whole self involved in what you are wanting to do and create. It means you'll have more fun, more energy, feel happier, come up with great new ideas, and likely finish what you set out to do or you'll come up with an even better idea.

There is a magic about it. You start from this place inside of you in which you feel really good about who you are, a love and appreciation you feel for yourself. There is no end to this love and appreciation. It is like the place where water flows up from underground to create the beginning of the McKenzie River in Oregon. That river keeps flowing and flowing and flowing and has for hundreds if not thousands of years. It is because there is a source that keeps providing new water minute after minute after minute, and on and on and on.

You have a source inside of you that is like the source of the river. It is that love and appreciation you feel in your heart for yourself. You can keep feeling that love and appreciation minute after minute, day after day, on and on for the rest of your life.

There is a story about Sunny. Sunny was like a bright light. Everyone liked her. She liked herself. Birds would flock to her and often land on her shoulder. Cats loved to snuggle up close to her sometimes as many as ten at a time. Finally a friend asked her how come she was happy and fun-loving and peaceful most of the time and why everyone liked her and why birds would land on her shoulder and almost all the neighborhood cats would come to snuggle up to her?

Sunny closed her eyes and waited for a few moments before she answered. Then, like a swift wind that just blew in through an open window, she said, "I love myself the way I am. There's nothing I need to change, because I am made of God's light. Every little cell in my body is happy. Every little cell in my body is well. Because I feel this and know this, I become like a warm fuzzy blanket."

October 17

Beholders

"May the beauty that we are be the beauty that we do."
—Evan Hodkins

Is it true that beauty is in the eye of the beholder? For me, it would be closer to the truth to say that beauty is in the heart of the beholder.

Beauty is experienced because we are able to feel something deeply. That particular feeling could have elements of love, serenity, joy, warmth, passion, mystery, and wonder held within it. Beauty is the result of being able to feel deeply about something we see, touch, taste, read, create, hear, smell, or imagine.

It runs the gamut from eyeing a newly bloomed wild trillium on the sunlit forest floor to the exquisite solving of a very complex math problem to a whisper of affection from a loved one. Beauty arises from our deep hearts being inspired by what life reflects back to us.

We are designed to deeply connect with the multifaceted universe in all its wild, pristine, infinite majesty. This truth is central to our collective story. Our deep hearts are powerful receivers and broadcasters of this never ending revelation. May we not take this for granted.

Be in the presence of your heart-breath today. Let beauty touch you, heal you, inspire you. Behold it everywhere.

OCTOBER 18

Channeling Rumi

"Sometimes you hear a voice through the door calling you....
This turning toward what you deeply love saves you."
—Rumi

See your past complete like a door closing behind you and see a door opening toward what you love. What if you were to love the life that you are now creating? What if?

I have thought, felt, and said this sort of thing in a thousand ways. So have you. The Divine Presence has always remained in your midst reminding you in countless ways about turning toward what you deeply love. Settling for anything less is a self-inflicted wound.

Often you cannot save yourself from yourself. You make choices that deny your essential golden self.

Get a hold of the moment. Ask your true essence to come to you, to abide in you, to strengthen you, and to awaken you. Come around... come around to the place you aught to be. It's never too late.

To paraphrase Rumi, "Why do you stay where you are when the door is so wide open?"

OCTOBER 19

Swallow Magic

"Leaders lead by telling stories that give others
permission to lead not follow."
—Michael Margolis

Witnessing thousands of violet green swallows fly in acrobatic high speed synchrony along the cliffs above the Colorado River as it rushes into Eastern Utah was awe inspiring. In this stunning geologic museum of towering ochre-colored canyon walls in front of a blindingly blue sky backdrop, all eyes were on the swallows as we neared the end of our whitewater raft trip.

I couldn't help but wonder, "Who's leading?" It seemed to be orchestrated, yet spontaneous, as if there was an imperceptible, ingenious, guidance system at work. Whatever would keep the movement coherent, they would do it. They all seemed prewired to inspire and move in unison as if conducted by an invisible maestro. I could only describe it as divine symmetry in action.

Being in leadership positions doesn't mean we are effectively leading. Through all my stumblings of being in a leadership position, I've found that one quality in leaders that stands out and truly calls others to lead and not just follow, is the capacity to inspire.

Leadership guru Lance Secretan provides detailed insight about those he calls "Higher Ground Leaders." In his superb book entitled Inspire: What Great Leaders Do, here's how he describes higher ground leaders and the ripple effects they create.

"Higher Ground Leaders make a loving connection with others. We can all see and feel the difference in a heartbeat. We sense the presence of a motivator—their manipulative and self-focused agendas are often so transparent. So, too, is the commitment to ego and personality, to the superficial and to the material. Higher Ground Leaders love others so genuinely, they cannot resist serving them—and followers are at once inspired by this congruence. The result is a connection of souls, of people doing soul work, and of the creation of a sanctuary. These are magical moments and magical places in which to live and work because Higher Ground Leaders are fully present. In these exhilarating states we become inspired. And to the great joy of those around us, we are inspired to offer our greatest gifts—we are called to release all of the music within us."[10]

Genuine love for one another is the golden key to creating the ripple effect of what Lance describes above. I call it "swallow magic"— inspiration, finely-tuned orchestration, and spontaneity are abundant. The invisible spiritual maestro takes over. It's glorious to be a part of it.

Lead with genuine love and the magic will follow.

OCTOBER 20

Eye Contact

"We've become so focused on that tiny screen that we forget the big picture, the people right in front of us."
—Regina Brett

Here's a powerful story I heard Professor Michael Nagler tell at a public lecture I attended.

"I was leading a seminar on non-violence for a group of students studying to receive a master's degree in peace studies at UC Berkeley. One particular male student seemed very troubled by what I was teaching. He asked several very penetrating questions and left hurriedly once the seminar finished. It was some time later and I went to the graduation ceremony for many of these same students who had attended the seminar. The student who had been disturbed at the seminar saw me and pulled me aside. He then said, 'When I heard you talk I thought it was pure bunk. Two months later I found myself in Rwanda and had to arrest a child soldier who had just shot a man. There he was... holding the rifle. I reached for my sidearm. But, then the thought popped into my head—maybe Nagler isn't bunk. So I left my sidearm in the holster, made eye contact, and slowly walked up to him. I gently turned away the rifle, feeling that the barrel was still hot, and took hold of him. I found someone who spoke Kinyarwanda to explain to him that he wasn't going to be punished (he was crying by that time) and everything would be alright.' The implication behind his words was... you saved my life or his."[11]

The power of making eye contact must not be underestimated especially when we find ourselves in stressful moments with another or in moments we are wanting to truly connect with another who may be troubled. It communicates that the human being in me sees and feels the human being in you. It truly helps to ease any sense of separation or threat.

Feeling and breathing into our hearts while making eye contact deepens the connection even more and widens the possibilities that this connection could bring to both. I know this for a fact as I suspect you do. This isn't bunk.

OCTOBER 21

Adrift and Rescued

"Someone had taken sex out of God and God out of my body."
—Gabrielle Roth

As a child and teen I received no education, no wisdom passed on to me, no profound understanding of sexuality and how to express it. I was left to my own devices. When left to my own devices, I took my sexuality and held it in the shadows, in secrecy. It's as if I was thrown overboard and left adrift in a sea of shame and misunderstanding about the body.

Most of you can relate. Shame and guilt became associated with the movement of sexual energy through us. It even became sport to agitate others to feel their shame and guilt as well. Strange. Our bodies became an objectification of this sad distortion. This has been a betrayal of who and what we truly are. We feel such raw emotion about all this. It's never too late to save ourselves from this bad dream.

There is a deep and profound spiritual dimension to our sexuality. It is no accident that passion is a word that describes both sexual union with another and the heart of the mystic seeking union with God.

Bring a sincere expression of forgiveness into your heart today—a great big sigh of self forgiveness for all the ways you have acted out this misunderstanding about your body. Embrace yourself, your body. It truly is a sacred temple, a divine vessel of the fullness of love for procreating divine ripples through you and those you are with.

OCTOBER 22

Crossovers

"The realm I experienced...allowed me to see my
own magnificence, undistorted by fear. I became
aware of the greater power I had access to."
—Anita Moorjani

Fear often becomes so ingrained into everyday life that we don't see how it gradually obscures our magnificence...yes, our magnificence. Magnificence as a quality of an individual soul, describes someone who is able to access their inner light and turn that light into acts of love and generosity in our world. Magnificence is an ever-present field of amplified creativity. All of us have equal access to this plenty, yet fear and conditioning often render us powerless to access this abundant resource.

The art of living with heart is to feel the fear but not allow it to stop us from diving deeply into the fullness of life. It is very much like climbing the ladder to the high diving board, feeling the fear and trepidation of launching forth into the deep waters far below, and doing it anyway. We do this not to inflate our egos. We do this in order to minimize fear's illusory power and to feel the presence and power of magnificence streaming through us.

Our calling is to crossover these daily thresholds from fear to love, from fear to creativity, from fear to healing, from fear to laughter, from fear to magnificence, and to encourage our friends and loved ones to do the same. The more you and I practice these crossovers, the more fear recedes into the backwaters of life. Vulnerabilities become access points to the field of magnificence within and around us.

Look more closely behind the veil of fear. A magnificence is there. This you know.

OCTOBER 23

Shadow Bag

"I give you all of me."
—John Legend

In <u>A Little Book on the Human Shadow</u>, poet Robert Bly declares that each of us has a "shadow bag." He further writes that in childhood, little do we know that we are stuffing our shadow bags full, while we learn how to be "good." By early adulthood, the shadow bag is often heavy with the weight of insecurities, greed, lust, rage, resentment, envy, loss, and other unacceptables of this ilk. Not only do we haul this shadow bag around and experience the weight of this load, strangely enough we typically develop strategies to insure that each anti-goodie in the bag is preserved.

There is the expression from the infamous German philosopher Friedrich Nieztsche: "What doesn't kill me makes me stronger." To advance this idea more closely in alignment with this book, I would say: "Become aware of what you carry inside of you that is killing your aliveness. This is the first step toward a new life."

When my first marriage ended quite suddenly, it was as if all the stored up feelings from all my life's episodes of rejection rose up to be felt all at once. I was experiencing the heavy weight of my shadow bag. I was inadequately prepared. I was hit with rage, fearful insecurity, resentment, and grief. Over the following ten to twelve years, with the help of others, I examined, felt, and slowly developed a wise understanding of these shadows. My shadow bag became lighter. It was very healing medicine for me and provided greater access to my aliveness.

You can become a beast of burden, moving slowly, carrying the heaviness of your shadow bag. You don't like carrying that extra-heavy weight, but on you go anyway. You assume this is the way it is and there's nothing much you can do about it. That's part of your shadow— accepting that there is nothing much you can do about it.

Now picture removing your heavy shadow bag from your back and shoulders. Feel the relaxing relief of no longer carrying this heavy weight. Standing next to a flowing river, you empty out most of the weight into the water and watch as the contents flow downstream and become part of the river. Take several minutes to breathe deeply and feel the impact of this release for your heart, mind, and body.

Carefully, you pick up your shadow bag and place it back on your shoulders. It is very light. The burden you have carried for decades is released. You feel so grateful.

OCTOBER 24

We are the Future Today

"I loathe the now culture where you just live for today."
—Penelope Keith

Are you wondering what the future will bring? If so, you are not alone. Futuristic themes abound in spiritual, religious, political, and economic circles. Interpreters of the Mayan calendar concluded that a 5,125 year epoch ended in the last month of 2012. It passed and predictions for this new era ranged from being one of chaos and destruction to a thousand years of peace and cooperation.

Is there any sense of urgency on your part? The Mayan prophecy and its predictions of this new era suggest we will play a substantial part in what manifests for our divine-human descendants far into the future. What responsibility do we have to these new souls coming in? John L. Petersen, one of the foremost futurists in the world, writes in his book, A Vision for 2012, "We are at once citizens of different nations and of one world in which the local and global are linked. Everyone shares responsibility for the present and future well-being of the human family and the larger living world."

What a time to be here! Choices we make now are clearly difference-makers for the lives of our children's children's children. If you are holding one child in prayer, also hold all children in prayer, both the children of today and of generations to come. As you care for one elder, hold in your heart all elders in all lands, the elders of today and of generations to come. As you serve one person who is hungry or homeless, remember that your love extended to one serves the whole of our world's hungry and homeless.

Pray (or whatever practice fits for you) from your heart with the deep feeling and focus that all people experience being loved and cared for and that hunger and homelessness vanish from the face of the earth. Together, we have an enormous capacity to make a difference now more than ever.

OCTOBER 25

The Heart-Brain Train

"Every moment of every day your heart is
having a conversation with your brain."
—Gregg Braden

Most of us went to school primarily to learn to use our heads. What if the children of today were sent to school to become literate in the powerful subtleties of energy within and around them, which they already have a feel for, as well as learn how to use their brains? We'd likely see them growing into adults who would naturally and readily connect heart-to-heart with others and have a profound understanding of the many emotional, psychological, and physical benefits of doing so. This would be seen as normal not paranormal.

Some days I feel like I'm back in first grade learning how to use my head as I wildly attempt to get a decent brain-hold on the rapidly moving technology rocket that is flashing by.

Before you get sucked in too far by the brain-rattling, light-speed force of this evolving technology phenomenon, we always have the option to do what I have suggested throughout this book and heard yesterday from best-selling author Panache Desai: Stop, slow down, and rest in the awareness of your breath. This helps us reconnect with the heart and its ability to put the subtle energies in our midst into action. Then, the heart and brain can dance together. Everything slows down. This minimizes the brain's stress response and improve it's cognitive function. This cohesion also ensures that we feel more connected, loving, and inspired.

Let's all, children and adults, climb aboard this growing heart-brain train!

OCTOBER 26
The World of Your Choosing

"The whole of life depends on the life of the
individual. It is here in my deepest, most private, most
personal self, that I make the world I live in."
—Carl Jung

I find it helpful to recognize, as renowned spiritual teacher Krishnamurti put it, that "I am the world." In other words, we are not a tiny cog in a very large wheel. Each of us is the universe in miniature. The creative genius inherent in the universe (God) is in us.

Most all of us have been soaked in the polluted waters of an old Newtonian cosmology and worldview which accepts that planet earth and you and I are just minuscule parts of a gigantic machine that can be controlled, quantified, predictable, and rationally defined. This is the very thing that incites individuals to speak out and have their voices heard.

There is a radically different and powerful viewpoint: We are beings of purpose, uniquely indefinable and immeasurable. This viewpoint and revelation could be described as "spiritual capital." Instead of investing our hearts, minds, and beliefs in the outdated premises of Newton and his disciples of scarcity, we invest our hearts and souls in what a wise teacher boldly stated about 1,985 years ago, "The kingdom of heaven is within you."

Applying the insight of Jung, "What world are you making and living in?" Is it a remake of Newton's world which leads you to believe that power is scarce and only a few have it? Or, is it Jesus' world which calls you to venture out onto the edges of where you have been and look further, stretch out, and allow the unquantifiable presence of Spirit to live and vibrate in you? If it has been your pattern to align with Newton's worldview, then I say to you, as <u>A Course in Miracles</u> strongly suggests, "Choose once again."

OCTOBER 27

Your Whole Garden

"I will soothe you and heal you, I will bring you
roses. I too have been covered with thorns."
—Rumi

I married my first wife after less than four months of dating. I truly felt I was in love with her and believed she was in love with me.

It was about fifteen years later while I was feeling the pain of our marital breakup that I began to see clearly what I had been blind to before. The scars of my premarital life were now being uncovered by feeling the raw pain of my wife and best friend taking leave of her relationship with me. I discovered that our relationship raced into marriage so quickly, because I unknowingly was driven to cover over my personal feelings of inadequacy, hurt, and aimlessness which I brought from my past. I completed this unconscious hidden agenda by securing her affection as well as attempting to rescue her from personal wounds and painful events of her own. This awakening seemed to intensify the searing pain I was already feeling.

As my spiritual life has matured through all things painful and purposeful, I have come to know that I have powerful mystical leanings. I am certainly far from alone. The mystic in me is clear that everything I have felt, experienced, created, and learned have combined to literally kick the hell out of me and open me to being transformed through love and acceptance. Everything contributes to this shift. What has covered over my essential goodness and inalienable value as a divine creation gradually gets burned away. This is the reality of the fiery path of the mystic heart.

Consciously connect with your breath. Slow everything down. Ask the Divine Presence to be with you. Now gradually, in your inner awareness, hold space for a very large garden that represents the whole of your life: all of your sorrows, joys, missteps, relationships, spiritual wisdom, creations, work, trees, ashes and remains of old feelings and experiences, favorite plants, pets, you, etc.

Rather than attempting to imagine every detail of your life, simply ask your inner awareness to help you hold space for everything. Take a few moments to get a deep sense of this garden of your whole life. Now, with love, let your awareness of this amazing garden slowly drop into your deep heart. Allow the Divine Presence in your midst to flow love through you. You fully accept all that is in your garden. Everything and everyone has its place. Stay in this awareness and feeling state as long as you like.

The Threshold

This is from writer Mitch Ditkoff. It's excerpted from his blog, "The Heart of the Matter."

"A few years ago I found myself standing in my closet, madly searching for clean clothes in a last minute attempt to pack before yet another business trip, when I noticed my four-year-old son standing at the entrance. In one hand, he held a small blue wand, in the other, a plastic bottle of soapy water.

'Dada,' he said, looking up at me, his eyes wide open, 'do you have time to catch my bubbles?'

Time? It stopped. And so did I. At that moment, it suddenly made no difference whether or not I caught my plane—I could barely catch my breath. The only thing that existed was him and that soulful look of longing in his eyes.

For the next ten minutes, all we did was play—him blowing bubbles and laughing. Me catching and laughing, too. His need was completely satisfied. His need for connection. His need for love. His need for knowing, beyond a shadow of a doubt, that absolutely everything was perfect just the way it was.

He is fourteen now. His bubbles are digital, but his need is still the same. And so is mine—and yours, I would venture to say. Scratch the surface of our differences, remove the cultural masks, and all of us— regardless of age, religion, politics, gender, or astrological sign—are seeking the same thing.

And this 'thing' is a feeling—a feeling of contentment, a feeling of peace, a feeling of deep freedom, fearlessness, and joy. Spiritual practitioners have been attempting to name this feeling for centuries, but ultimately it doesn't matter what it's called."[12]

As Mitch goes on to say, this thing you seek, is discovered by making the short move from your head to your heart. He's right. Make this move with someone today who you normally relate to from your head. They too are in search of the same thing. Watch what happens to both of you.

OCTOBER 29

Targets of Judgment

"Judge not, lest you be judged."
—Jesus

I heard this piece of wisdom yesterday: "Live life independent of the good opinion of others." This is a kind, somewhat tongue-in-cheek way to say that we are far better off when we don't allow the opinions or judgments others have of us to determine our self-image and how we live our lives.

This past year, inaccurate stories about me spread around the community I live in. They grew out of assumptions and judgments several people had of me as a result of a decision I had made and actions I had taken. A number of individuals believed the rumors, assumptions, and innuendos to be true and shunned me.

Here's the most damaging part. I allowed these actions and judgments to affect me. When I would see one of these individuals in public turn the other way upon seeing me, I would sink. I began to resist even going out in public. I was feeling the pain of being rejected, shunned, accused, and judged. Most importantly, I knew that the reason why I had opened to take in "the good opinion of others" was because I started listening to my own voices of judgment inside myself. Like attracts like.

In these common scenarios, everyone loses and is harmed, unless the one being judged learns to be independent of the judgments of others. Science and ageless wisdom teachings confirm that holding feelings of critical judgment about ourselves or another creates not only harmful biochemical and neurological effects in our bodies, it also disturbs our spiritual core.

I leave it to the deep wisdom which abides in you to work out any issues of this kind in your own life. The secret is staying heart-connected...for there the truth is known and felt and will lead you into right action where love and healing take place.

OCTOBER 30

Pressing the Pause Button

"At the center of life, the world stands still."

Our collective longing for time to stand still is expressed and experienced in so many powerful ways: paintings, photographs, songs, sculptures, architecture, deep silence, holding a gaze into another's eyes, inspired words, pure love. We yearn to press the pause button. We want to feel being at the center of something beautiful and true and capture it in such a way that it would place an everlasting mark on our souls before its momentary glory merges into eternal light.

With this said, we realize life is progressive, always moving through space and time to fully embody the vision of standing forth in full divine radiance. Birth and death mark but the opening and closing of the gates of this particular earthly experience.

The reasons we are here on Earth are to have the experiences and to learn to serve in ways that are necessary to assure us of progress in our soul's ongoing contribution, as well as assist in the spiritual awakening of every child, woman, and man into the fullness of unconditional love. The release of the body, when it comes, is merely another step on that path of development. Our challenge is to release all fear of this doorway and embrace it as one more golden thread of love's divine weaving.

Don't let today pass by without pressing the pause button. Allow your eyes and your heart to fall upon something beautiful. Experience it as eternity pausing alongside to say hello.

OCTOBER 31

I Am With You Always

Warm winds from a southern direction
breathe bold whispers of irresistible greeting
as if rumbling up from ancient sanctums and
calling all souls to this magical meeting.

All kinds of earthly godlings gather
and lean toward sounds of mysterious repose.
Ears are opened and hearts attuned
as a sudden light appears in golden glows.

Not in words or phrases of the mind
does the light of the living one speak
but in melodies of electric rapture
that to ripe hearts are easily bequeathed.

These celestial tones of magical marvel
whirl and arc in blissful splendor,
harmonizing all ills, shattering all fears,
and form an oasis so utterly tender.

Gradually joy descends from expanses above
and ascends from the depths of earth below.
All sound then merges into waiting silence,
deep stillness arises into which all things flow.

Then a message emerges so beautifully clear
as if stamped upon the hearts of all those living.
The golden glow unmasks the truth for all to hear:
"I am with you always, forever forgiving."

NOVEMBER 1

Shame-Free Zone

"It felt like seventh grade all over again."
—Anne Lamott

I heard about a local group which meets monthly called "No Shame Theater." For individuals performing, anything goes as long as you abide by the following rules: What you create has to be original, it can't be any longer than five minutes, and you can't break anything including the law. Well now, what's not to like about this?

Even more daring is to improvise in the moment—no forewarning, no preplanning, or notes. There was a period of about two months in which every talk I gave on those Sundays was spontaneous. I did it not only to exorcise lingering inhibitions and self-consciousness, but to mirror to all those present the beauty and creativity which gets freed from within if we're willing to move through our fear of shame and ridicule.

We all could benefit from entering and spending time in shame-free zones. It's a basic need and requirement. There are twelve-step groups, support groups, and other venues which do their best to keep shame outside their doors. But, if shame is off limits, we likely bring it through the doors anyway. We simply keep it to ourselves. And, that's the issue. We're still privately drinking that sickening spiked punch.

So, I ask you, "Is there a place in you in which shame is off limits?" Often the purpose of practices such as creative visualization, meditation, wilderness excursions, and the like is to create an inner space where there is no shame, to open you to your soul's return. In your soul, your deep heart, you are shame-free.

Pause for a quiet moment. Improvise. Feel the energy of a radiating golden light in your solar plexus. Keep your full attention there. This represents your soul, your shame-free zone. Let it expand and radiate throughout your being. Open your heart so that you may see.

NOVEMBER 2

The Work

"I was born when all I once feared, I could love."
—Rabia

I realize that I've been "working on" several aspects of my life for many years. The biggest one is about moving in the direction of living the life I am called to live—my authentic life. I'm still working on it. This evolutionary impulse grabbed ahold of me long ago and hasn't let go. Being evolutionary, the journey to living an authentic life will never end.

I get it. My life unfolds as an upward-moving spiral. I am learning that it turns with an inspiring sound and feeling, when I am attuned to loving what I have been wrestling with about me.

What if, rather than "working on" our incompletions and imperfections, we love them? We accept and don't resist our incompleteness that for years has kept us awake at night. Lisa Nichols, inspirational author and speaker, calls this "falling in love with our humanity."

What about you are you working on? Rather than working on these aspects of you, I offer you this question today: "What in you needs to be loved right now?" Consider this in your heart. Your real work is to love what remains unloved.

NOVEMBER 3

Bright Moons

"You darken the sky when you leave."
—Emil Adler, Julie Flanders

Love is life longing to be all it is meant to be. Souls have come in and gone out, each one creating a unique reflection on the waters of my life. I'm feeling them today.

Human love, the deeply divine version of it, can send us beyond the usual boundaries within. We enter the wilderness of love in which only beauty, awe, and radical aliveness assemble. It's two souls deeply committed to wanting only the very best for the other and feeling that tide flowing back into their own hearts.

Pay homage to all those who have been the bright moons shining over the waters of your soul. Even touching feelings of loss that may be present can soften the outer hardness of your pain. Open to the restoration of all the ways you have experienced love as a pristine shining light upon you whether for a moment or a lifetime.

Return to love. It is still there within you, even if you've exiled it to a hard to find place. To paraphrase a well known teaching: tis' better to return to the love in your heart and feel the loss, than to resign to never feel love again. You are born to love. Be still and give thanks.

NOVEMBER 4

Devil of Change

"What lies behind you and what lies in front of you,
pales in comparison to what lies inside of you."
—Ralph Waldo Emerson

Often in contemporary spiritual teachings there is much said and much attention given to the practices and longings to change our minds or our attitudes or our beliefs in order to progress, heal, or be acceptable. This is also a cultural message. These little devils of mental and emotional caretaking are often found perched on our shoulders chirping out words of advice or admonishing us for still being the same old self.

I've been around this inner self-help watchdog for forty years. You can count me as one of those who's been an advocate and teacher of this approach to life for most of that time. This annoyingly soft but persistent assault on our being presumes we're defective, thus creating a pressurized mental and emotional undertow that is unforgiving. Even in the guise of being something positive like "change your thinking, change your life," there is an air of needing to fix something that is judged broken.

Frankly, what I've consistently observed and experienced with myself and countless individuals through the years is that creating lasting change is daunting. Through all the talk, spiritual practices, and courageous acts of self-exploration, long-term habits and inner patterns create waves of resistance to lasting change and healing. We may, for the most part, feel formed and shaped for life.

Feeling this powerlessness explains why so many of us and our descendants have turned to some form of immersion in a Divine Presence, a higher power, in order to arouse an inner spirit and be reborn. Whatever it takes, each morning we are at the starting line again, reaching inside ourselves to give birth to something new, relieving the suffering we and others feel, and opening to the presence of love.

I'm inclined to offer you this option today. This is written for a Sunday. Any day will do. Take a sabbath. What I mean is, take yourself off the hook. Decide to cease and desist from all practices that support the need to change something about yourself, make your mark on the world, and/or accomplish some task.

This is not a day of doing for doing's sake. Abide in your heart. Feel your light. Put that compulsive little devil that is on your shoulder to bed. It's obsessed and exhausted and so are you. Simply be. Save the urge to change or judge for another day.

November 5

Appreciation is Power

"Appreciation...eats the stress response for breakfast."
—Doc Childre, Howard Martin

My grandfather Doc lived a life of appreciation. He expressed it freely and genuinely whether he was with a client or family member or someone he met for the first time. He was doing what came naturally.

Unknowingly, he was applying what HeartMath calls a power tool of the heart. The measurable benefits of sincere appreciation are powerful in the ways they settle our nervous systems and chill the stresses we feel. The brain-mind is a poor substitute for what the heart-space is naturally designed to create.

My grandfather's life was not easy. Throughout most of his sixty-four years of being a chiropractor, he faced financial hardships and harsh ridicule from a society largely disparaging about chiropractic treatments and philosophy. What emanated from his heart is what carried him through and what drew people to him. His voice was single and his message clear, "I am here to help ease your pain so that you feel more vital and alive." This he did for me and so many others.

The more consistently you live from the heart, the more consistently you will experience harmony of body, emotions, mind, and spirit and the greater access you will have to the power tools of life.

Read The HeartMath Solution by Doc Childre and Howard Martin.

November 6

Start Right Where You Are

"We shall not cease from exploration, and the end of
all our exploring will be to arrive where we started
and know the place for the first time."
—T. S. Eliot

At a friend's suggestion, I reserved a "deluxe yurt" for five nights at a state park along the Oregon Coast for some much needed personal renewal time. I left home and began the two hour drive one January evening.

About halfway there, it began to snow heavily to the point where it appeared I was driving into a blinding snow scene painted solid white on my windshield. I had no perception of where I was going other than a faint hint of the highway's edge out the lower right side of my windshield.

After about an hour of this twenty mph insanity had pushed my stress meter into the red zone, in an instant, I drove out of the white flood of falling snow now turned into rain. "Whew! I made it!" I exclaimed to myself. "Now on to my haven of rest and peaceful retreat."

I parked as close as I could to my deluxe yurt of choice in a downpour with streams of water tumbling down the path leading to its front door. Finally inside with all my stuff, I removed my drenched shoes, socks, and pants and put on some dry clothes. Something I noticed right away was the noise of the rain hitting the vinyl roof of the yurt. I thought to myself, "Once I get settled in and warmed-up and comfortable, I'll likely not even notice the noise."

On day one I took as many walks as possible in the cold-water-world outside in order to get away from the thundering sound of the monsoon rains endlessly slapping the deluxe roof overhead. Even when the rains let up for a few hours, the winds would keep gusting and shaking the trees overhead causing loose debris and snapping limbs to come crashing down over and over onto the roof with loud smacks and thuds. It was the perfect soundtrack for a classic horror movie.

This continued unabated into day two. I tried earplugs and listening to music on earphones, all to no avail. I headed for the nearby sand dunes for a change of scenery. Upon gazing out into the low dark clouds and cascading rains and winds on these giant mounds of sand, I had this vision of the end of the world. That was my cue to turn around NOW and hoof it back to the deluxe house of noise.

By midday, no end to the rains, winds, and deafening decibels were in sight. Waters were rapidly collecting outside. I began to look for buckets for bailing, thinking my deluxe yurt could soon be floating away into a nearby lake and become the world's largest and most well-equipped life raft. I succumbed to the reality of being powerless and hurriedly tossed everything in my car and sped out of Noah's stormy wood.

Several hours later I was back home. I made note of the quiet, looked out my bedroom window, and felt very glad to be where I began, comfortably dry and warm. My renewal would take place within this space most familiar to me. I appreciated the unexpected twist of insight.

November 7

What Do You See?

"At the start when there's an empty canvas, you
see your whole life looking back at you."
—Georgia O'Keefe

What would it be like to experience our lives as an empty canvas at the beginning of each day, knowing too that we are composites of our past? There are always carryovers from yesterday or yesteryear. And, like a tapestry still in the process of being completed, something new gets woven into us every hour of every day. I understand the spiritual and creative benefit of focusing on the untouched part of the tapestry each day, to explore the new instead of that part which is finished. Seen rightly, it would be like gazing into the eyes and opening our hearts to a new lover each day. Embers of inspiration would alight.

The cynic and naysayer continues to bite into or be bitten by the past. Their canvas is rarely empty, their heart consistently closed, their tapestry an almost endless set of repeating patterns, and their light and colors dimmed. I've been there and so have you.

Heart-wisdom as a way of life carries with it a different air. You look onto the empty canvas of each day and see your whole life looking back at you, yet see it with your heart. You see and feel the angles and curves of love that have molded you. You touch your humanity and feel threads of compassion for yourself amid all of your life's difficulties. You honor the muscles of courage and perseverance that have carried you this far. You see and value all the ways you have added your light to a troubled world. You truly feel gratitude for all who have generously given of themselves to you.

You intend to fall in love with life all over again.

November 8

The Drawbridge

"There are waves of forgiveness and waves of regret."
—Ann Hampton Callaway

While I was sipping on a hot drink in a coffee house one early winter afternoon, a mother and her young son came in and sat down next to me. She was visibly angry with him and he was clearly directing anger toward her. Finally, she told him to put on his coat and go sit outside for a cool down. I even felt a bit of energy rise up my spine. I recalled the sparring days with my mother. It grabbed my attention.

Anger and resentment are like this. They grab us and get our attention. They may kidnap us and exile us to an inner prison cell in the back of our brains. We remain captured there for awhile by the energy of these strong feelings. We feel as if we've severed our connecting cord with our humanity.

At times anger or resentment become so large we remain stuck there for decades. It's akin to being in a tiny isolated village surrounded by high walls and a deep mote with no apparent way to get out. It's getting rancid in there. We need help breaking out and finding our wholeheartedness again.

This is the role of forgiveness. Like a drawbridge, it opens our inner spirit to reach out for help. It frees us from the prison of our own making. Whatever the reason for resentment or anger, if we're waiting for someone to do the forgiving, we may be delivering ourselves a life sentence.

Forgiveness takes place, because you quickly, or after many years, decide to take down the wall inside which has isolated your angry, hurt, resentful self. This awakens the wise and willing healer within you to come to life and take action. No one can do this for you. You may need help and encouragement, but ultimately it is a conscious, courageous, inner choice only you can make. Begin to take down that wall. How about today?

NOVEMBER 9

Helpmates

"They say there's a place where dreams have all
gone....It's miles through the night just over the
dawn on the road that will take me home."
—Mary Fahl

We are home to dreams of all kinds...silly dreams, scary dreams, senseless dreams, enlightening dreams, prophetic dreams, lucid dreams, beautiful dreams, repeating dreams, daydreams, and more. Dreams provide a hallway into our past, present, and future where we reconnect with loved ones, friends, or foes as well as special places we have visited in our everyday lives or imagination. There is often a helpful handout of insight, if we look closely enough.

I've often felt that I'm not alone especially when I enter into sleep world. At times it seems like I am in an endless school of learning and gifted with my very own master dream teacher. This wise and playful spirit is choreographing anecdotal tales with both obvious and hidden messages that assist me in finding my way through all things.

Imagine calling together all your inner and outer connections to assist and guide you through this day and the days to come. You then become like the hoop dancer among native peoples whose goal is to remind all of us to return the responsibility for all our problems and fears to the Divine Presence in our heart-space.

You are not alone. You have so much help. Gather together in your heart-space your helpmates of spirit and human form. Feel their support and undying love. While fully awake, dream this dream today.

Unstructured Time

"Instead of getting into being bothered, get into being free."
—Michael Singer

Structures are necessary. They need not be all-consuming. It's not good for our health.

Western civilization, and I reluctantly put those two words together, is overflowing with overwhelming time commitments. So many of us have so much that occupies our time, we have become puppets of this widespread social engineering.

Here's a very common example: My female companion and I were talking last night about the patterns of her life as a single working mother with a six-year-old daughter. The question arose about whether her daughter should start a sports activity that would involve practices and games or to continue to have consistent unstructured time.

Most days, her daughter has unstructured time to explore her own creative inclinations...to draw, to play outside, to go to a friend's house, etc. Being free to develop a stronger relationship with her inner spirit prior to being propelled into the world of structured activities almost every day of the week makes so much sense. Her daughter agreed. The mother sees and knows the importance of this because of her own opportunities to feel the freedom of her inner spirit when she was a child.

This awareness for the mother became a mirror that brightly reflected back to her how she conserves little or no unstructured time for her soul and spirit. She's not only bothered by it, she's feeling the life-force being drained right out of her. Her scales are too heavily weighted to one side. Like many others I have known, this imbalance becomes so ingrained, she struggles to act on her own behalf.

Unstructured time and space to explore, create, breathe, and relax into the moment are native to who you are. Reclaim it. Put it on your daily schedule. Renew your love for your whole life.

November 11

The Sun is Shining

This moment is my refuge and strength.
As the sun descends toward the bright blue horizon,
light warms the air and filters into the late afternoon spaces.
There's a softness about the moment.
Only fools let the moment in...all of it.
So, I push the fool's button.

I feel sleepy, a bit resistant, yet peaceful and full.
My eyes are playing with the colors around me
and my inner stream of consciousness is swirling within me,
somehow spiraling together to be the experience
of light as me on this canvas of oneness.

I realize I'm re-centering, following my own suggestion
to join with the now moment.
Many passages, symbols, and practices
speak to this simple movement.
Right now, what re-centers me is one-pointed attention
on a distant, towering, maple tree with red-tipped leaves.
How about you?

Each of us lives in the macrocosm of infinite options at any moment.
Re-centering is one choice, a homecoming, a
still-point, a movement of the heart.
The sun drops a bit further, no longer shielded by a nearby tree.
I appreciate its presence.
It feels like the center of our small corner of
the universe is highlighting me.
May this day lead you into center of all life where the
light of love is always brightly shining for you.

NOVEMBER 12

A Fitting Welcome

"The creation of human beings
contributed to sparks gathering."
—The Kabbalah

"I'm beginning to see the blessing of knowing who's coming in advance. We can then name the child months before it is born. As the child is developing in the womb, everyone is calling our child by name in whispers and in prayers, in song and in joy. Certain phrases that include our child's name are repeated over and over such as 'I love you _____'; '_____, I look forward to your arrival'; '_____, you are so beautiful'; '_____, I'm so glad you are my daughter (son)'; 'Ohhhh, _____, you are strong.'"—Thoughts from a parent-to-be.

This becomes a ritual blessing of acceptance and affirmation for this incoming soul. As a result, the child's name becomes a positive emotional anchor for their future self-identity.

What about you? Have you ever received a ritual blessing of acceptance and affirmation? Has a parent, friend, mentor, or loved one ever set aside the sacred time and space to celebrate your unique presence and affirm the gift of you in this world?

Through the years I have performed and been the beneficiary of several of these kind of welcoming ceremonies for adults who have carried the effect of not feeling welcomed into this world with open arms and open hearts by their parents. It is often the case that parents do not usher their children into this world in this open-hearted affirmative way, because their own emotional unmet needs as a child arise before, in the midst of, and after their child's birth. This causes the parent to lose sight of the great importance of welcoming their child into the world with an outpouring of love and joy.

So, for all of you reading this, I take this moment to extend a blessing of acceptance and joyful affirmation to you. Take this to heart:

"Welcome to this world. I celebrate your arrival. You are truly beautiful. You are truly loved. I am so glad you have come."

NOVEMBER 13

Sweet, Sweet Music

"Music is my religion."
—Jimi Hendrix

I sat spellbound listening to Beethoven and Chopin being elegantly performed on piano in the 800-year-old Saint Julien le Pauvre Church in Paris. I knew I was having a spiritual experience. Somehow the masterful blend of composition, performance, imagination, and well-aged sacred space swung my heart open. It felt as if the gods had gathered to communicate that there are no limits to the beauty that can be created through us.

Take a precious moment out of your life today and acknowledge something which may long be overdue for you. Call up from your heart a big "thank you" to all the musicians whose music has enriched and framed so many memorable moments of your life. There is exquisite beauty, passion, joy, and inspiration that comes to us through music. Musicians are divine messengers and muses that unhinge us from life's tragedies and fuse us with heavenly joys.

Music and the arts are the nectar of the gods, a pure and boundless expression of love and imagination that has no end. Today, let's be exceedingly grateful to know that this is so.

November 14

Out of the Fog

"The ones who are reluctant are the juiciest."
—Bo Eason

Today is another day of fog like the past week. This Oregon valley frequently becomes a foggy bottom.

About a mile from where I live is Spencer Butte, a local landmark. Today, I climbed the 1.2 miles to the top. Not far along the path I emerged out of the fog. Once I arrived on the summit, I was in bright sunshine with a 360 degree view of the fog-shrouded valleys all around. I couldn't stop smiling, as I sat for some time on a large, flat, sun-splashed rock.

Reluctant as I was, I called my first wife who I had been estranged from for almost twenty-eight years. Our marriage had ended suddenly and a wall went up that had never come down. I felt there was an opportunity to begin to bring down this thick wall between us. Fortunately, she accepted my offer to come and spend part of a day with her and reconnect and begin to talk about ways we could join together in support of our children and grandchildren.

Several weeks and two plane flights later, I was sitting with her in her home and talking with her face-to-face, one-on-one, for the first time in twenty-seven years. This persistent fog of confusion and loss which had surrounded me and affected so much of my life began to lift. Being together was awkward and uncomfortable much of the time. However, the time spent was worth it. We have committed to move forward in a new and connected way as friends and parents of our amazing children.

Notice in your life where you remain reluctant to take action and change certain circumstances and follow your heart. It may feel like resigning to being stuck in a fog-shrouded valley. Connect with the truth that one simple and likely uncomfortable step can radically alter your relationship with your past and your present and thereby shine a new light onto your future. Rather than waiting for the fog to lift on its own, move toward what you truly want.

November 15

Daytime Dream

Beleaguered by aching remnants of past mistakes,
I'm on constant heightened alert,
Waiting to be overtaken once again by voices of perfection.
What sort of mad illusions of my mind will
feast on guilty gamesmanship?

A dream appears...
I'm in a strange world of low-hanging overripe fruit.
I can't resist removing them from the tree.
But, rather than feed them to the swine or leave them to rot,
I consume them as if I were starving.
It leaves me disturbed and sickened.

Hypnotized, I drift aimlessly in the heavy heat of this endless orchard
Finding more of the same...
Aging trees, overripe and rotting fruits.
Nothing else grows in this place,
Or, so it seems.

I'm the only one here.
My eye catches a glimpse of a tree in the distance with no such fruit.
It grows separate and away from the others.
My heart beats faster, my breath quickens as I approach.
I begin to run toward her as if my life is at stake.

Almost breathless, I arrive.
There is grass that thickly blankets the ground beneath.
It smells and feels of virgin green.
Shaded by her outreaching arms adorned with sun-glistened leaves,
I fall down and stay down,
Stretching out, cooling off, giving myself over completely to gravity.
I feel not the past but only a soft silky
breeze gently brushing my skin.
Safe and light and guiltless, I feel my heart,
my deep heart loving me through and through.

NOVEMBER 16

Awe and Wonder

"Praise then Creation unfinished!"
—Ursula K. Le Guin

Who hasn't had the thought, "How did I get here and why?" For me, it's as if I was looking for that something which lies at the heart of existence soon after I arrived. Thousands of times I have attempted to put some stamp of insistence on the moment, demanding that the world in some magical way answer my questions. We, the explorers, seekers, and non-conforming outsiders, may have to come to terms with the bitter reality that we may never find what we so desperately are searching for. So be it!

Ironically, as we stir the waters of what is largely unknown and make new discoveries, there appears to be less and less certainty and more and more vulnerability. This is what makes our evolving universe so fascinating.

Make note of the following translation of Jesus' very first teaching in the gnostic Gospel of Thomas: "Those who seek should not stop seeking until they find. When they find, they will be disturbed. When they are disturbed, they will marvel, and will reign over all."

This cryptic revelation offers up something rather simple and direct. Seeking is not futile, but it will always lead to the same truth: The more you discover and the more that is revealed, the more you come to understand that this universe and its organizing principles will always stretch far beyond what we can know and control. That may be disturbing to a number of us.

You are then left to simply open wider and see with the eyes and feel with the heart of awe and wonder and allow yourself to be overtaken by the marvel of this discovery. Become as a little child.

This reminds me of the famous philosopher and paleontologist Pierre Teilhard de Chardin's prophetic words: "Someday, after mastering the winds, the waves, the tides and gravity, we shall harness for God the energies of love, and then, for a second time in the history of the world, man will have discovered fire." So be it!!

November 17

Choreographer Needed

"I came to believe that a power greater than
myself could restore me to sanity."
—The Twelve Steps of Alcoholics Anonymous

I've come to know that balance is not the crazy-making attempt to stand delicately in between two strengths in an attempt to give them equal room to express. Balance is not some mushy watered-down blend of the two.

Balance in its most powerful understanding is a choreographed dance. Each aspect leads when needed and stands aside when needed. This is done in a way that honors and acknowledges the value in each . strength. Imbalance often occurs when the two compete for power and supremacy. This pattern usually places us in some state of guilt, confusion, or frustration.

For example, I innately want all things to work out well for others, while at the same time I place importance on attending to my own personal needs and well being. Many of us have experienced a lot of stumbling and struggle while developing the wisdom to know when to serve and give to others and when to step back from that and serve and give some love and care to ourselves.

I have come to realize that this inner wrestling is where the heart, the inner choreographer of all our unique polarities, is much needed. The aim is to allow what we say or do to arise out of being attuned to the wisdom of the heart. This heart-directed awareness can be applied throughout life to navigate vulnerabilities, utilize and grow our strengths, heal wounds, and create balance where needed.

Remember that the heart is an expanded energy field connected to and extending out in a large circle around you. This heart-space is your guide. Breathe into and feel its amplitude and power circulating through you like blood through your veins. Take this keen awareness with you throughout your day. See what happens.

NOVEMBER 18

Two Become One

"I wanted to put myself back together again!"
—Gabrielle Roth

Let's heal the separation between the sacred and the human body that has systemically taken place over the last several millennia. Western civilizations and religious traditions have largely promoted and taught that bodies are godless, shameful, and sinful. Like dance pioneer Gabrielle Roth, we all want to put ourselves back together again and experience Divine Presence in the body. Science, sport, dance, and some spiritual schools focused on health and healing are helping to rectify this split as they reveal the evolutionary marvels and beauty of the body human.

In the Gospel of John it is written, "In the beginning was the Word, and the Word was with God, and the Word was God....And the Word was made flesh, and dwelled among us, full of grace and truth." (John 1: 1,14) Consider that the vibration of the transfiguring Spirit of all life (the Word) is made visible as flesh not just in one body (Jesus), but in every body. Let's put ourselves back together again!

Today, as you place your clothes on your body, feel them enveloping you with Divine Presence. Hold this awareness as you place your arms and hands firmly around you. Sit in this Presence for a few minutes breathing into your heart. Give your body the love and sacred respect it deserves. It is an incomparable wonder.

November 19

Wonders Never Cease

"I am not washed and beautiful, in control of a
shining world in which everything fits."
—Annie Dillard

As a boy, for years my father and I were two of the very few who had access to a secluded wild section of the Trinity River in North Texas which meandered through private property only a short distance from busy city streets. Underneath a familiar waterfall was a large fossil bed. I loved scouring through it and holding three-hundred-million-year-old remnants of creatures in my hand. I'd run my fingers over the ridges and indentations and attempt to imagine what that area had been like when waters covered the land or when dry land appeared and scary mammoth animals roamed and thundered through those savannas.

I still can't consciously grasp billions of years of evolution. I get little twinges of insight much like a few stray drops of water dropping off a ledge into the Ganges. Such is wonder. It converted me into a spiritual naturalist. Many of us earthlings have had parallel fascinations with our natural world and its near endless life cycles.

This same sense of wonder eventually led some of us into exploring the ageless inner landscape. Remnants of a Divine Presence have been found there. Everything points to grand design and infinite uncertainty.

Grasping such things has been a well used path that leads to more questions. I like it that way. Too many claims of certainty whitewashes the path into a permanent hellish encampment for minds all made up.

Scientific discoveries and spiritual wisdom are parallel meandering rivers flowing onward toward the same great sea. Both reveal the wonders of creation. Each of us is designed to be a practitioner of wonder no matter where we are or what we are doing. Let's cherish the time we've been given to explore the wonders of this life on Earth both within and around us. May the placard for our lives declare, "Wonders never cease."

NOVEMBER 20

The Less Traveled Way

"Somewhere, something is waiting to be known."
—Dr. Carl Sagan

The way of heart-wisdom is a path that is not well-worn. These words of Robert Frost left an indelible mark on my consciousness as a boy. "Two roads diverged in a wood and I—I took the one less traveled by, and that has made all the difference."

I grew up in the heart of Texas and experienced its traditions through the lens of my extended family and post-World War II social trends and longstanding pre-World War II religious and cultural traditions. I was a reluctant participant in many ways. Socially established hierarchies based on financial wealth, race, popularity, religion, and what clique you belonged to, were the accepted norm. Within churches, religious conformity was the gold standard.

I tried to fit in. No matter how determined I was to have those ways of life be mine, I couldn't fit into those shoes. I experienced a slow suffocation of purpose and direction. Something else was waiting to be known in me.

Heart-wisdom induces movement **toward** the unknown rather than away from it. You become less prone to accept someone else's version of truth or conform to convention or be stopped by fear. Mystery is given breadth and depth to flourish and answers are questioned. Wisdom is shaken from the branches of new discoveries.

Feel appreciation this day for all you have passed through to be who you have come here to be. What is still waiting to be known in you? Ask your deep heart to assist you in bringing this into expression. Namaste.

November 21

A Grateful Heart

"Gratitude is the memory of the heart."
—Jean Baptiste Massieu

There is a true story of a man who was informed by his doctor that he had six months to live because of an incurable condition. Most everyone in his life wanted to commiserate with him. When asked "What will you do?" he replied, "I will do what I have always done: live with a grateful heart one day at a time." Ten years passed and the man in question was still very alive and well, living one day at a time with a grateful heart.

This real life story reminds each of us that gratitude truly is a causative energy. It is a vital expression of consciousness that keeps us in alignment with a more divine flow.

A grateful heart that keeps on giving thanks, not out of obligation, but simply out of the recognition that every day is precious, is certain to experience even more to be grateful for. You have a decided choice how to color your life.

NOVEMBER 22

Being a Flute

"If Kokopelli has lured you with his magical flute, it is
time to listen to his song. This song is one of fertility."
—Jamie Sams

Dating back as much as a thousand years, images of the Kokopelli have
been found carved into rock all across the southwest. This mythical
flute player has captured the imagination of recent generations as it did
me when I lived in the arid lands of western Colorado.

Seven years ago I decided to get a Native American flute. The
"little horse," the name given to it by its maker Butch Hall, for the most
part, remained in its bag. About once a year, I'd break it out and try to
play it. The sounds I created were not pleasing to the ear or the heart.
So, back in its bag it would go.

Not long ago I was inspired to pick up the little horse again and
play it. This time, it was as if something in me knew what to do. The
sounds coming from the flute were pleasing to my ear and my soul.
You might say, the Kokopelli was luring me with his magical flute and
awakening me to new dimensions of life.

The flute is a magical instrument. You are also. What if you let
(rather than try) yourself be an instrument expressing a beautiful
purpose? Nature is always standing by as an inspiring instrument
of creative amazement expressing itself beautifully. What have you
always wanted to do but, for whatever reason, stopped short or backed
away?—play a musical instrument, ride a horse, write a short story,
write a letter to someone?

Let the beautiful music of your life play through you now.
This is a productive time. Do you hear the Kokopelli's song? Listen
closely.

Core Values

"The core of any family is what is changeless, what is
going to be there—shared vision and values."
—Stephen Covey

What are core values? They are your personal beliefs, mission, and philosophies that are meaningful to you and serve to be central to your purpose for being alive. My personal core values are derived not only from family and mentor influences, but also from the depths of my soul.

One of my core values that I derived from family is to help to end suffering wherever and whenever possible. I have been greatly influenced by my paternal grandfather in this regard. Growing up in rural Western Oklahoma in a homesteading family of eleven children, via an ad in a magazine, he decided he wanted to be a chiropractor. At the age of nineteen, he rode his bicycle eight hundred miles to Davenport, Iowa to attend Palmer School of Chiropractic. He graduated in 1919 and headed off into the world as a chiropractor.

In that day and for several decades to come, chiropractors were either being jailed or scoffed at by society and the medical profession. No matter, "Doc," as he was affectionately known, went on to help relieve the suffering of many for the next sixty-four years until his passing in 1983.

On the day of his passing, he had adjusted four patients that morning. He then lay down and called his daughter and asked her to come over. He told her he was unusually tired. She arrived within the hour and found him lying on his bed. He reached out a hand to her, closed his eyes, and left this world.

Growing up, I paid close attention to my grandfather and noticed that he was often willing to say "yes" when someone needed his assistance in relieving suffering. He expressed a joyful demeanor at being able to serve others in this way. His value became my own.

Write down three of your core values on paper. Take them with you. Post them in your car or somewhere visible at home or work. Let what you truly value pull you forward into the rest of your life.

NOVEMBER 24

Full of Light

"Is it true that our destiny is to turn into light itself?"
—Hafiz

Jesus' words were direct: "If your eye is single, your whole body will be full of light." When all aspects of us are anchored in the heart of love, we shine. The word for light in Jesus' Aramaic language was *nuhra* meaning "the illumination of what is unknown." We come to earth to experience transforming the unknown into the known. This is enlightenment.

We see in spiritual masters how the vagaries of universal mystery become embodied with rare and brilliant clarity. Soul-infused individuals are bright shining stars. They turn into light itself.

For most of us, we are magnetically drawn to holding a newborn very close. It feels like basking in the sun. We perceive a radiance, a halo effect that is irresistible. For those few moments, we believe an angel of light has been sent to soften what has become hardened inside us. Then, while still holding the child, someone says to us, "you look different." As Hafiz wrote, those closeby "notice my happiness and delight in pointing toward my beauty." Light begets light.

Carry a small child with you in your heart. See their face. Feel their light and warmth. As I look upon the photo of me at the age of two posing in my sailor shirt, I see a light. I feel different. You very well may have a picture of you as a small child or toddler. Take a close look at you before the world may have dimmed your light.

Hold vigil for this light in you. Settle into your heart for a moment and breathe deeply. Call for the light to return. Open to be guided in ways that allow you to be the light that you are born to be.

November 25

Your Life is Your Message

Many of us know that Mahatma Gandhi was asked by a journalist, "What is your message to the world?" He responded by saying, "My life is my message." Clearly, how he lived communicated his message.

This is so straightforward. No matter what I say or write, how I live will be the true measure of my message.

The living book of life turns page by page each day. For many of us, hundreds, if not thousands of pages are turned and hardly noticed. If life passes unnoticed, then slowly over time we become forgetful. We forget why we've come.

The message in all this is to get connected to what inspires you and allow that inspiration to guide you through your life. Then, not only does your inner light radiate beautifully, your one-of-a-kind human imprint cascades out of you to make your authentic mark on the world.

Today I leave you with this vision: Send yourself messages that help unlock your light. Frame each day with a conscious beginning and ending that inspire you.

Use the tools you have—prayers, poems, art, music, silence, exercise, writing—whatever frames each day in ways that strengthen and stretch your spiritual muscles. Spiritual strength and expansion allows you to generate and turn on more light in your cells and in your self-expression. Your message is not so much about what you do as it is how you shine.

The View from the Milky Way
by Dennis Rivers

"Over the years I come back again and again
to a perspective I call 'the view from the Milky Way.'

I have been deeply influenced by the emerging
story of how we all got here,
especially the way that all the elements in our bodies
were fused together in the hearts of stars,
all the carbon and iron and oxygen.
Then those stars, pregnant with the elements
that would eventually become you and me,
blew up in titanic explosions,
spreading their rich harvest of elements across space
to become the seeds of future stars and beings,
rivers and trees and toddlers on tricycles,
all part of the extraordinary breathing out of
some cosmic creativity and fertility
that I can barely comprehend.

From the point of view of the Milky Way
all these forms pass away and all are renewed again and again.

I always find it startling to shift perspectives
from wanting an infinite future to having an infinite present.
What matters then is not how long I last
but how well I love in each of these amazing moments.

Then I start to feel timeless
and part of something much larger than myself.
That is the message that the night sky brings to me:

that we are part of something much larger than ourselves which holds our time-bound existence in its hands.

The view from the Milky Way.[13]

November 27
Everyday Sabbath

(Sabbath is) "the presence of something that arises
when we consecrate a period of time to listen to what
is most deeply beautiful, nourishing, or true."
—Wayne Muller

Recently, in those moments in between commitments and appointments and relationships, I have been feeling unable to settle all the way. There is a loud buzz going on in me even late into the night.

When this buzz shows up from time to time, it's almost always an attention getter. Like a wandering bell ringer, a familiar inner presence comes back around and wakes me up. My mind goes into pause and I listen to this presence. It's so often about balance and taking complete care of myself. I settle all the way into deep rest for a while. I feel a low hum all around me. This space opens me to receive love, renewal, appreciation, and a spiritual message.

I send these words out to all of you and call to your spiritual attention the importance of settling all the way into a restful, calm, and uninterrupted state of consciousness. It soothes the soul, restores the nervous system, and calms the inner chatter. This is the remembrance of keeping the sabbath.

Be an instrument of thy peace.

NOVEMBER 28

Your Secret Heart

"There is a treasure hidden in a field."
—Jesus

Consider this teaching of Jesus in my own words: "praying in secret carries a reward." As scholar and mystic Neil Douglas-Klotz expresses it: in the privacy of your own heart "the swell of the divine ocean can move through you." Through the power of creating a certain *quality of deep feeling,* a previously undiscovered dimension of being you is revealed.

No matter what form your prayer takes, surround and imbue yourself with a heart-centered feeling and your reward shall be great. Rather than pray for love, *be* love. Let yourself remember the feeling of love you have had in life's special loving moments. Simply allow that feeling to radiate from your depth. Rather than pray for healing, feel full of life. Be filled to overflowing with the remembrance of feeling fully alive, vibrant, and healthy.

Bring this depth of feeling to your concern or need. Prayerful silence infused with this quality of feeling energy, generates what Jesus described as "even greater things." You experience the vibration of the Divine Presence that is within and all around you and in every part and particle of this universe. In this prayerful awakening, you discover and create a true intimacy with your depth in God… the reward arising from your deep heart. Go to a quiet place and begin.

November 29

Awakening

"I awake inside myself. It's like a flame forever burning or a diamond
in a mirror turning or a cathedral when there's no one there."
—Steven Walters

In the 1990 film "Awakenings," patients who had been catatonic for
decades gradually awaken after receiving doses of an experimental drug.
These patients have to relearn what it's like to be in a conscious state
in a world that has radically changed and be in their bodies walking,
talking, and feeling. One patient named Leonard completely awakens
and continually resists the restrictions placed on him. He wants to
experience life for all its worth. Gradually, the awakening effect of the
drug subsides and, sadly, Leonard, along with all the other patients,
return to their former catatonic states.

This movie had a powerful effect on me. My cells were vibrating
differently when I left the theater. It was like a surge of electricity. I
was getting the message that the energy of life moving through me is
precious and miraculous, so stay connected and grateful.

We all can relate to those times in our lives when we have become
so anesthetized by circumstances that we go numb. We are like
sleepwalkers, unable to feel what it's like to be energized, creative, and
connected to and appreciative of the moment. We lose consciousness
of ourselves.

Each day is a container for waking up in your body—to feel
aliveness moving through you! The key is to remain conscious of life
as a priceless creation. Feel it vibrating, pulsing, and flowing. You are a
temple for its passage through time and space. Every waking moment
stands poised to receive your loving attention. May you wake up to
what you are and what you've been given.

November 30

Groove

I'm the long gone. I'm the immediate here.
This beautiful spirit slings out of my body to the left and to the right
on a wild roller coaster ride.
I feel joy and gratitude to have such a party to dance in.
Let me say, let me shout without a doubt—
There is a great light, the alpha and the omega,
burning bright, burning high and burning low
and burning through the piece de resistance of everything.
And what's left?
It's one presence, one power, one seismographic,
mesmerizing, intelligizing, unmistakably now arising
in every dark corner, on every high mountain,
in every winged bird, rumblin' and tumblin'
through every human heart, every living thing—
the beat, the sound, the vibration, in every nation
of Love—the divine kind,
the only kind in the one mind.
What a find that unbinds and unwinds all the tension
in suspension and did I mention that
we are the ones, the daughters and sons of the Most High—
out loud and humbly proud, irreversibly wowed
by this groove that so truly soothes this soul and body
and sings only one song, one verse, one stanza, one rhythm
with just one word—Love.
Yet, we're back at the wheel, the karma kind
that turns around and around.
And this squeaky wheel is always an appeal
to wake up, to slow down, and take a good look around
and within, for it is there that we'll see divine mirrors
placed perfectly to give us the insight that we are alright
even if we are uptight.

For we are the living breath, the heavenly sound,
the universal 'it-ain't-a-rehearsal' blend of flesh and flow
of life that is soooo...cosmic.

DECEMBER 1

Our Love is Strong

"Round and round we go, we hold each other's hands, and weave
our lives in a circle. Our love is strong, the dance goes on."
—Unknown

I recall singing this song on several occasions through the years at
Dances of Universal Peace gatherings. When sung in a round, it is
especially powerful. Singing the phrase "our love is strong" takes on
an extra dimension of energy.

As winter and sacred holidays approach, our attention is drawn
more into the inner realm. May our thoughts, prayers, feelings, and
visions generate more small moments of love. May there be more
occasions for us to hold another's hand and reaffirm the strength
provided by love's embrace and our unbreakable eternal ties.

There is a great love in this world and in the universe that shall
always be. Sense the golden cord that weaves this love through your
spirit, soul, and body. Let the universal spiritual law of love-action do
its perfect work.

In truth, there is only one Presence and one Power in our lives and
in the universe, Love Divine. Thank you for adding the love that you
are to this grand circle. Today, let the phrase, "our love is strong," be
your mantra through which you see, hear, and speak.

December 2

The Mystic's Sword

"What are all these insane borders we protect? What are all
these different names for the same church of love we kneel in
together? For it is true, together we live; and only at that shrine
where all are welcome will God sing loud enough to be heard."
—St. Teresa of Avila

I love setting aside time to completely be with another in the moment
and simply drop into my deep heart and ask the one I'm with to do
the same. Prayer may be too loaded of a term to describe what happens
when I'm connecting with another in this way.

From this slowed-down inner space, I allow myself to open and feel
what's present and gradually give that feeling a voice. It's as close as I
can come to authentic expression. There is no agenda, no have to's, no
hyperactive impulse to control what happens or impress. This makes for
a powerful connection with each other and with the amplified heart-
space. It's one way the Divine Presence breathes its way into human
life. Countless times, these sacred moments have carried me and others
over painful thresholds and released us into a vibration that is ripe for
greater things.

When we choose to get connected with others in this way, we are
making the choice to use one of our most powerful spiritual tools—the
mystic's sword. This spiritual sword heals by cutting away all neurotic
illusions of being disconnected from the Divine Presence and each
other and restores our sacred connection. We awaken to the strength
and power of One. The more powerful our connection to the web of
life, the stronger and more expansive we are as individuals.

Breathe deeply and connect with your deep heart and the Divine
Presence. From this sacred connection, pick up your mystic's sword.
Centered in this powerful consciousness of divine union, ask with
conviction that all thoughts, feelings, and energies which disconnect
you from the eternal truth about you and the world around you, be
spiritually and mentally cut away. Feel the release of what no longer

belongs to you while continuing to breathe deeply. Give thanks for this spiritual sword of healing that is transforming you now.

DECEMBER 3

Your Hearth

"I thought God was a dancer."
—Anna Halprin

It has been said that art may very well have been the original religion and served as a way to access the presence of the gods in our midst. It still does.

For a number of years I have been drawn to the word "hearth" and its messages. I have explored the synergy of this word...a convergence of heart, art, and earth. For most of us, hearth invokes images and feelings of a place to gather where there is warmth and meaningful conversation, a sense of home. It is a way of connecting with others and yourself, where your heart opens to express and uncover tender and powerful truths that lead to discoveries of new ways of being, like a painter awakening to new shades and brushstrokes of light and shadow. New expressions of art come into play.

Hearth is an invitation to find your art, the art of being you. Whatever it is, your heart and mind are fully engaged and your passion is pouring through you. You express yourself like an ecstatic dancer who cherishes having both feet caress the earth as well being unbound and flying free.

In this movement of life, your preconceived limits become unchained. You find the ground of your being in which the Divine Presence is taking you to places inside yourself previously unexplored. Creation is inviting you to explore Jesus' core conviction that "greater things than these shall you do." There is a music, a frequency, a way of being that is your heaven, your hearth.

Like a powerful, passionate dancer, breathe into your deep heart and find a body pose which feels like the artful expression of who you have come here to be now. Let it flow out of you. Hold that pose for a few moments. Feel it. Sound it out. Take this energetic awareness with you always.

December 4

She

"She is near. She is near in the body and the breath."
—Kalia Bethany, Marie Garry

There is a powerful feminine energy which is moving through our world now. I felt it so strongly as I stood gazing at a larger-than-life golden statue portraying Mary Magdalene being lifted, protected, and adored by angels atop the high altar in The Church of St. Mary Magdalene in Paris. Noticeably, she was pregnant. Yes, pregnant. Her presence was mesmerizing. I was so deeply moved.

This collective feminine presence and power is giving birth through hearts and souls everywhere with a prominence never witnessed before. We are the bearers of her message.

Malala Yousafzai, the Pakistani girl who survived being shot in the face by members of the Taliban for publicly speaking out for girls' education, is a living example of this feminine voice and energy. At the age of sixteen, she spoke before the United Nations Youth Assembly and said, "We call upon our sisters around the world to be brave, to embrace the strength within themselves, and realize their full potential....We will continue our journey to our destination of peace and education. No one can stop us. We will speak up for our rights and we will bring change to our world." This energy is everywhere present expressing across gender, socioeconomic class, religion, ethnicity, culture, and system of education.

If you are reading this it is likely that you too realize the potency of the feminine emergence which is passionately giving voice and expression to a new vision for the world our children and grandchildren will experience. Every time you stand for compassion, forgiveness, justice, union, celebrating the body, peace through non-violence, safe communities and education for all, or you express a fierce and caring heart, remember that you are being called by this collective feminine power and passion to do your part. Thank you for heeding this call. She is healing and inspiring our world.

DECEMBER 5

We are Many

"A god that could frighten is not a god—but an insidious
idol and weapon in the hands of the insane."
—Meister Eckhart

Mounted on the wall in my kindergarten Sunday school room was a large poster of a loving Jesus holding a tiny lamb gently in his arms while tending his flock. I loved to gaze upon this picture every time I was there.

I distinctly remember my Sunday school teacher standing in front of this portrayal of Jesus one Sunday and proudly declaring that anyone who did not believe that he died for your sins would be sent to hell for all eternity. It frightened and upset me. Hell was a scary place and why would people be sent there forever? Jesus was about love and this was not loving. Sending anyone to hell seemed mean and wrong. Years later I came to the conclusion that my Sunday school teacher's message was not only mean and frightening, it was insane.

I am grateful that I have been given the opportunity to present a very different view of the Divine Presence to many people through the years. This Presence is not consciously seeking to create more suffering. Rather this Presence is Love Itself. I took what I divined from that kindergarten poster and made it my own and let it into my heart. Call me insane if you want for cherishing the spiritual movement and teaching which declares that Love, not fear, is divine. In this movement, we are many and we are here to stay. So be it.

DECEMBER 6
Emotional Intelligence

"Blessed are you who are weeping now: you shall laugh."
—Jesus

These words of Jesus remind each of us that life is intended to touch the full spectrum of emotions. Most importantly, emotions have a purposeful place in everyday life whether it is joy and its accompanying laughter and lightheartedness or mourning and its flow of cleansing tears. What a gift of wisdom this could have been for me as a boy. All emotions offer a sacred possibility, even anger. Anger can serve to be the motivation to resolve injustice or protect the vulnerable from harm.

A golden thread of wisdom is that emotions can be used to generate a flow of energy that can serve to collapse our mental barriers that halt expression of our full potential. The overall intent is for our emotional nature to more cleanly serve this inner jail break. Emotions are one of our inherent transformative tools.

You and I are free to choose how to channel them--for ill intent or for the greater good. The secret is this: "Do emotions be you or free you?" There can be a tendency to over emotionalize when stirred up. Next time big emotions are ready to flow, remember this: set your heart on dissolving all ill will as well as having the flow of emotion contribute to spiritual freedom for you and all those you're with. Namaste.

DECEMBER 7

Co-Creation

"The artist is always beginning."
—Ezra Pound

Sexual procreation has been with us for eons and has been the most powerful evolutionary energy on earth. Sexual drives stay with us throughout most of our lives. The fullness of creation, of which procreation is a part, takes on more luminous aspects and is always with us.

Futurist and visionary Barbara Marx-Hubbard wrote: "Immense, loving, nurturing energy has gone into sexual procreation—birthing and caring for children—much of this energy will increasingly be available for a new purpose: 'suprasexual co-creation'....The vast, dormant potential of the human race is about to be liberated en masse as we shift from maximum pro-creation to co-creation, from reproducing ourselves to evolving ourselves. We are born on the cusp of a new life cycle."

As the Christmas season emerges, I invite you to see through its traditional messages and mythology. It could very well be that Jesus' physical birth and soul emergence served to usher in a collective spiritual birth, or, as Hubbard said, a new life cycle that has been 2,000 years in the making.

The juices of co-creation, when expressing through our hearts, minds, and bodies, give form to the Divine Presence and support a greater good for all. We are then active participants in birthing a tangible reality which reflects Jesus' vision of a transformative love that literally recreates who we are, how we live, and our purpose for being human.

Enjoy the cultural and sacred traditions which are so much a part of this time of year. Remember that there is hidden wisdom within these traditional messages. There is a gift for you awaiting your discovery. Inwardly prepare this season to receive new insights into the part you play in our collective story of co-creation. You are born into this world for a noble purpose.

December 8

Get Your Growl Going

"I love and respect you, but if we get chased
by zombies I'm going to trip you."
—Unknown

I was a very sensitive child. Very sensitive children become very sensitive adults.

See if this describes you or someone you know. There is a tenderness that easily allows buttons of vulnerability to get pushed. Sensitives feel deeply what's going on in another, or the family, or world, and emote easily. Their outer shell is porous and readily lets in the whims and influences of others. They can get lost in all that is going on around them and forget how to take care of and protect themselves. They suffer because of it. They tend to go off and be by themselves, because they feel safer and love their time alone.

Like all vulnerabilities, being very sensitive or being chronically afraid to express our true feelings can arouse in us the audacity to face our fears and chronic tendencies that keep us stuck in our default position.

My second year of college I could not get through a speech class. About six weeks in, I dropped the class. My terror of public speaking, or, more accurately expressed, my fear of embarrassment and how others might judge me, was overwhelming. My over-sensitive inner child was in charge and letting fear take over.

Fourteen years later, I was staring into the heart of this vulnerability and sensitivity as I was facing the decision of whether or not to make the attempt to become a minister. I felt paralyzed by fear again.

My dog Lancelot always bears his teeth and growls when another dog dares to get near his food bowl, because he fears that his food will be devoured by the rival dog. I knew I had to bear my teeth and growl at my fear of public speaking and embarrassment that had nearly devoured me on many occasions or my dream would have been squelched. That powerful growl proceeded to help carry me through more than twenty-seven years of speaking presentations.

Your greatest strengths and most audacious gifts may very well lay just underneath your most paralyzing vulnerabilities! Out of love for yourself and the adventure of life, get your growl going. Grrrrrrr.......

DECEMBER 9

A Tribute

"There is music in our hearts."

I was richly blessed to know and hear David Tipps. David's long wavy hair was a throw back to the sixties. He was a blue-collar singer and guitarist, a raw and skillful talent, often practicing songs over and over and over again to get them just right. He could sing with passion and bravado, but yet he had a tender and raspy tenor voice that could touch the heart. Many, many folks had come to deeply appreciate David, his music, his heart, his honesty, his compassion for others, and his infectious smile.

Each year at an annual Christmas concert, he would conclude the evening by singing John Lennon's "Happy Christmas" sometimes known as "War is Over." David owned Lennon's song like it was written for him. He sang this song with an unforgettable spirit which placed a one-of-a-kind mark on the hearts of hundreds of folks who would flock to this great concert each year. You couldn't help but leave feeling hope for the human family along with a swelling of joy—the true spirit of Christmas.

David recently left this earthly existence on December 9 fittingly only a day after the anniversary of John Lennon's passing. I have David's songs and smiles and soothing Texas twang in my bank of grateful memories.

You know someone who has touched you deeply over and over again with the gift of music. This divine gift has been brought to you with such profound spirit and love, you are certain that your life has been permanently changed for the better. Whoever that may be for you, remember them today. Send them a message of appreciation and blessing for their powerful inspiration of music and song. 'Tis the season.

DECEMBER 10

Your Verse

"Imagine a Divine conversation in which you are
asked to help in some great endeavor."
—Lance Secretan

After much contemplation, I've concluded that my reason for being here is: "To open humanity to the sacred wonders of the heart." Some would call it my destiny.

As influential poet Walt Whitman wrote, "The powerful play goes on, and you may contribute a verse." What is your verse? What is your primary reason for being born into this world? There is a singular inspiration that lives within you and only you. It's as if you've been summoned to leave a legacy that will outlive you, a legacy that truly helps to create a world less fearful and more wise, creative, and caring. Pulitzer-Prize-winning poet Mary Oliver puts it this way: "Tell me, what is it you plan to do with your one wild and precious life?"

I have always been greatly inspired and intrigued by those who have persevered through great difficulty or tragedy and have continued to love fully, create beauty, and give their hearts to the world. This unique and outstanding quality of these exemplars has helped point me toward my soul's reason for taking birth that I shared above.

What inspires you more than anything else? Let your deep-hearted meditations take you there. These inspirations have common qualities that point you toward the marrow of "your one wild and precious life."

Know yourself and why you have come. This clarity is powerful. You will shine more brightly and steer more easily through all things. And, our world will give thanks.

December 11

Listen to the Trees

"A few minutes ago every tree was excited, bowing to the roaring storm, waving, swirling, tossing their branches in glorious enthusiasm like worship. But though to the outer ear these trees are now silent, their songs never cease."
—John Muir

As I peek out my window at home, the trees are silent, bending with the weight of new fallen snow. This silence calls to me as does the deeper message of Christmas. Drawing inward, I see images of happy moments still living in my memory. I also remember sad images and moments. All serve to compel me to get quiet and be still and let it all be. Nothing to do, nothing to change, nothing to master.

Even with all the swirling movement of life, allow the song of silence to sing its melody to you. In that undoing, discover the divine resting place in your inner heart. Allow all of your life and its images past and present, happy and sad, to dissolve in the heavenly peace of the Great Spirit's birth within and all around you.

During the days upcoming, find a way to reach through your earthly concerns and call to your inner heart. Hold another's hand, be silent before speaking, behold each person with presence. Love with your soul, ears, and eyes wide open. Listen for the melody of our shared humanity that is a clear and powerful message during this time. Feel the roots in you go down into the earth. Listen to the trees.

DECEMBER 12

Hereticking

"He was not a loony. He was the sanest
man I ever knew in my life."
—Ted, from the movie "The China Syndrome"

Author and religious reformer John Shelby Spong commented, "First the heretic gathers enough followers so that there are too many people to burn, then the ideas become a movement and eventually a reformation." Heretics decide what part of the collective story needs to be kept and what part needs to be put to rest. They then speak their truth to power. This daring directly confronts conformity.

What's this have to do with everyday life? There's a quality in the heretic that many of us would love to cultivate. It's the quality of "having heart"—pouring energy into helping change something for the better even when the odds for success seem small, the status quo is entrenched, and no one seems to be listening. Heretics act even when feeling inadequate or unqualified.

Heretics don't get an education in hereticking. There is no training that specifically qualifies someone to be a heretic. They (We) rise up and make choices that are consistent with the evolutionary impulse of their (our) hearts and souls. The heretic's integrity stands ready for these choices to be made.

I thank you and all those who have the heart to be a part of the human-inspired movement to evolve and make our world a better place for many not just a select few even when the odds don't seem favorable.

Even if you are a lone voice in your family or community, you are not alone in your heartfelt desire to put old paradigms to rest. May your voice be heard.

DECEMBER 13

Relieve the Suffering

"Unseal a spring of love."
—Sogyal Rinpoche

The reminders of the uncertainties of the human experience are humbling. Through all the life changing disasters of loss and trauma, there are those of us who remain, who are therefore called to carry on and to continue to let our light of compassion shine within us and upon others especially in times of great loss.

Go ahead and feel any pain or sadness you may have as a result of the suffering others are bearing, but don't take on their pain. Thankfully, it's easier to do when we are not in the midst of a disaster. Those of us in these outer circles of light that connect us with those affected by life-changing events, have a significant part to play in their healing journey as we radiate feelings and vibrations of love and compassion from our hearts. As these circles of light form, this light and spiritual strength and focus radiates back to those we hold in that center circle wherever disaster has struck.

This exchange of light and love is no small matter. It is Divine Presence being activated. Distance is not an obstacle to the real power of our bond as a human family. Science confirms this truth.

Hold vigil today for those in the midst of human suffering. Several minutes helps. Take a few moments to slow your rate of breathing by taking full, long, deep breaths. Feel an inner sense of calm and peace. Now, breathe into your heart and feel the suffering. Then breathe out healing love and compassion for our brothers and sisters wherever they may be. Breathe in the suffering. Breathe out the feeling of healing love and compassion. You are bringing healing to the human family as well as to yourself.

DECEMBER 14

Plant Your Life

"If we keep everything locked up in our hearts for our own personal use, nothing will happen. It will perish and die with us."
—Mahatma Gandhi

I remember watching in elementary school an old newsreel of Helen Keller with her teacher Anne Sullivan who was showing how she had taught Helen to speak. We were learning about her remarkable life. Clearly, Helen, who was deaf and blind and the recipient of the American Medal of Freedom, demonstrated what it means to bring to life what is inside of us. The spirit in her was large.

One thing that gets in the way of letting our light shine is fear of rejection or rejection itself. Scientific research now shows that the effect of rejection is strikingly similar to physical pain. We can survive living solitary lives, but we can't thrive. We are created to bond, belong, and interplay.

Episodes of rejection have been hurtful. I've noticed that I can tend to give way too much attention to the rejection event. This has been a challenge throughout my life as it has been for most of us. When this occurs, we become like a seed locked up inside of us without soil.

Helen Keller said, "Often we look so long at the closed door that we do not see the one which has been opened for us." You and I have many seeds for planting, an abundance of soil available, many doors that are open, and many ways to understand what happens in our lives. We are always so much more than what the voices of rejection say about us. If you look into your heart, you know this is true.

December 15

Keepsakes

"Most of our troubles are due to our passionate desire for and
attachment to things that we misapprehend as enduring entities."
—XIV Dalai Lama

Recently I completed a major purge of personal belongings even down
to going through boxes of old photos and discarding about ninety
percent of them. Of the things I kept, most were practical necessities.

Then, there was my son Zach's bike. I've been hauling it around
for twenty years. It was custom made for him. The maker was a small
bicycle company called Clark Kent. Yes, Clark Kent, Superman's alias.
Shortly after Zach won a national championship on this bike in 1993,
I ended up with it. Zach went on to even better bikes.

I hung on to the Clark Kent. In 1997, I had it overhauled and
began to ride it myself along the roads and hills where I lived. Since the
year 2002, for the most part, it has been hung from a hook or found
leaning in a corner somewhere. It still seems to have some strange kind
of special power over me.

I realize that the Clark Kent represents my feelings of love for
Zach as well as it being a bright blue carbon fiber expression of the
axiom "be strong." Through all the changes of my life, I've appreciated
having this reminder alongside. My son has been a mirror of strength
and courage for me.

Much of what we hold onto has had its place in time. The cycles
of life are urging us forward, yet accumulation of attachments can
mightily pull back the reins. Beyond the practical necessities, if what
we keep helps us feel truly surrounded by love, strength, and gratitude,
it's a beautiful thing. It's a keepsake. If that's not the case, then what
are we waiting for?

December 16

The Miracle of You

"Life itself is the miracle of miracles."
—George Bernard Shaw

Exploring how healing works especially what has come to be known as miracle healing is like searching to uncover the truth behind a great mystery. It has been said that miracles are natural and disease isn't. Ironically, this natural state seems more elusive than illness and disease.

Many of us are adaptive creatures. Some of us have adapted to life in this culture and in our families even when what we experience is harmful to our wellbeing. Others of us have not adapted very well and find ourselves in resistance to what we have come through. The resistance is understandable, but it has its own hazards. There is a third way. This third way is being in harmony with one's natural state.

It shows up much more rarely and is connected to a central metaphysical theme in the traditional nativity story. Before giving birth, Mary, accompanied by Joseph, returned to Joseph's ancestral home. The birth of spiritual healing, living in harmony with your natural state, takes place when you return to your ancestral home. Spiritually speaking, your ancestral home is your most natural spiritual state rooted deeply in you.

This is the third way. Often it is described as "the spirit" of a person and it is this spirit which keeps you attuned to the subtleties of your naturally whole and powerful self. Miracles naturally arise when one person is fully clothed in their spirit, their divine likeness. Even those who are close-by experience the ripple effect.

Each breath is taking you closer to your ancestral home in spirit. Open to this vision today. Feel and notice how your attention shifts and your state changes as the miracle of being you finds its way into your heart once again.

December 17

The Naked Truth

"I want to know...if you can look back with firm
eyes and say 'this is where I stand.'"
—David Whyte

In this life I've broken promises and vows. Others have broken promises and vows made to me.

There are wise and protective reasons for breaking a vow or promise. It very well could be an act of love for yourself. It may also be an act of love for the one you're with.

The pain of loss is real. Lives come apart, yes. What also comes apart are the illusions and dishonesty we try to maintain. It may take some time for that illusion to break down, but once it does, we stand staring at the naked truth. From this truth, we birth the beginnings of an authentic relationship with ourselves and hopefully with those we love.

May your heart reach out in love to all those you know who have made these life-changing passages. We are many.

December 18

Measure of Good

My maternal grandfather reflected on the powerful connection we have with one another in a letter he wrote to my mother during World War II on December 18, 1943 when she was seventeen:

"I rarely ever sit down to a meal, or get really warm and comfortable, without remembering the many thousands in and near our battle areas who are neither fed, clothed, nor properly housed. There is always in my mind's eye a picture I saw in a recent issue of Life—four children, ranging from about three to eight in years— one little girl, in particular, about eight years of age—all standing against a wall somewhere in Italy, all perfectly nude, and all showing distinct evidences of undernourishment. I all but burst into tears merely gazing at the pictures. So, knowing that you and your sweet mother are housed, and clothed, fed and loved, and are living in such a good land as all of us in America can enjoy, is sufficient in the way of Christmas cheer for me."

This letter of real emotion is a heartrending touchstone for all of us. The ravages of war and poverty, as well as unstable economies and geopolitical gamesmanship continue to leave the vulnerable ones in deplorable situations whether far away or close to home. Experiences and feelings of isolation, injustice, and powerlessness are universal. We can all connect with these shared human experiences.

There's the expression, "There, but for the grace of God, go I." Whatever your spiritual point of view may be, your personal circumstances reflect some measure of good. Without judgment or evaluation of how little or how much you have, give a piece of your heart today in appreciation for the basics you receive—warmth, food, companionship, health of mind and body, clothing, love, freedom of movement, and income.

In the midst of your feelings of appreciation, let your attention turn to someone you know who is struggling to have their basic needs met. Give them some room in your heart today as well. We are in this together.

December 19

Pattern Break

Every once in a while I decide to break the pattern
or actually it's the planet Saturn
that's opposite my natal moon.
So I'm a buffoon, but Taurus is rising
and my sun is energizing that creative spark
that flies out of the dark and into this moment
right here, right now.
Do you ever get stuck in the muck

of what other people think?
It's like takin' a drink
that only causes you to sink into the stink
of your own fear.
Yes, fear. This is the year
for all of us to clear those fears,
fears gone wild since we were a child.
You see, life is the greatest gift and
Love is its Source, Love its Mother, its Father...
call it God...I call it Love.
It is everything fear is not.
It is kind. It is powerful.
It is healing every feeling of emptiness, loneliness, shallowness.
For Love is here, fully, completely present
in our midst and in the twist of our DNA.
And in that fist where you hold on tight
and fight as if the world is against you,
I remind you that you are here to be a part
of this awakening in every heart
of this eternal vibration sensation,
that magnification without limitation
of pure being.
Ho! Amen! Yes Ma'am!

DECEMBER 20

Brainridden

"The ego does whatever it can to keep me small
and hidden so that I don't get eaten."
—Unknown

I can't remember where I heard or read the quote above. It seems like
something right out of the Neanderthals. I have had this pop up for

me throughout my life when my introvertedness has collapsed around me. It's one thing to be shy. It's another to feel almost suffocated by it. There have been times when I have wanted to be so small and not be noticed, because I was feeling this oversized fear which insists that something awkward or embarrassing or mean will happen to me if I crawl out of my inner cave.

All of us have basic aspects of our unique human identity that can't be disposed of. They are such things as being shy, or outrageously funny, or having a never-ending love for learning, or often seeking out ways to connect with others. We are who we are when it comes to these things.

When these aspects become distorted into ways of being small or compulsive or destructive, we're usually under the spell of a strong visceral fear of some kind. We're living almost entirely from our brains much like our Neanderthal ancestors did 50,000 years ago. Ugh...ugh.

This explains why I'm passionate about the heart and its powerful electromagnetic energy. If left to our brains alone to run our lives, you and I become brainridden—controlled and stopped by the brain's fearful reactions. We either tend to withdraw and try not to be noticed or we are consistently defensive— flight or fight. Sound familiar?

Fear will show up. When it does, give the power of your heart a chance. It's a simple step of attention. Stop, breathe into your heart, and slow down. Remember, there is a mind in your heart. At these times, you can learn how to think and respond from your heart which moderates and balances the brain's impulse to try and escape from the fear of being eaten. Rather than you being eaten, your fear gets devoured. Bon appetit!

December 21

Homing Instinct

"Colorado, everywhere I go, I'm in your shadow."
—Chuck Pyle

We all have favorite places. Colorado is one of mine. It's always been my home away from home. From Ouray to Grand Junction to Denver to Lake City to its rugged snow capped mountains and flowing streams and blue skies, it has always felt like where I belong. It is where I feel most alive with the exception of being in the arms of the ones I love.

Each of us need a few moments each day to remember and connect with those spaces and places that feel like home. They may or may not be where we live, but they are always with us like the turn into a new day.

Return home today, wherever or whatever that may be for you. Some say your aim needs to be to feel at home in each moment. Okay, yes. And, there are times when it's likely that you want to envision and experience something more tangible, creative, and bold.

What matters is regenerating the power and feeling of being comfortable in your own heart, mind, body, and soul. Right now, listening to the rainfall on the roof takes me there. Life has endless home entry points. Beautiful.

December 22

My Handle

"'So you may know that the Son of man has the power on earth to forgive sins'—then he said to the paralytic, 'Arise, take your pallet and go home.' And he got up and went home."
—Mark 2: 10-11, 12a

This form of spontaneous healing, which includes the elimination of physical illness or disease, comes about because a profound transformation has taken place at a cellular level. Jesus' method generates this cellular metamorphosis through creating what could be described as an energy field of amplified love. In this field, those present and receptive are freed from the paralyzing neural circuitry which is linked to hardened thoughts and repetitive feelings of guilt, shame, and the like. The result is a healing or re-patterning.

What all this really says is that forgiveness is a very powerful remedy for what ails and paralyzes us. It provides a handle for us to be able to firmly grasp the eternal golden thread of life which is always connected to this amplified presence of love. In this divine quality of love, we are freed from past impressions, heartbeat by heartbeat, breath by breath.

Repeat throughout your day these words: "Arise, take up your pallet and go home." Attune your heart, mind, and body to what these words convey. Whatever you have been lying in, arise, and feel the pull of the golden thread of love. Take hold of this handle, and go where it is leading.

DECEMBER 23

A Love Revolution

"I was there in the beginning and I was the spirit of love."
—Rumi

One soul, one life is precious. There is the story of Ryan, who was born and lived outside his mother's womb for only two days. This story was told before an international television audience. Spiritual author and teacher Gary Zukav addressed the grief and loss of the parents. For the millions who listened and witnessed, it was as if the very brief incarnation of this one soul had greatly contributed to a powerful turnaround in their own lives. Those who viewed the exchange of compassion between Zukav and Ryan's distraught parents were once again shown the priceless miracle of being a soul coming into human form.

This time of year, the incarnation of one soul, in the form of a newborn, by design, is to teach us again that this event marks something miraculous and unparalleled—a soul being born into this world. This annual nativity brings to us once more that there is a Divine Presence that moves, creates, and sets the stage for each of us to have this experience and be celebrated. Often, when a child is born, we reconnect, celebrate, and hug with our hearts and bodies. We remember that all life is precious.

Take a moment to recall looking into the eyes of an infant. Feel the light coming through. Let the spirit of a child come alive in you this day. Say a prayer of thanks for the hoop of life which turns through you.

DECEMBER 24

There is a Light

"Breath of heaven, hold me together. Be
forever near me, breath of heaven."
—Chris Eaton, Amy Grant

Traditions merge into this season of goodwill, joy, and hope. Symbols and visions of light fill us with new possibilities.

Many on our small blue planet enter this resplendent time of year with significant life challenges. We are attuned to this earthly reality in our community, country, and around our world. Jesus brought forward a bold vision for this world even in the heartbreak, poverty, and persecution of his time. He felt the breath of heaven upon him as did others around him.

That breath lives on. It is the act and prayerful intention of calling forth the light in every person—an elegant vision with a real world application. What are the small things that are always within your reach that you could lovingly do and be? Consider yourself divinely provoked to go forward into this season and the year to come with the affirmation and feeling that the breath of heaven is behind you, within you, and all around you.

Open to this spiritual energy supporting you in bravely shifting priorities. If your life is a bitter pill to swallow right now, channel your helplessness into helpfulness for others. If your life is sweet right now, share that sweetness with your neighbors and friends in need. The breath of heaven is guiding and uplifting you as you bring loving intention to each present moment and do your part to call forth the light in every person.

Begin with you. See a golden light enfolding you. Then say and breathe these elegant words of truth: "I am the breath of heaven, a bright light. This breath and light extend out from my heart to everyone I am with today. I gratefully shine and breathe light into the world."

Speak these words from your heart. Feel the light of a beautiful spirit shining through you. Be still and hold this presence close like a newborn child.

DECEMBER 25

The Twelve Days

Drawing from a very old European tradition, the Christmas "season" begins on Christmas Day and continues for twelve days through January fifth. Hence, these twelve days have become known as the "Twelve Days of Christmas." I offer my spiritual version of the popular Christmas song, "Twelve Days of Christmas." "My true love" represents the Divine Presence.

On the first day of Christmas my true love gave to me (MTLGTM) life unendingly.
On the second day of Christmas MTLGTM two miracles and...
On the third day of Christmas MTLGTM three power prayers...
On the fourth day of Christmas MTLGTM four children's gifts...
On the fifth day of Christmas MTLGTM five golden things...
On the sixth day of Christmas MTLGTM six grand visions...
On the seventh day of Christmas MTLGTM seven lights a-glowing...
On the eighth day of Christmas MTLGTM eight hugs for spreading...

On the ninth day of Christmas MTLGTM nine gratitudes...
On the tenth day of Christmas MTLGTM ten magic moments...
On the eleventh day of Christmas MTLGTM eleven letting-go's...
On the twelfth day of Christmas MTLGTM twelve joys to share...

This is about energizing your spiritual generosity and vision. For example, one of the five golden things could be a "golden aura of healing light enfolding every soul." Or, one of the four children's gifts could be "unconditional love freely given to every child."

Create your own list of gifts for each day. The song details the growing number of gifts that are to be given as each day passes. The first day is one, the second day is three (two plus one), the third day is six (three plus two plus one), etc. The total spiritual and imaginal gifts given through you when you complete the twelve days is 364, one gift for each day of the year except for one day and that is reserved for unexpected abundance. This is a powerful practice for initiating a new consciousness of gratitude and abundance for you and our world.

Happy Christmas to you and those you love.

December 26

The Mystery of G

"There is a difference between the experience
of God and the explanation of the experience.
Religion tends to assume they are the same."
—John Shelby Spong

More and more of us are moving toward embracing God (G) as mystery and away from God as a fixed historical concept or an extension of our human fixations or a grantor of wishes. Mystery, in this sense, means G is not some riddle to be solved. Rather, G activates and cultivates aliveness, yet relationship with this presence of aliveness never completely settles in a well defined place. G is elusive, yet captivating.

When we say with conviction "Be still and know that I am G," we are directing our random mental activity to quiet down. We are energizing the heart, mind, emotions, and body with the aliveness of the G, the bearer of eternity within and around us. We are amplifying the G code that is programmed into our DNA. We are remembering that we are more than human flesh and bone—an expression of the eternal spirit of G. This is captivating and real and accessible to anyone. Yet, G, the one Divine Presence and Power in the universe, taken as a whole, remains elusive, far beyond the grasp of any one of us.

Deeply appreciate that you have this playground in which to dive into the spirit of G. Anything that touches the aliveness of the universe—a river, the sky, expressing deep affection, a joyful moment with a child, stillness in meditation, helping someone in need, inspiring words of wisdom—is G's mystery reaching through time and space to open your heart and refresh your soul. Understand that these experiences are not G. G remains unknowable. Getting wind of G now and then is priceless.

Move through this day and ask the mystery of G to show itself to you. Open and connect with your heart today. Notice that it may feel as if G has hands that are literally touching you and leading you through this day. Enjoy the mystery of it all. Smile each time you feel G's presence.

DECEMBER 27

The Dream of You

"There's a place for us, a time and place for us."
—Stephen Sondheim

Sobonfu Some', a foremost voice in African spirituality, tells the true story of the West African tribe called the Dagara and how each mother dreams their children into being. Some' details how the life of the child begins before birth on the day that the child becomes a vision or thought in the heart and mind of the mother.

Once a mother-to-be feels the time has come, she walks off into the neighboring woods and finds a particular tree. She then waits until she hears inside herself the song of her child. As soon as she hears it, she returns to her village and decides who will be the father of her child and teaches him the song. She teaches it to the other women of the village.

This song is sung when the child is born, when the child becomes injured or sick or does something noble, when puberty arrives, at the child's marriage ceremony, during adult sickness, and finally when death is near.

Singing a song is powerful medicine. It is like praying twice. Every time a member of the Dagara tribe hears their song, they are called back to the marrow of their identity whether they want to or not. The song is a lifelong reminder that there is always a place for them in their home community and world, a place that cherishes and nourishes their heart and soul.

Very rarely do we in the west experience such things, but this fact doesn't prevent us from bringing our favorite song, poem, sacred verse, memory, or reading into our awareness today. I call you back to the dream of you held in someone's heart long ago before you were born.

What is powerful spiritual medicine for you and quickly reconnects you to the essence of you? Serve it up today. Feel your place and value in this world. You are a dream come true.

December 28

Release and Resilience

"Let your soul be your pilot."
—Sting

Anthropologist Victor Turner wrote about what he called the space between "no longer" and "not yet." He calls it a "liminal" period in which familiar attachments and beliefs change or dissolve altogether creating disorder for awhile. In this liminal space, we usually have no idea where it's all leading.

Relationships have tossed all of us into this tar pit. "Who am I now and how can I go on without this person?" is the refrain. The answer comes back, "I don't know!!" Stumbling forward into the unknown, we feel the agony of needing to let go. So much of our identity feels like it's on life support.

Truth is, we are remarkably resilient. Love doesn't cease to exist. It is merely hiding inside of us for a period of time.

Like some kind of nasty burned on crust, we feel old feelings and visions stuck to us. Bit by bit, in our willingness to begin to open to the life beyond, all manner of loving angels arrive and assist us in scrubbing off what is stuck. Much of this is painful, some is pleasurable. The urge to reach into the past in search of heart-holds lingers on. Even when we feel like we are suspended between trapezes, we are mandated to trust that there is a wise and powerful spirit within us that is assisting.

Liminality is what I've felt when being in the midst of feeling fear. I have been discovering what I am truly made of—the soul of me.

Cherish the gift of resilience that has carried you through it all. There is a Great Spirit within and around you always. Breathe into your heart and give thanks for this enduring Spirit that blows at your back.

DECEMBER 29

Field of Prayers

"Churches are good for prayer, but so are garages and
cars and mountains and showers and dance floors."
—Anne Lamott

I've come to know, as one of my spiritual teachers Eric Butterworth expressed, that "prayer is not a position but a disposition." It is what overtakes us when we let our whole being lean into the mystery and wonder of the infinite. From this disposition, an inner corridor opens and this Infinite All invites us in to listen and receive.

These interactions with the Infinite All have been uttered and felt by countless souls for ages. We live, move, and have our being in this rich field of prayer. I've attuned to it in cathedrals of stone and nature. I have felt it when deeply communing with others and with music and art. So have you.

In Buddhism, it is said that during many previous lives the Buddha made five hundred vast and profound prayers to awaken and free all beings. In the Bible, it is written that Jesus prayed, "Father, I have made your name known to them and will continue to make it known, so that the love with which you loved me may be in them." Mahatma Gandhi said: "I am praying for the light that will dispel the darkness; let all those with a living faith in nonviolence join me in the prayer." These prayers of the enlightened ones still live on and vibrate today in the consciousness of the Infinite All.

As this writing comes to a close, I do so knowing that you and I are right now joining together in turning the timeless soil of infinite compassion, love, and wisdom. Prayers, bits of heaven, have been left there for us to harvest and share. Now let's scatter some seeds of our own into this sacred and fertile field. Thank you for opening your hearts to give in this way.

DECEMBER 30

Let it Burn, Let it Go

"I am in the world but not of it."

As the new year draws near and this year comes to a close, be still, and let the wisdom and experiences of this year settle more deeply into that quiet awareness of amazement and non-judgmental presence. You're here. You have passed through many episodes of life's weavings this year. Whatever you may feel about what has taken place this year for you and for all of us, place it all in your inner fire. Let it burn. Give thanks you have made this passage.

Now, feel and see the edge of a new field of experience and expression coming to you. Welcome it, even with all its unknowns. The journey of life as a soul moves on and on and on.

You are so much more than all the chatter in your mind. You are the movement of eternity expressing itself as resistance or flow. If you choose, embrace this prayerful vision with me: "With heart, I flow wisely and in sync with all things moving into and through my life. The infinite energy of Divine Presence awakens me to all that I am and all that we are together. In service to the whole of humanity, I live for the benefit and blessing of all. And so it is and so it shall be."

December 31

For Love of the Earth

"We are the hearts. We are the hands. We are the voice of Spirit on earth. And who we are, and all we do, is a blessing to the world."
—Karen Drucker

It was twelve noon Greenwich mean time, December 31, 1985. My family and I gathered with about twenty friends in a rural home near Bozeman, Montana at 5 a.m. local time. Inspired by John and Jan Price's vision of a World Healing Day (which officially began Dec. 31, 1986), we joined with others around the world to hold sacred space for our world and its future. Prayers were offered and words of inspiration were shared. We truly felt our love for our wondrous planet and all its inhabitants. I still feel the golden thread of powerful love that was created that morning through our shared commitment.

For many years after, on December 31, I, along with millions of others, participated in World Healing Day.(WHD) During that period in the late 1980's, at the height of global participation in WHD, we did experience enormous political and global changes that greatly lessened world tensions.

At the core of WHD was the palpable awareness of the love that we have for our planet. The name for the event was apropos—World Healing Day. We truly yearned for the healing of this living organism that we share and will pass on. Through the years, with the advent of the internet, this awareness and yearning is far more widespread. We love our planet big time. We are connected to the ancients who felt the same way.

Today, I invite you to turn your heart and attention toward our shared home. Pour your heart out in appreciation for what our ancient Mother provides and all that She has been, is now, and shall be.

ENDNOTES

1   Excerpted by permission from Thinking Allowed with Jeffrey Mishlove: An interview with Stephen Levine, Conscious Living, Conscious Dying (#W343); thinkingallowed.com

2   Excerpted by permission from "My Homage to MLK" by Michael Nagler; Tikkun Daily Blog, Jan. 20, 2014; www.tikkun.org

3   Reprinted from Workbook, Lesson 21, A Course in Miracles, Third Edition, Combined Volume, 2007, published by The Foundation for Inner Peace, PO Box 598, Mill Valley, CA USA 94942, www.acim.org

4   Reprinted by permission from an article by Dennis Rivers, "Joanna Macy and The Work That Reconnects: Exploring A Path Toward Compassionate Resilience," April 2010; ecobodhi.org

5   Reprinted by permission from Dennis Rivers, ecobodhi.org

6   Excerpted by permission from Glenda Green, Love Without End by Glenda Green, Heartwings Publishing, Jan.1999; www.lovewithoutend.com

7   Story used by permission from www.opendemocracy.net/transformation and Michael Nagler, May 2014 article, "Humor but not Humiliation: Finding the Sweet Spot in Nonviolent Conflict Resolution"

8   Story used by permission from Gregg Braden; Secrets of the Lost Mode of Prayer by Gregg Braden, Hay House, January, 2006. For more info contact: www.greggbraden.com or info@greggbraden.com

9   Uhl, Christopher. With Dana L. Stuchul. Teaching as if Life Matters: The Promise of a New Education Culture. pp. 145-146. © 2011 The Johns Hopkins University Press. Reprinted with permission of Johns Hopkins University Press.

10 Reprinted by permission from Lance Secretan; Inspire:What Great Leaders Do by Lance Secretan; Copyright 2004 by The Secretan Center, Inc. Published by John Wiley and Sons, Inc.; www.secretan.com

11 Story used by permission from Michael N. Nagler, Ph.D.; Story by Michael N. Nagler; www.michaelnagler.net

12 Reprinted by permission from Mitch Ditkoff; www.ideachampions.com; "The Heart of the Matter" blog posted Dec. 11, 2010, entitled "A Message for Dads Who Travel."

13 Reprinted by permission from Dennis Rivers; www.karunabooks.net/dennis_rivers.htm; 2009